RURAL DEVELOPMENT THROUGH COMMUNITY TELEVISION

Concept's International Series in Communication Education and Development

Concept's International Series in
Communication Education and Development-1

General Editor : **BINOD C. AGRAWAL**

RURAL DEVELOPMENT THROUGH COMMUNITY TELEVISION

Raja Pokharapurkar
Professor and Head
Audio Video Centre
Yashwantrao Chavan Maharashtra Open University
Nashik

CONCEPT PUBLISHING COMPANY, NEW DELHI 110059

About the Author

DR. RAJA POKHARAPURKAR, M.A. Ph.D is currently Professor of Communication and Head of Audio Video Centre at Yashwantrao Chavan Maharashtra Open University, Nashik. He was also Assistant Professor of Research at Film and Television Institute of India, Pune for 15 years. Earlier, he gained an extraordinary experience while conducting research for Satellite Instructional Television Experiment (SITE) at the Space Application Centre, Ahmedabad. At the Film and Television Institute, Dr. Pokharapurkar had displayed a remarkable range of interests both in media as well as in the choice of themes. He has published many papers on communication research and educational television programmes. His experiences in Distance Teaching through audio video programmes is a contribution to Open Learning.

His efforts on writing plays on science fiction have been highly acclaimed. His play "Flash Forth" has been awarded prizes of Best Play, Best Lighting, Best Sound effects and Best Direction for 1988 play competition at Pune.

ISBN 81-7022-450-0

First Published 1993

Published and Printed by
Ashok Kumar Mittal
Concept Publishing Company
A/15-16, Commercial Block, Mohan Garden
NEW DELHI 110059 (India)

Lasertypeset by
Printing Express
H-13, Bali Nagar
NEW DELHI 110015

GENERAL EDITOR'S INTRODUCTION

Rural Development Through Community Television is our first volume in the "Concept's International Series on Communication Education and Development". A number of scholars in Asia, especially in India have been toying with the idea of bringing out a series of monographs in which their first hand experiences of communication intervention in education and development can be documented for wider international dissemination. It was felt that such monographys must be based on field researches carried out in Afro-Asian and Latin American countries. I have taken lead in this direction with the help of M/s Concept Publishing Company, New Delhi.

Keeping in view the importance of this venture and to have expert advice of the national and international scholars in the field of communication education and development, we have proposed an "International Advisory Board". The proposed editorial board consists of eminent scholars and communication researchers. While many have agreed to be on the board, a few have yet to confirm their participation. I have taken the liberty to indicate all the names of the scholars to whom I have written to be on the advisory board for the present. I hope there will be no change in it.

The present volume contains the doctoral work of Dr. Raja Pokharapurkar. Dr. Pokharapurkar has worked for over fifteen years at the Film and Television Institute of India where he was involved in research and teaching of television communication with specia; reference to formative communication research. His indepth understanding of rural India is well reflected in this book and also the utility and limitation of community television for rural development. Reader will find his approach of analysis refreshing and useful for future research.

BINOD C. AGRAWAL
General Editor

PREFACE

Culture and communication are two of the basic attributes of all human societies. Man is a social animal only insofar as he can communicate himself to others and to the natural environment in a meaningful manner. All his communication is mediated through his environment. With the process of evolution from savagery to civilisation the mechanisms of communication have been constantly and drastically modified. What we have today at our disposal is a set of different audio-visual media of communication that could be out to use for further development or for involution. In other words, the media have always been and still are as neutral as scientific knowledge. It is our choice and the need of the time that determines the charge with which the media are utilised.

Communication in a developing society has to face not only its internal and operational difficulties but also the extrinsic, perceptual problems. It has to fulfil a two-task of entertainment and education or rather it has to educate the people into entertainment and entertain them while educating. Television is one of the most advanced media that we have at our disposal today, has certain definite advantages over other channels of communication. Communication cannot bring development by itself; it can only accelerate it if properly administered.

Immediately after I had completed my post-graduate training at Tata Institute of Social Sciences, I invested a good part of time in studying the media. The various experiences that I gained in advertising, research, in the Satellite Instructional Television Experiment (SITE) etc. Finally my discourses at the FTII have helped me considerably in conceptualizing the theme of my present work. My engagement at the SITE lent me an opportunity to visit as many as 2400 villages where I could get my first hints about the factors that inhibit effective TV communication. After producing more than 100 and odd TV programmes for our rural audience and after having constant contact with the villages in Maharashtra, I was beginning to understand that there is a great range of variables which create such situations resulting into the mutual loss of effect on the part of both the messenger and the receivers. The Rural Broadcasting Department of Maharashtra State has been building a network of Community TV sets in a large number of villages. The villagers are also greatly interested and enthusiastic in having this link with the society at large. While this mutual enthusiasm is at work, however, the objective of TV in a developing society as an instructor and educator is becoming more and more distant. It is high time that we check our promises on which we have been trying to spread the network of communication. Such thoughts as these influenced my decision for undertaking a study which would incorporate the background of the viewers, the functioning of the Community TV, the physical and demographic set up of village and also the choice profiles of the viewers. However, even after completing this present work I can not claim that I have covered even a part of the problem.

RAJA POKHARAPURKAR

CONTENTS

LIST OF TABLES

LIST OF MAPS AND FIGURES

1

INTRODUCTION

Communication and Social Sciences

Social scientists were interested in the study of communication for a long time. Communication is to be related to the studies in social structure, to culture, to the psychology of the people, to the economic organization of the society. This has been the major consideration of Sociologists.

All living species have certain means to communicate with their fellow members. What distinguishes human-beings from the rest of the animal kingdom is not only that they interact through communication but also they have developed a capacity to communicate to themselves in the process of communicating with others. In other words, with culture as something to share commonly in terms of knowledge, beliefs and ideas, the human beings are constantly interacting with each other in their social activities.

Every culture evolves certain means of communication with which its participants are informed and educated. Starting from an African tribal culture where "talking drums" are used as a medium of distant communication, modern societies have evolved different modes of communications. Social Scientists interested in communication studies have a great variety of communication media to tackle with. In each case one of the means of communication, the structure of communication is more or less constant. It is the "message" that is to be passed on by the sender to the receiver, which remains a constant principle in case of talking drums of Africa or the institution of gossip in rural areas or newspapers, telephones, radios or television in urban areas. While the process of communication might be complicated, basic idea and the aim of communication has not changed as we move from the talking drums to the television.

Communication media are an inseparable part of socio-cultural life of people. People can communicate only through the five senses :

sight, hearing, touch, smell and taste. The more senses one uses to communicate a message, there are greater chances that it will be understood. Let us short list different stages of evolution of human communication.

Man must have attempted to communicate for the first evertime through simplest incoherent sounds expressing feelings like fear, pain, anger etc. The tradition of such oral communication evolved through millennia although limiting itself strictly to verbal signs. The communication in this area cover forms of '*Harikatha*', '*folk songs*', '*puppetry*' etc. Superseding oral communication is the primary of varied types of written or printed signs. Power of written message weighs itself on the sense of sight and knowledge of language of more sophisticated, more impersonal and far reaching medium of communication evolved by man has been audio signalling i.e., radio, cutting across a territorial as well as politico-geographic barriers and overcoming the problem of illiteracy of recipient the radio has proved to be very powerful medium of communication. Lastly, at the summit of communication media is placed the greatest innovation of man i.e., electronic communication or television.

Objective of Television in India

When TV was introduced in India, the Government of India aimed at achieving specific objectives. There was a great debate as to whether a poor country like India can afford the tremendous expenditure on TV broadcasting. However, the advantages outweighed the economic considerations and LPTs were installed for quick dissemination of information. The main objectives visualized by the Government of India according to the advantages they would bring about to the society were enumerated below:

(a) to act as a catalyst for social change,
(b) to promote national integration,
(c) to stimulate scientific temper among the people,
(d) to disseminate the message of family planning as a means of population control and family welfare,
(e) to stimulate greater agricultural production by providing essential information and knowledge,
(f) to promote and help preservation of environmental ecological balance,

(g) to highlight the need for social welfare, measures including welfare of women, children and the less privileged,
(h) to promote interest in games and sports,
(i) to stimulate appreciation of our artistic and cultural heritage, and
(j) educating the masses.

Television

Indian Government wanted rural development to be achieved at the quickest possible time. For this, science and technology is to be utilised in heralding the economic development of the country. has an unique advantage over other mass media, while it provides words with pictures and sound effects like movies, it scores over the latter by its high intimacy and reaches the largest number of people at the shortest possible time. The visual facility it has, has the advantage over the radio. It can deal with topical problems and depict the messages in various formats. It can also provide solutions for the problems discussed. People learn through the eye and the ear will remember things better because of its audio-visual effect. Its impact is long lasting. Through television the information relating to the new and better agricultural technology can be disseminated. Any exposure through two or three sensory organs has better chance of registering the message and it may convince the farmers to adopt better farm practices. Apart from the evidence seen by their eyes, farmers respond readily to what is said by other farmers. Television provides the ideas into the receptive environment. TV programme lead to awareness, provide information, which creates curiosity in the minds of rural viewers. Agricultural programmes on TV can contribute for the betterment of rural viewers' life-style. Timing, frequency and length, format or design, content and the treatment used for putting the content across are the important factors in TV programme. The Government's motive in introducing rural TV programmes is mainly for rural development. Communication through television could be effective because of following strong capabilities namely: (a) can be universalised, (b) can cross cultural bonds, (c) universal interest set up, (d) wider area covered, (e) more participation of beneficiaries can be obtained.

Considering the above facts television can be considered as the best effective media of communication for rural development. The rapid expansion of LPTs and proper building up of TV network by Government indicates the need for the positive steps to be taken in the area of rural development. Experiments like SITE, and linking of all Low Power Transmitters (LPTs) in Maharashtra could give us fruitful results for rural development.

The main aim of Government in introducing TV networks in the country is for heralding rural development effectively within a short span of time. So let us look at the concept and theories of rural development.

If development is to be viewed as a cohesive, tightly-knit pattern, development should not be assumed. It seems more fruitful to specify a number of major dimensions of social change and ascertain their trends and interrelationships. If changes tend to cluster in a demonstrable fashion, it would help to define the concept of development or modernisation.

It is necessary to integrate the country's developmental plan with the educational system, transportation planning, internal communications network, mass organisation systems, etc. This is true because most developing countries tend to treat communications without proper emphasis or understanding about its role in planning. The communications strategy requires imaginative appreciation of the political strategy, from those in power, initially, and the consensus to make it work.

Communication and Social Change

Sociology of Communication

Communication is not only an essential element to the persistence of social order but to look at it more positively, one may say that communication can be an effective means to developmental change. Aristotle had defined the study of communication as "the search for all the available means of persuasion". By this he meant that the prime goal of communication was to persuade the other people to accept the speaker's point of view. Sociologists have made great efforts to record the instances of distorted communication also. But more positively they have also studied as to how communication has contributed enormously to the acceleration of developmental processes. This thought of analysing the role of communication in the developmental process, although it was given a systematised expression as late as 1960s, since then it has been given an appropriate consideration in almost all social science disciplines. A separate branch of interdisciplinary research in this field has come to be called as development communication. Experts in the fields of economic development, sociologists and communication scholars have dealt with the task of contributing to this newly emerging field.

Development communication deals with the developing societies. As Quebral has put it aptly "development communication is the art and science of human communication applied to the speedy transformation of a country from poverty to a dynamic state of economic growth that makes possible greater economic and social equality and the larger fulfilment of the human potential". Taking the above statement in sociological senses, we may conclude that the development communication carried at expediting the process of social evolution. Here social evolution has to be considered in a teleological sense whereby the meaning of progress can be looked at in terms of the following factors:

(i) economic development,
(ii) social justice, and
(iii) personality fulfilment.

However, the field of rural development which is the prime concern of the present work is in itself a multifaceted subject. It involves various processes and mechanisms such as those belonging to the interest of economists, agricultural researchers, politicians and sociologists.

Needless to say that it is not possible to cover such a great range of diversified subjects in a single research project like the present one. More importantly, since our prime concern is to explicate on those processes of communication with reference to TV programmes, which are supposed to be rural development-oriented we would be restricting ourselves to the perception of rural viewers.

Communication Theories of Development

There are two aspects to the process of development or modernisation – invention, or the original process of change, and innovation, or the process by which invention is spread, copied or disseminated. What is important, so far as diffusionists are concerned, is not what has been invented, but its process of dissemination – diffusion of the innovations.

Lerner found in the Middle East that mass communication helps the "mobile" emphathetic personalty (Daniel Lerner, 1958). By this he means a personality who can accept change and take demands in his or her stride. This he says is the personality pattern in modern life, developed by urbanization, literacy and spread by mass media. He concludes that mass media communication is the greater multiplier in the development, providing the services that can spread new ideas and knowledge more rapidly.

Pioneering ventures in this direction by Rahim (1961) in Bangladesh, and Deutschmann (Deutschmann & Danielson, 1960) and Bonda (Deutschmann & Bonda, 1962) suggested that new ideas spread among peasants in villages in a generally similar pattern to their diffusion in more media-saturated countries such as the United States and Western Europe.

Studying two villages in Asia, Rao (1963) found that mass communication was more important in spreading development among socio-economic groups. He concluded that there is an interaction between communication and economic development and that it is constant and cumulative.

Holmsberg, studying village culture in the Andes Mountains, decided that a real problem exists in bringing these villagers into life, attitudes and stored knowledge of the nation, and that in this task mass media play a leading role as soon as the first face-to-face explanation and demonstrations are over (Holmberg, 1960).

Dobb (1969) decoded that communication was at the very "center of existence" for developing Africa.

Communication, according to Schramm (wilbur Schramn 1964) is a basic social process, and therefore, at the very centre of existence for any society:

> "Whatever dangers or opportunities need to be reported, decisions need to be made, new knowledge needs to be taught or change is imminent – there information flows. It is not surprising, therefore, that the efficiency of communications is a consideration in determining the speed and smoothness of national development, where all of these needs for information are vastly intensified.

The role of communication in developing countries has previously been emphasized. Here literature on the type of communication considered necessary for development will be reviewed.

Pye (1966) feels that mass communication has been over-emphasized in considering the impact on national development. He advocates the use of mass media only if it is fully supported by informal social communication channels which are intimately related to basic social purpose. Bowers (1974) agrees with Pye. He urges the use of extension (person-to-person communication) and information (communication through mass media) as effective means of communication to a rural audience.

After a review of the types of communication necessary for development, the need arises for a comprehensive strategy for development with the help of communications. Foote, Hudson, and Parker (1975) suggested the implementation of telecommunications infrastructure on a developmental priority list for planning and operation of any economic system. According to these scholars, rural development plans which utilize local people as their change agents through comprehensive strategies involving training, developing on-going services independent of outside enterprise, and capital have been effective in some areas in Northern Canada and Alaska. There is potential for this type of communication in other areas with similar needs.

Arora (1975), advises that policy-makers should have a thorough understanding of the various farming systems and provide strategies aimed at different audiences, such as subsistence farmers and modern farmers. The use of mass media, interpersonal communication, and more attention to rural change agents is suggested.

Boyd (1975) firmly believes that the level of rural development action is the project level, since it is where the participation of the people affected by the plan can occur.

Cowlan (1973) indicates that the potential of existing equipment and services should be thoroughly examined before any new and expensive items for communication are considered.

Cooperation between the planners of the modern system and those who coordinate the delivery of products is essential. Once a demand for something is created, the means to satisfy the demand should be available. The social effects of the media should always be kept in mind. Fore-thought during building construction is necessary, even when electricity is not currently available, schools should be wired for electricity to save later higher expenses. Media equipment should be selected by professional, and "political purchases avoided". He concludes by stressing the need for credibility of media. He feels that if they are used for obvious propaganda, the messages will be ignored and achievement of development goals hindered.

Lerner's theory (1932) which stressed literacy, urbanization, and mass communication as the three important variables for diffusion, has been previously cited. The most important part, however, is played by mass communications in swiftly spreading new ideas and knowledge (Lerner, 1932). Several authors have confirmed this theory in their work with developing countries. The works of Pye and Bowers concerning the role of communication as a major device to aid diffusion have been considered, they investigated the role of inter- and intra-personal communication in national development.

It is pertinent that communication practice is viewed from the perspective of communication theory. Middleton describes communication planning as, "the application of theory to reality, in order to reach decisions about what to do, when, and how" (John Middleton, 1978). It is with this theoretical background that India's communications and development problems are tackled.

Role of Television in Rural Development

Assuming that development (more specifically rural development) is as Bordenave (1977), suggests – "a matter of changing attitude, increasing productivity, improving the quality of the individual's life (through education, better health etc.), encouraging rural populations to remain on the land rather than flock to urban areas, giving rural peoples the tools to develop their own political, social and cultural potential". – What is the role that a medium such as television (and that tool in a community viewing situation) can aspire to play? Before tackling this question let us examine some inhibiting factors that hinder the process of development.

Factors Inhibiting Development

Variegated Concepts of Development: It is a well-known fact that the rural development programmes do not originate with the people most concerned – the rural population themselves. In our case the major sponsor of development is the Government itself, though there are several voluntary agencies in the field too. Their presence, however, is too scanty to be of any substantial significance. What becomes clear after closely examining the situation is the fact that those who formulate the plans for development, and those who are supposed to implement them are, by and large, alienated from the realities of rural life, however, well-meaning they might be. The entire process of planning is so highly centralized that it leaves very little scope for participation at the grass-root level.

Besides, more often than not, political agencies take precedence over the real needs of the rural population, when it comes to fixing up the developmental priorities. In implementation the developmental process gets diversified to the extent that it losses its thrust and direction. Different government agencies involved in the process, conceptualise development in different ways than originally perceived by the planners:

> "It happens rather often that the various agencies collaborating in a given programme do not share the same basic concept of the nature and purpose of rural development and of rural communication" (Bodencave, 1977).

People: The Objects of Change: The essence of the development of a society is change – "a process of moving from what it is to what it aspires to be" (Inayatullah, 1964). It is, therefore, not "a matter of technology or gross national product but the growth of a new consciousness, the movement of the human mind, the uplifting of the human spirit, the infusion of human confidence" (Everott Klein Jans, 1960). Any developmental model should be centred on the people concerned and recognise them as the subjects of change. Our system is so structured that it ends up treating people as passive objects. The entire developmental process is sponsored, directed and managed by people who represent the elitist interests and preoccupations which automatically get reflected in planning and executing the total developmental programme. In this manner the development endeavour takes the shape of some sort of charity that some well-meaning people grant the masses.

The Bureaucratic Impediment: Over the years our bureaucracy has grown in strength to become the most effective barrier in the process of development, frustrating the efforts of the protagonists of change. This section of people who hold the real reins of power, generally are the least concerned in as far as the development of the poor and the needy is concerned. They are highly enthusiastic and forthcoming when it comes to benefiting people of their own standing and status – and absolutely indifferent and apathetic where they should be the most sympathetic and zealous – assisting the people at the bottom level. In fact, they do everything to perpetuate *status quo*, as it suits their own interests the most.

The Neo-feudalistic Rural Set-up: Every village has a clique of the higher-ups who are the *de facto* masters of the destiny of almost the entire village population. In Kheda (Village) this group generally comprises the *Sarpanch*, the *Mukhi*, the *Talati* and the Chairman and Secretary of the milk cooperative – the so-called agents of development – and a few other privileged ones. More often than not, the Village Panchayat works against the objectives it is supposed to fulfil. Panchayats in reality are anything but a decentralised institution for self-government and participation. Highly politicised and caste-based as the Panchayat system is, it suffers from draw-backs that make it anti-change. The development agencies involved in rural development find it extremely difficult to penetrate this interest-group to reach the grass-roots. Even when some benefits of development trickle down, it is a result of the favour this group shows to some people whose support they need or who belong to their own community or caste. The real benefits of development are concentrated in the hands of this privileged class because of their access to "resource, instruction, credit influence and power". The people at the bottom stay where they are (Bordenave, 1977).

Fatalism and Inertia: The process of acculturation and indoctrination as carried from generation to generation through the institutions of education, religion, literature and communication, generates such values and attitudes among the masses as lead them to become fatalistic. Paulo Freive (1969), a Brazilian educator describes the present communication and education systems as tools of domination and domestication of the masses. He points out that "merely transferring content from a knowledgeable and authoritative source to a passive receiver does nothing to promote the receiver's growth as a person with an autonomous and critical conscience capable of contributing to and influencing his society". The hapless majority finds itself ill-equipped and resourceless to stand up to the exploitation that they are subjected to at all levels of their struggle for survival and growth. Besides, the divisive nature of our rural society makes it impossible for them to organise and unite themselves into a collective force. The defeatist tendencies are so deep-rooted that even the strongest stimulus from any source fails in securing any positive response or reaction whatsoever.

Information Gap: There is no dearth of developmental schemes sponsored by various government as well as voluntary agencies. The benefits of these programmes, however, fail to reach the people who need it the most. One reason for this situation is the lack of proper and adequate information to the masses about these schemes. The information either gets held up or is yielded in such a manner as would weaken the spirits of even the most enthusiastic activist. The terms and conditions to acquire these benefits are so impractical and unrealistic, and the process so complex that one would rather feel safer keeping away from such ventures.

These and many other factors hinder the process of development in rural India.

Media Behaviour: Communication Gaps

What role can be assigned to TV in such a dismal situation? Any attempt to answer this question one has to look to certain historical and existing perspectives in terms of the behaviour of our media into consideration. Some aspects of media and mass interaction create unbridgeable communication gaps, causing doubts about the possibility of the media acting as relevant and effective tool of development.

Communication Media – Wild horses let loose?

A critical analysis of our media – the manner in which it operates the programme content that they generate and transmit, makes the absence of a clearly articulated, development-oriented, people-based communication policy. Our media run more on the basis of unspecified precedents – a hand-out of the colonial heritage – than a well-defined strategy with clear statement of purpose. The result is that instead of acting as catalysts for stimulation, activation and mobilisation of the audiences, they provide them with programmes that are escapist in nature, and produce an opiating effect. Thus TV communication media in India looks like wild horses let loose.

I give, you take

The whole attitude of mass-media tends one to believe that the masses are treated as passive receivers. Even in case of the specially designed education or developmental programmes the media-planners and practitioners consciously or unconsciously endorse the inappropriate concept that of "communication as instruction and persuasion through a one-way transmission from sender to receiver" (Bordenave, 1977). Thereby perpetuating the concept of 'I give, you take'.

Wide Gap between the Promises and Practice

Media-practitioners, guided by the consultancy from different developmental agencies produce messages that arouse expectations, while there is no system of follow-up to check whether the infrastructure availability or the buying power of the people is commensurate with them. "Communication programme, no matter how brilliant, in an area where no attacks on under development are in evidence is bound to be a waste of time. In fact, arousing expectations through the media that cannot be met by existing services can have disastrous effects" (Bordenave, 1977).

The Remote Control Mechanism

Our media men are city-based and urban-oriented. Most of our media-practitioners come from elite background and stationed as they are in big cities. They have little interaction with their audience. The programmes are, therefore, not only biased but devoid of content-based on local needs, dialect and culture. Besides the management of our radio and TV stations is highly centralised and more often than not the programme producers have to go by the directives of a single personality whose priorities may not be developmental necessarily.

The Training Lacuna

The orientation and training that is provided to the media-practitioners is directed more towards providing functional skills than developing pedagogical insights. "Too often change agents are trained quickly and superficially, as if mobilising and educating people for rural development and making good use of communication in this process were as simple a matter as showing people how to build a latrine or fertilize soil. In most cases, their change agents are taught a pedagogy of a transmission and persuasion, rather than shown how to help people to learn to reason, ask questions, make decisions" (Bodernave, 1977).

Impracticality of Community Viewing

In a highly caste-based socio-political culture like ours, a homogeneous village community is nothing more than a far-fetched ideal. Physically as well as socially, the village population is clearly fragmented into castes and sub-castes. At the time of elections (the only occasion when the masses are involved in the democratic process) the caste and community sentiment is exploited to the core by almost all the candidates. This strengthens the process of separation and alienation. The ultimate losers and sufferers are the lower castes who are economically backward. All institutions of development are controlled and manipulated by the rural rich. In such a situation if the community viewing poses a threat to the interest of this privileged class, they will make sure that the "target audiences" have no access to it. For all practical purposes the sets will become non-operational.

This is a very grim picture of the situation noticed in rural India. But this is the way things are in reality.

The question that arises thus, are in such unfavourable circumstances, how can a medium like TV play some meaningful role in assisting and accelerating the process of development and change? While there are no ready-made recipes that one can prescribe with certainty and authority, there are some possibilities that could be put to test. Author shall now try to share some of his thoughts regarding these possibilities with the assumption that though no revolutionary changes in the nations' socio-political structure are envisaged in the near future and that no drastic changes are expected in as far as our communication policy is concerned. Yet author feels TV can still be an effective and meaningful tool to help the developmental transformation of our society.

It needs to be emphasised that by itself TV or for that matter any communication media cannot produce development though they can indirectly contribute in the process quite substantially. They can contribute "toward the creation of an ethos of change and progress" (Dube, 1975). Within these limitations and constraints the role of television seems to have been perceived by the policy-makers.

Libertarian Education: TV can be used as a means of educating the masses by organically integrating it with such processes as conscientisation, organisation and politicisation. For achieving these the participation of the audience is essential. Through participatory programmes it becomes possible to create a dialogue between the people and the media-practitioners and among the people themselves. "Without a dialogue there is no communication, and without communication there can be no true education" (Paulo Friere, 1969). The dialogue can be fostered through several formats involving the audience directly and indirectly. This necessitates making TV accessible to rural population and letting them have their say.

Media-practitioners change-agents and the decision-making authorities who have been acting as sources of information and knowledge will have to learn to become receivers. Media can in the initial stages help people to learn to formulate and articulate their own ideas and feelings about matters important to them.

In such a situation the audience is to be considered as the user and the media-practitioners as change-agents. Have-lock and Have-lock (1969) describe the five essential points for a user-oriented model of communication as :

> "*First* that user need is the paramount consideration and the only consideration and the only acceptable value stance for the change agent;
> *Second*, that diagnosis of need always has to be integral part of the total process;
> *Third*, that the outside change-agent should be non-directive, rarely, if ever, violating the integrity of the user by placing himself in a directive or expert status;
> *Fourth*, that the internal resources, already existing and easily

accessible within the client system itself should be fully utilized; and

Fifth, that self-initiated and self-applied innovation will have the strongest user commitment and the best changes for long-term survival."

TV as a link between the people and the decision-makers : One very important role TV can play is that of providing unambiguous, simplified information regarding several developmental projects available for the benefit of the people. Basic facts about, "how to do", and "what to do", to acquire the benefits of a particular scheme ought to be communicated in lucid and comprehensible manner.

Similarly TV can also bring information regarding the problems and difficulties faced by the people to the decision-making authorities. This can help making communication a two-way process and removing bureaucratic blocks in the path of development.

TV as a vigilance keeper: Different developmental activities that are launched by different agencies need some kind of monitoring. To make sure that the benefits of a particular scheme are reaching their ultimate destination – some sort of vigilance is required. As different stages of operation of a particular project – TV can follow the progress made or otherwise and bring it to the notice of the concerned authorities, so that the required corrective measures can be taken in time.

Localised Programming: Nothing interests the audience more than their present problems and pre-occupations – a consequence of their encounter and interaction with their immediate environment. It becomes imperative, therefore, to make sure that content of the messages is relevant to the problems and needs of the audience. Programmes must be based on local culture and use local dialect as far as possible. The content material should be presented in a form that appeals the audience and ensures their undisturbed attention.

TV in non-transmission mode : The mobility due to the latest innovations in TV technology makes it possible to carry and operate TV equipment in the remotest places. This enables the media-practitioners to do in-depth study to measure the impact of a particular programme format or pretest prototypes for launching an effective serial.

In this mode it is also possible to study developmental projects carried on at different places by some groups or individuals dedicated and committed to the cause of social change.

Sometimes some very sensitive issues can come up during dialogue with the audiences. The content of the dialogue may be of great substance and significance to audience, but may cause problems if transmitted. In fact transmitting such material may do more harm than good but a proper analysis of this material may lead to some fresh insights insofar as the problem solving effort is concerned. Such material can be of immense use to media-practitioners as well as concerned decision-making authorities.

The above suggestions fall within the purview of the Government's declared policy of using TV for entertainment information and education. These possibilities are over and above the conventional use of the medium for instruction, demonstration and entertainment. Putting these suggestions into practice, does not necessitate great structural changes in the existing set-up.

When the researcher looks back over the period since his work began that is, since 1981, he feels that a drastic change has come about right in the very purpose for which the television was accepted in the policy. It appears as if that the objective of information and education has been replaced by a sheer entertainment and revenue collection. To put it more explicitly as there is an exponential growth in the number of sponsored programmes the number and the quality of the educational programmes has been found to be on a sharp decline. The telecast charges of the sponsored programmes are quite high and add to the profitability of television. The policy-makers found sponsored programmes (owned by the Government) as a new source of revenue. The present situation, therefore, reveals the fact that there has been a sharp diversion from the educational and informative programmes with development as a theme or as an orientation, has changed to advertisements and revenue collection. With the result what we find that the original purpose of television as an effective medium of development communication has been defeated. However, this is only a very recent development could, therefore, be controlled if it is brought to the notice of the policy-makers that if this system remains unchanged the television would loose all its significance for the developing country.

Review of Literature

In the present section, our aim is to critically examine some of the

earlier researches accomplished in the field of mass communication and see how far we have advanced in understanding TV and what are our areas of ignorance. This exercise will help us to understand the state of affairs existing at the moment that is noticed by the researchers in this field and also that has a direct bearing on the present work.

There has been a very great corpus of research material in the field of communication, its sociology and its planning for rural development in particular. In the study, on 'Education for Rural Development : Case Studies for Planners', we find that topics such as general education, improvement of rural life conditions etc., have been covered. The anthology involves presentation of 17 case studies discussing the role of communication for the grassroot level leaders as well as workers and motivators. It is aimed at examining strategies for non-formal education at a cross-cultural level. It, however, gives an appearance of a study including a wide variety of problems faced by communication and education but with a loss of depth and the insiders perception (Ahmed, Manzoor and Philip, 1975). However, a few other studies (Allen Dwight W, and Philip R. Christensen, 1973; Aurora, 1975) could be mentioned as an example of in-depth researches in the fields of hardware and programming, general educational considerations. Particularly Aurora observes that a very general communication strategy cannot be adopted for a country like India because different types of communities representing distinctive stages of development but different types of demands on the communication media.

Yet another study completed by Balcomb John *Communication for Development: From Propaganda to Dialogue* (1975), is worth reporting here. This study stresses that communication need no more be considered as a means of persuation, the emphasis generally falling on the perspective that the communication especially aiming at development needs to be a two-way process. He discusses Tosh's three models for introduction of innovations, namely, "Industrial Process Model", "Social Interaction Model" and the "Problem Solving Model". He has argued that the industrial process model is found to be unsuccessful in most of the cases. Some of the programmes involving mass media have been described as achieving the desired goals, the examples of which could be found in the countries like Ethiopia, Tanzania and Zambia. One important suggestion worth mentioning in this context is that the experts in communication having a foreign background should necessarily have an experience of living and working in the rural setting before their expertise is diverted towards development programmes.

There have been a few studies exploring the ways to achieve better policy planning and more efficient transfer of technology. Barzaky, in his work, *Policy Making and Technology Transfer : The Need for National Thinking Laboratories* (1979), discusses the subject-matter inherent in the title of the work emphasizing the need for establishment of national thinking laboratories. It is indicated that such efforts could promote in an organised manner the transfer of technology which could act as catalysts to organise policy-making. Such attempts would be more useful particularly in the developing countries. The often discussed area of communication gap is examined by a few researchers. One such noteworthy study, *Talking and Listening : Problems of Communication in Rural Communities in the Developing Countries*, by Bell Geoffrey (1971) discusses that the project administrators and communication specialists usually miss the point that the rural person's point of view is distinctly different from their own, the former being frequently town-based. The word of appreciation has been extended towards the Institutes of Mass Communication in India and Philippines which use the methods involving feedback from the community.

Some examples of misuses of communication like non-communication, mis-communication and confusing communication that have occurred in development projects have been pointed by Boyd in his article, "Causes and Cures of Communication Neglect in Development Planning" (1975).

An interesting study in the field of educational television has been reported by Carpenter, et al., *Analysing the Use of Technology to Upgrade Education in a Developing Country* (1970). The study involves the development of methodology for educational television (ETV), conducted in a developing country like Columbia. It is suggested that a system using ETV, needs half the number of teachers to attain the same level of education, suggesting further that without increasing the number of teachers the educational system can be considerably improved.

A study aimed at agricultural development through mass media has been discussed by Chavan, (1973), in his work, *The Mass Media : Their Use in Agricultural Training, Education, Extension and Information Services*. A new type of educational policy has been found necessary and the need to accept the recommendations of the 1970 World Conference on Agricultural Education and Training. It is further stressed that the teachers should receive training in communication techniques and in human and social aspects of cultural environment.

In a paper, 'Indian Project – SITE, Bombay', 'Indian Space Research Organisation', 1971, Chitnis, E.V. et al., Seal with the Proposed India – U.S.A. SITE Programme concerned with direct broadcasting to augment television sets. The pilot projects undertaken for research and development are given along with the problems related to development of instruction material are discussed by the authors. An important paper on communication resources and strategies for rural development has been published in the form of proceedings. "Communication Strategies for Rural Development : Proceedings of the Cornell – CIAT International Symposium" (March 17-22, 1974). CIAT Headquarters, California, Columbia, South Africa, Ithasa, New York, 1974). The Working Group Report summarises the implications and applications of communication strategies and also gives specific recommendations on research and training aimed at rural development.

We have seen above that a large number of studies have already been done highlighting the role of mass communication and more particularly that of television in the development of rural community. The studies reviewed so far make a general impression that they are directed more towards evaluating the impact of communication media on the masses while a few others represent a corpus of knowledge on an abstract level, the effectiveness and the need of the media itself. Many of the studies in the field have been accomplished in the interest of the policy planners and they could, therefore, be found out to be presuming a 'from without' rather than a 'from within' view point. In other words, although these studies are quite important, what they lack is the sociological analysis.

The present study hopes to tackle some of the important issues in development communication with a sociological insight. It may be said that the present research programme is different than the available works insofar as it attempts to incorporate the viewers' perceptions for different specific programmes. An attempt has also been made to locate the otherwise neglected issues arising out of the gap between the communicator, the message and the viewer. The present study also attempts to take into consideration the role of the custodians of the CTV as a controlling agency of communication and also as a common viewer. Furthermore, the study has been designed in such a way as to overcome all the criticism that is generally made in regard to the sample size for it is based on the data obtained from as many as 304 villages.

Aims and Objectives of the Study

In this section we would elaborate some of the salient objectives the researcher has undertaken. As has been mentioned earlier, the problem related to rural development in India form an area of interest of the discipline like development, planning, political economy, rural sociology etc. However, development communication as a newly emerging field of research has a lot to exchange with sociology. In so far as this is accepted, it becomes at once relevant that a sociological study of television communication would take a form of a kind of feedback analysis in its formative stages. With this view in mind, the investigator undertook to survey how the television programmes were perceived by the rural viewers in the given area. At a more general level, however, it has been one of the chief concerns of the researcher to understand the role of television in the present-day rural life. Furthermore, it was thought that the present analysis would enable the researcher to arrive at the understanding of television in the larger framework of mass media.

In the earlier discussion it has been made clear that television as one of the communication media contributes to the process of development in a meaningful but a limited way. As regards social change, television, or for that matter, any other communication medium cannot be considered as a direct agent of social change. In other words, the media should be considered as a catalyst rather than an agency of social change. It is, therefore, our concern to understand how and to what extent do the people regard television as a source of education and information in a positive manner.

With this background, let us proceed to formulate some of the salient objectives of the present study:

(1) To make a general survey with regard to the television viewing by the rural community with reference to the frequency of viewing.
(2) To make an attempt to understand the preferences of the rural

masses in regard to the television programmes. It is attempted to find out the linguistic aspect of such preferences in the context under study.

(3) It is further investigated to find out if certain programmes are preferred by the rural community and if so the types of such programmes are noted down.

(4) It is also considered whether the programme timings were convenient to the rural viewers taking into consideration their agricultural and allied occupations.

(5) It is aimed at studying the relationship between the socio-cultural and economic background of the rural viewers with their programme preferences and avoidances.

(6) It is further explored whether the expectations from the television programmes are fulfilled.

(7) It is attempted to investigate carefully whether there exists any gap between the policy planning and community reception, particularly with regard to rural viewers.

(8) There is a controversy between academicians and programme designers as to the effectiveness of instructional, informative and educational programmes. An attempt would be made to infer the viewers' perception of the medium, from the field data.

(9) To evaluate to what extent this medium has been successful in offering an alterative to the channels of traditional entertainment.

(10) To understand the status of physical conditions of community TV and other related physical factors.

The books has been divided into eight chapters starting with an introduction on objectives of TV, theoretical consideration and review of literature.

Chapter 2 deals with an historical account of TV in India, highlighting the developments, plans and expansion of this medium site experiments, INSAT communication, introduction of colour TV and Sponsored Programmes.

Chapter 3 is on Methodology of the study, the design, tools and techniques adopted in the study.

Chapter 4 deals with demographic and communication facilities available in the villages.

Chapter 5 concentrates on the socio-economic profile of the respondents.

Chapter 6 deals with the analysis of the viewers' preferences and avoidance of the Doordarshan Programmes. It also discusses the results of the experimental study of the viewers perception.

Chapter 7 is an integrated analysis of the various parameters cross, tables with the socio-economic characteristic and programme references. It gives an overview analysis of the entire study.

Chapter 8 concludes the study and establishes the hypotheses and gives suggestions to planners for improving the programmes for rural development. On the basis of the study further studies are suggested.

To sum up therefore, the present research has a nature of a feedback study rather than an impact study. It is hope that the findings of the study would enable the researcher to formulate certain propositions for the policy-makers. It is thought that the present study would represent a consolidated perception of the rural viewers who are the targets of our developmental policies and programmes.

2

TELEVISION IN INDIA : An Overview

Television was introduced in the country on September 15, 1959 by setting up a centre at Delhi with the aid of UNESCO, and with the prime objective of promoting socio-economic development of the people. In the initial years, transmission was limited to Delhi and adjoining rural areas and the rural viewers were provided with community viewing sets funded by the Ford Foundation. Over the past 27 years (Map – Doordarshan Transmitters). Doordarshan has expanded both its network and the scope of its activities.

In 1956, the Indian delegation to UNESCO submitted a proposal regarding the establishment of a pilot television centre to further education and community development. The UNESCO General Conference authorised the organisation of pilot projects which would assist member states in, ". . . the fuller the use of press, film, radio and television and educational scientific and cultural purpos" (*Telecommunication Journal*, 1965). For a period of six years (from September 1959 to July 1965) it remained in the experimental stage. During this period only educational and informational programmes were telecaste. The centre was established in Delhi and the transmitter and studio were completed in August 1959. With a total of 71 sets, 40 of which were supplied by UNESCO, television came to Delhi. The original transmitter had a range of 24 kilometres (15 miles) and served selected schools and community viewing centres in Delhi and a few neighbouring villages.

Two experiments were conducted over the Delhi television during the period 1959-65 – one with the support of UNESCO, and the other with that of Ford Foundation. The UNESCO experiment dealt with the theme, "Responsibilities of Citizenship" and the other with class-room instructions (October 23, 1961). These experiments demonstrated the social and educational potential of television in a

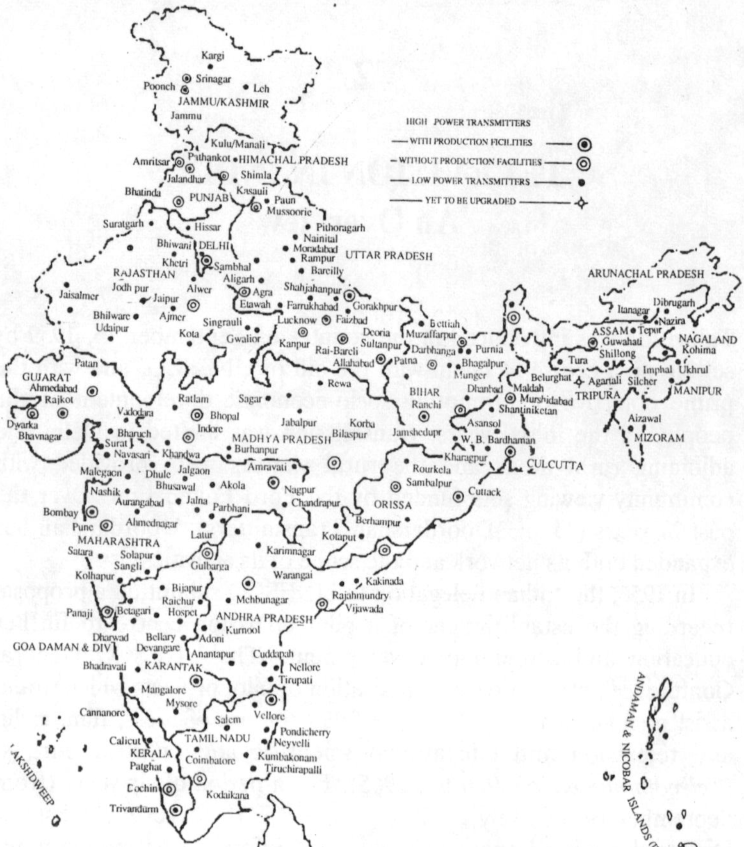

Notes (i) H.PT.'s shownin Capital letters.
(ii) Base Production unit of Jaipur, Raipur and Muzaffarpur is at Delhi.

FIG. 2.1: India: Doordarshan Transmitters.

developing country such as India (Ranjan Borra, 1972). The Educational service was mainly envisaged as a supplement to regular education in schools keeping in view the limitations of school education such as overcrowding, lack of laboratory facilities, shortage of trained teachers etc.

Up to August 14, 1965, the Delhi television station was involved in experimental transmissions related to social and cultural education and in-school instruction. Daily one hour General Service Programming began on August 15, 1965, and covered 37 miles, mainly the area of New Delhi City and its suburbs. Besides a variety of programmes, e.g., news, drama, agriculture, health and cultural programmes, it catered to community viewing programmes for schools. School television lessons were broadcasted for grades seven to eleven in physics, biology, chemistry, social studies, English and Mathematics (Ramesh Chander, 1972).

In January 26, 1967, the Delhi TV station introduced agricultural telecasts twice a week, each of 20 minutes duration, named, "Krishi Darshan", meaning, "Agricultural Television". The programmes were increased to three times a week in 1970. The project, started initially to assess the effectiveness of TV in improving agricultural productivity and also with a secondary objective – to gain insights into the social and organisational problems of using TV for development tasks (Prasad Vepa, 1969). The Department of Adult Education of the National Council of Educational Research and Training (NCERT), undertook the systematic field evaluation in 1968. Evaluation confirmed the value of TV for an effective dissemination of improved agricultural techniques. The experimental programmes were produced at a cost as small as Rs.3,000, but also demonstrated the problems involved in organising an effort of this nature in India. For example, it took 11 months to install 80 sets where there had been a two-month time-table, normally 10 per cent sets were out of order with the figure going up to 20 per cent during the monsoon months. In addition, poor consideration existed between those responsible for physical requirements such as seeds, fertilizers, insecticides, etc., and the telecasts.

In the late sixties some affluents of Delhi imported TV sets and according to Mehra Masani (1976) they formed a pressure group for inclusion of entertainment programmes in TV Broadcast. The Delhi TV centre succumbed to the pressure and some entertainment programmes were included in the telecast in the year 1971. The entertainment element subsequently went on increasing only at the cost of education and informative programmes.

The growth of TV has been slow in India, but consciously so far, it was felt that TV must grow in such a way that not only the context would be ingenious, but TV would have a close identification with the Indian personality (Gujral, 1972). The important landmarks in TV development are given in Table 2.1.

TABLE 2.1: Landmarks in Doordarshan

Events	Date
1. TV Experimental Service Inaugurated by the President of India	15th Sept. 1959
2. School Television Project launched	24th Oct. 1961
3. Daily One Hour General Service started	15th Aug. 1965
4. Krishi Darshan — the First Rural Programme Started in Delhi	26th Jan. 1967
5. The Second TV Station Inaugurated at Bombay	2nd Oct. 1972
6. Satellite Instructional Television Experiment (SITE) introduced in six States in 2,400 villages	1st Aug. 1975
7. Introduction of Commercials in TV	1st Jan. 1976
8. TV separated from All India Radio	1st Apr. 1976
9. Satellite Instruction, Television Experiment (SITE) completed	31st July 1976
10. First Post-SITE Centre commissioned, Jaipur	1st March 1977
11. Launching of INSAT-1A	10th Apr. 1982
12. Operationalisation of INSAT-1A and Inauguration of National Programme and Colour Telecasts (INSAT-1A abandoned on 6th September, 1982)	15th Aug. 1982
13. Commissioning of 20 Low Power Transmitters and Coverage of IX Asiad through TV Network	19th Nov. 1982
14. Coverage of Non-Aligned Meet through TV Network	7th—12th March 1983
15. Launching of INSAT-1B	30th Aug. 1983
16. Operationalisation of INSAT-1B	15th Oct. 1983
17. Coverage of CHOGM through TV Network	22nd—28th November 1983
18. Programme of Higher Education	15th Aug. 1984
19. Silver Jubilee of Doordarshan	15th Sept. 1984
20. Inauguration of 2nd Channel in Delhi	17th Sept. 1984
21. Inauguration of 2nd Channel in Bombay	1st May 1985
22. Inauguration of INTEXT Service	19th Nov. 1985
23. Terrestrial Transmitters in Maharashtra are linked with Bombay	9th Aug. 1986

The tremendous increase in TV sets over the years 1962 to 1985, from a meagre 41 sets in 1962 to 67,50,000 in 1985.

The number of TV sets for which licences were obtained in different states of India. It is seen that urban metropolis like Delhi has a maximum number of sets (6,41,462).

Plans for the Expansion of Television

Until the beginning of the Fourth Five-Year Plan in 1969, television in India enjoyed a low priority. Although introduced in 1959, it was to remain confined to the New Delhi area until the inauguration of the second television station in Bombay on December 2, 1972.

This was an important landmark in the history of Indian TV, because Bombay Television Station was the first station to be designed and out into operation as the full-fledged station for professional service.

AIR proposals for the expansion of television in India were first presented in 1964-65 to the Bhabha Committee which surveyed the status of the mid-1960s, future potential, and scope of governmental initiatives for the development of electronics in India.

In 1967, ISRO, then a division of the Department of Atomic Energy, commissioned a study on the cost and significance of a synchronous satellite to link isolated rural communities and distinct centres of population in India through a national system for mass communication using television. The study team had the cooperation of the National Aeronautics and Space Administration as well as the participation of specialists from establishments and departments of government. The team investigated the feasibility and cost of five system alternatives:

(1) Limited to and extension of local radio,
(2) Ground-based TV,
(3) Direct broadcast from satellite,
(4) Re-broadcast of a satellite signal, and
(5) A combination of ground stations and direct broadcast from satellite.

The study concluded that a hybrid system with direct satellite reception in thinly populated rural areas and traditional rebroadcast stations in relatively dense areas as a possible alternative.

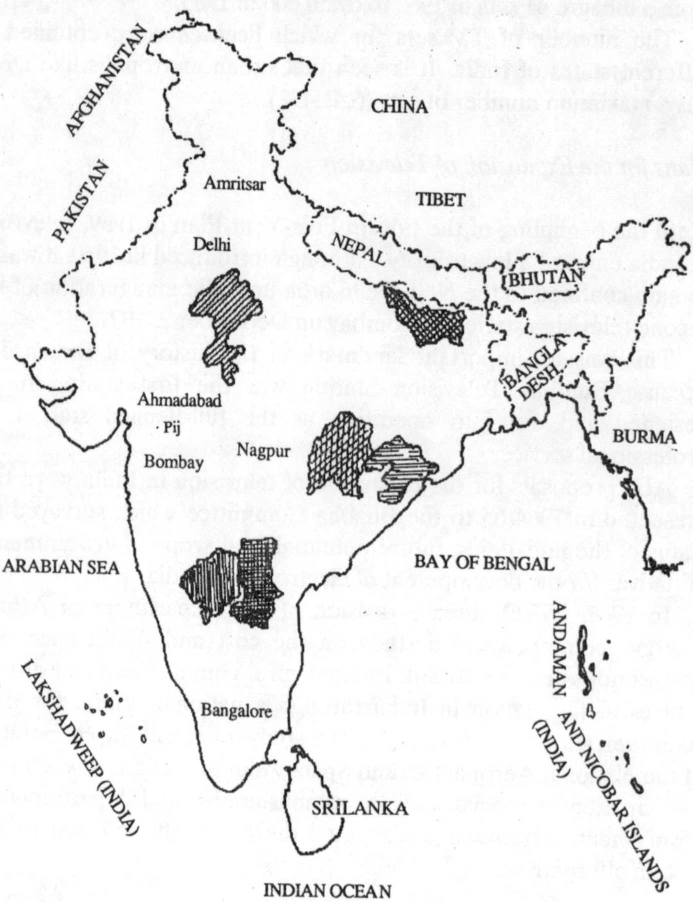

FIG. 2.2: Site Clusters.

Near about the same period, India undertook one of the most exciting and ambitious projects in the field of mass communication. That was the Satellite Instructional Television Experiment (SITE). With the help of an American satellite ATS-6, 2400 villages in six States of India got covered. Various evaluation studies appreciated the success of the SITE experiment for having contributed substantially towards the general consciousness and change in the attitude amongst the beneficiary viewers in the rural areas. At the end of SITE, a new SITE Continuity Project was initiated providing for the installation of six terrestrial transmitters in backward areas. Community sets were installed in villages by the State Governments for direct viewing by the villagers. The objective of programmes communicated through the SITE experiment was to mount development-oriented educational programmes directed to the most under-developed parts of the country. The SITE experiment rightfully claims a great success. The SITE experiment launched in six States on 1st August, 1975 (Andhra Pradesh, Orissa, Bihar, Karnataka, Rajasthan and Madhya Pradesh) has useful objectives like promoting family planning, improve agricultural productivity and to inculcate the feelings of National Integration. It also aimed at providing general school and adult education, improve occupational skills, improve health and hygiene and so on. Thus the plan had unique approach in attaining the developmental culture in the rural areas.

Commercial Service of Doordarshan was started on January 1, 1976 and reached a revenue target of Rs. 50 crores in 1985-86. On 1st April, 1976 Doordarshan was conceived as a separate department with a Directorate of its own and was separated from All India Radio, for administrative and functional matters.

INSAT: Communicate Through Television

A villager sitting in his hut in a remote village never imagined that he would be able to see 'live', the important events happening in his country. However, his dream became true when he saw the Independence Day celebrations telecasted from Red Fort in Delhi for the first time in 1982.

August 15, 1982 was a red-letter day in the history of communication in India, as it witnessed four major events through the INSAT facility (the Indian National Satellite) :

- Commencement of National Network for as All India relay
- Conversion of Black and White to colour Television,
- Utilisation of micro-wave links for television on a regular basis, and
- Distribution of television programmes throughout the country.

While INSAT served the purpose of country wide coverage through satellite, important metropolitan cities were also interlinked via land-based microwave systems for the purpose of exchanging television programmes. These microwave links are installed and maintained by P&T Department and some of the more important micro-wave routes existing now are :

(i) Delhi-Bombay-Panaji-Bangalore-Madras.
(ii) Bombay-Pune.
(iii) Delhi-Dehra Dun.
(iv) Delhi-Lucknow-Calcutta.

Recent developments in satellite communication technology in India have, in a way, provided media-planners with new opportunities for assisting those segments of population who are apparently lagging behind in the social and economic scenario of the country. INSAT service enabled us to provide National, Regional and Local Telecasts which in addition to the urban centres were received by community TV sets in remote and tribal areas.

INSAT-1B is a multi-purpose operational satellite system. It has an expected life-span of 7 years, which in addition to TV segment has capabilities of radio programmes distribution, providing timely disaster warnings and relaying of meteorological and oceanographical data on a continuous basis. For, TV INSAT system has the provision of two transponders which are utilised as two simultaneous channels for alternative programming.

Colour Television came to India during ASIAD, 1982, in the name of technology. Obviously there are two beneficiaries of this:

(a) Those who developed this technology as they got good market not only for the machineries but also for the colour TV receivers the import of which was liberalised during Asiad, 1982, and
(b) Those urban elites who could afford owning a colour TV set to get a lot more entertainment. This was, therefore, another fill-up to the entertainment orientation of Indian TV.

The first 20 LPT (Low Power Transmitter) centres of 100 watt capacity in the country were also commissioned to synchronize with the start of Asian Games on November 19, 1982. This was followed by coverage of important events like Non-Aligned Meet on March 7, 1983.

There are 183 TV transmitters out of which 11 are main centres producing and telecasting programmes. Five relay centres, 10 post-site/INSAT Centres and 157 LPTs linked with Delhi. These transmitters covered more than 64 per cent of the population in 1986. In 1985 it is estimated that 60 million people (8%) of the Indian population regularly view TV. A great deal of community viewing occurs especially in villages. The unprecedented speed with which the transmitter installations have come up all over the country is considered as a magnificent achievement in the annals of world television. Major political international event namely CHOGEM was covered on November 22, 1988.

Delhi got its second channel on September 17, 1984. Bombay was next to get it on 1st May, 1985, Calcutta – 19th November 1987 and Madras – 1st July, 1988. The second channels cater to the diverse interest of local viewers and to provide an alternative source of viewing.

Satellite-based Television Programmes

Area Specific Programmes (ASP)

ASP are being telecast for 35 to 40 minutes for each cluster produced by respective INSAT Kendras with the active cooperation of user-agencies like the Ministries of Agriculture, Health and Rural Reconstruction. The programmes are primarily based on needs and priorities of the people as assessed by Research Evaluation Cells through specific studies. A number of sets on ENG equipments have been provided at each INSAT Kendra with editing facilities to produce them quickly on the spot in the researcher-producer team mode.

To produce relevant and effective programmes for the rural viewers, continuous research inputs are provided. A number of programmes are pretested to judge its effectiveness in terms of its format, duration, content, density, presentation, comprehension etc. Besides preparation of Audience Profile and Needs Assessment studies, both qualitatively and quantitatively are taken up to evaluate the total impact. An automatised multi-sources feedback system has been developed at each INSAT Kendra to get continuous feedback of the viewing and on the hard-core items.

All the ASPs, thus produced at each INSAT Kendra are brought to INSAT Cell, specially created at Directorate General of Doordarshan for purpose of liaison and coordination. This cell remains in constant touch with all the INSAT Centres for continuous flow of programmes for telecast as per prescribed schedule. Normally, programmes for four weeks are made available in advance. All programmes are previewed and monitored by experienced programme personnel so that nothing is left to chance. The relevance and effectiveness, is in a way pre-judged before a decision is taken to air a particular programme.

The specific programmes for each cluster are fed from Doordarshan Kendra, Delhi to Earth Station at Secunderabad (U.P.) through the micro-wave. Thereafter, they are beamed to INSAT for further transmission to DRS and VHF sets in the areas at specific timings (diagrammatic representation is enclosed).

The present timings predetermined for the six clusters are as follows:

Ranchi	- 5.00 to 5.40 p.m.
Gorakhpur	- 5.40 to 6.15 p.m.
Cuttack	- 6.15 to 6.55 p.m.
Hyderabad	- 6.55 to 7.30 p.m.
Nagpur	- 7.30 to 8.05 p.m.
Rajkot	- 8.05 to 8.40 p.m.

National Programmes

In order to keep the countrymen informed about cultural, social and economic progress in various parts of the country and to bring home the message of unity in diversity as well as the spirit of national integration, a common National Programme was introduced for simultaneous telecast by all transmitters (including INSAT Centres) with effect from 15th August, 1982. These programmes are produced at various Doordarshan Kendras and reflect broadly such themes as national integration, communal harmony, family welfare, India's cultural heritage including dance, India's struggle for independence, science programmes as well as news and current affairs.

After the initial introduction of this common chunk, adjustments in the timings and contents of the National Programmes were made periodically to accommodate viewers' interests as well as regional/local programmes during the prime viewing time. National programmes are at present telecast between 8.40 p.m. to 11.15 p.m., including the National Hindi News Bulletin at 8.40 p.m. and the National English Bulletin at 9.30 p.m.

Educational Telecasts

The developments in satellite communication technology in India have provided education experts and media planners with new opportunities for distance learning. Though school telecasts have been in existence since inception of television system in the country, the satellite has further boosted the activity tremendously by providing its widespread application. As a result, it is now possible to extend educational facilities in all dimensions. It has, in a real way, reduced the cost of teaching and is far superior in quality to the traditional method of instruction.

Recently there are two educational services in vogue where satellite is used to disseminate the instruction throughout the country.

Educational Television (ETV)

ETV service is meant for primary school children of 5 to 11 years of age. The enrichment type of programmes included in it are presently planned and produced jointly by NCERT and Doordarshan. However, the total responsibility of producing ETV programmes will be transferred to NCERT in the near future as soon as the necessary infrastructure is created in SIETs in the respective states.

These programmes are of 45 minutes duration for each cluster and cater to the two separate groups of school children i.e., 5 to 8 years and 9 to 11 years age-group. Thus, a capsule for a day consists of two segments of 20 minutes each for the two age-groups, with the provision of 5 minutes change-over time from one group of children to another. A music filler of 5 minutes duration is given so that the interest is maintained.

Due to paucity of studio facilities, presently the programmes are produced first in Hindi and thereafter are dubbed in different languages, viz., Oriya, Marathi, Gujarati and Telugu. NCERT is also producing a weekly programme, 'Hints for Teachers' to refresh them in teaching methods.

Higher Education Project of UGC

Country-wide Class-room: INSAT communication facility has added one more dimension of distance learning in higher education. University Grants Commission (UGC) has planned and initiated higher education through INSAT. The programmes are produced at specially selected centres in some Universities in addition to selections obtained from overseas. It is expected that this would be a beginning of a country-wide classroom which will be expanded so as to occupy the pivotal role in the national educational system particularly in continuing distance education.

The main objective of UGC in utilising the satellite for higher education is to bring about an improvement in the quality of education. This to being attempted by exposing students to programmes which will stimulate them to think and thus broaden their base and improve the overall quality of education. The programmes collected from other countries such as UK, USA, Japan etc. are edited and tailored at a central point like Jamia Millia Islamia to suit to the needs and requirements of Indian students. Programmes produced by agencies such Educational Media Research Centres (EMRC) at Jamia Millia, Pune, University of Gujarat and Osmania along with borrowed items from abroad are put through INSAT throughout the country for one hour between 12.45 p.m. and 1.45 p.m. The same programme is repeated between 4.00 p.m. and 5.00 p.m.

Service Expanded

Over the years Doordarshan has widened its operation in terms of programme and duration, in order to benefit country's heterogeneous population. Presently, three types of services are being extended:

(i) Regional programmes produced in local language and transmitted at the respective programme production centres and beamed prior to the National Programme in the evening (i.e. between 5.45 p.m. to 8.40 p.m.).

(ii) Common National network programme between 8.40 to 11.15 p.m. telecast from Delhi to all television centres in the country; and

(iii) Area Specific and Development-oriented Programmes for the post-SITE and INSAT centres.

They are prepared for the respective clusters and telecast for a limited duration of 35 minutes and 40 minutes between 5.00 p.m. to 8.40 p.m.

Doordarshan has extended transmission hours throughout the country on weekends, that is, Saturday afternoons and Sunday mornings as well as in the afternoons. In not so distant a future 'breakfast television' will also be introduced. However, from 9th August, 1986 all the Low Power Transmitters in Maharashtra have been linked with Bombay and have started relaying programmes through C-Band Transponder, a process gradually to be followed by other States as a part of three-tier service.

Training for Media Personnel

Doordarshan has attached great importance to the creation of a trained cadre of professionals to meet the specific requirements of television. There are not only arrangements for inservice training, but facilities are also available at Film and Television Institute of India, Pune: Institute of Mass Communication, New Delhi, and Space Application Centre, Ahmedabad, which are utilised to strengthen the professionalism of TV personnel. A large number of experts in different fields like News and Games have also been invited for intensive workshop organised in house by Doordarshan from time to time. Employees of Doordarshan were sent for international institutes like Asia, Pacific Institute of Broadcasting Development, Kuala Lumpur for exposure and training.

Sponsored Programmes and Rural Developments

Another important deviation from its cherished path of socio-economic development of Indian people was making the TV commercial and allowing advertisements from commercial houses. Apart from consuming the precious moments of TV broadcast, these advertisements are promoting consumerism.

The thrust of normal TV programmes when shifted to entertainment bias the scope for sponsored programmes increased. The sponsored programmes indicated a strong desire to cater to the liking of urban audiences. The journey has been from Bombay films to Sherlock Homes and Spiderman. At present nearly 40 per cent of the programme content of Doordarshan, which is purely entertainment consists of sponsored programmes, song and dance sequences etc. To provide information, education and entertainment to the rural people, who are the target audience, the right kind of software is necessary. This is not forthcoming through sponsored expanded television programmes. Given the wide divergence in language, social customs, and tastes in rural India, programmes with rural development in mind should have a priority over sponsored programmes for prime time, subject, coverage etc. More often an action-oriented programmes in this area are really required. In the development of television in India, it is visible that original goal viz., development communication and educational programmes has drifted away to 'entertainment' for the urban middle or upper middle classes. It is because of commercial motives and pressures from the urban rich. TV commercials from commercial houses have started consuming precious time of TV telecast, by promoting consumerism. Programmes suitable for rural people are neglected by: (a) lack of imaginary presentation, (b) by unsuitable time of transmission, and (c) lack of participation from viewers.

Sponsored programmes have become an attractive feature of Doordarshan ever since they were introduced in 1984. They have not only widened the production base by tapping outside talent and resources, but have also helped in involving various agencies in preparing programmes of interest to the people. The danger of station which may creep into programmes entirely produced by personnel working in the organisation, is best avoided by inviting outside and non-official agencies to lend a helping hand. A degree of competitiveness also developed which will go a long way in improving the format and quality of TV programmes.

Increasing appeal of the rural viewers in sponsored programmes namely, *Buniyad, Hamlog, Rajani, Chote Bade* etc., indicates that television is defeating the purpose of rural development. The efforts to improve content, presentation style, relevance of subjects in rural development programmes is the utmost need of the time.

Among the serials on Doordarshan, while *Ghar Jamai* provides pure entertainment, *Srikant*, based on Sharat Chandra's famous novel familiarises viewers with the life-style of West Bengal. *Buniyad* having the maximum viewership among the present serials has almost taken the place of *Hum Log*, Doordarshan's maiden venture in Soap Opera. The serial is also reported to be extremely popular in the neighbouring countries such as Pakistan.

Some of the forthcoming TV serials are : *Shakuntala, Nakab, Rajya Se Svarajya Tak, Yatra, Akash Ganga, Chhota Babu, Ajeeb Musibat* and those specially produced for children namely *Appu Aur Pappu, Khel Khel Mein* and *Khoi Dishain*.

Incidentally, sponsored programmes are also an important source of revenue. All over the world, television has been an advertisers' paradise, and Doordarshan has monetarily benefited from the day it went commercial in January 1976. The revenue from advertisement has shown an upward trend from a meagre 0.77 crores in the first year, to over 62.27 crores in 1985-86. During this decade the revenue receipts increased to nearly 80 times. Even in a short period of three months from April to June 1986, the income earned 21.93 crores and it is estimated that it might touch 100 times of the 1976-77 revenue. But this lure for money has, in no way, distracted Doordarshan from its main goal of providing support to the National Developmental Plans and policies.

The role of Doordarshan is not only to entertain but also to inform and educate its viewers. To achieve this it has introduced formats from time to time to make viewers aware of the present days' problems and issues confronted by region/State/country in a futuristic perspective. The ultimate aim of these telecasts is to evoke interest among the viewers about the topical issues and motivate them to ponder over them.

With its rapid expansion Doordarshan is striving to grow a personality of its own which would be typically Indian. The Seventh Five-Year Plan makes small budgetary provision for creating necessary software. The following facets will receive urgency and eminent producers will be involved for the purpose :

(i) TV Films in different languages (60 minutes to 90 minutes),
(ii) Exclusive Video Films of local interest (30 minutes), and
(iii) Video Films for children, youth, women and Scheduled Tribes (30 minutes each).

Programme Exchange

A number of bilateral cultural agreements have been entered into by India with several countries. In addition, Doordarshan has separate protocol for exchange of programmes with TV organisations abroad. In view of the increasing interest in India's rich and colourful heritage, specially in the areas of dance, music, film lores, the demand from foreign countries for Indian TV material has considerably gone up. Even serials like *Hum Log* evoked interest among foreign buyers and organisations. A Programme Exchange and International Relations Cell has recently been set up by Doordarshan to meet these commitments.

The main aim is to communicate with the people in their own language and at the same time to make people in one part of the country aware of the rich culture and traditions of the people in other regions and to instil in them a feeling of integration with main stream of national life.

In order to achieve these objectives, a three tier service is envisaged.

Primary Service

Each major State will have its own primary service originating from the State capital in the regional language and made available throughout the State. This major studio centre in the State capital will be linked to all relay transmitters through microwave circuits or satellite.

National Service

This service will be available throughout the country with Delhi as the main production centre but drawing programmes from other States as well. It will emphasize aspects of national integration and a blend of information and entertainment so that it becomes acceptable to a wide cross-section of the society throughout the country. It will be a visually rich programme where language(s) will play a minor role.

Local Service

Local service in the local dialect/language would normally be relayed for a limited duration. Production facilities will be provided at relay transmitters in a phased manner, subject to availability of resources.

Present Utilisation of INSAT

In the end, let us present the status of utilisation of TV segment of satellite.

INSAT has facility of the transponders for telecasting

programmes simultaneously. Both the transponders are supposed to be optimally available for 16 hours daily (barring 8 hours sleeping time). Out of which Doordarshan is utilising transponder I and II approximately for 13 hours, 45 minutes and 12 hours 20 minutes respectively which are significant proportions of total utilisation (Table 2.2).

TABLE 2.2: Programmewise Daily Utilization of Two Transponders

Transponder I		Transponder II	
Service	Time	Service	Time
	Hrs.Mts.		Hrs.Mts.
ETV	3-45	Network	7-00
HETV	2-00	National Programme	2-50
ASP	3-40	News Conference	2-30
National Programme		2-50	
JDK	1-50		
Total	13-14 (86%)	Total	12-20 (77%)

This utilisation is likely to be increased further with expanding demand of the medium.

Community TV Scheme in Maharashtra

After long experimentation for 13 years, the Bombay TV Centre was commissioned in October 1972, with a coverage extending to 76 per cent urban and 24 per cent rural population. The State Government took the initiative to sponsor the Community Television Scheme, through its own Directorate of Rural Broadcasting, which has been administering the Community Radio Listening Scheme. Its technical staff were deputed for training with AIR and a separate TV division was created at Bombay for installation and maintenance of Community Television sets in the service area. Another Divisional Office was created at Pune, when the relay transmitter came up in October 1973 for extending the scheme to Pune Zone, covering 70 per cent rural and 33 per cent urban population.

The operational system of the Community TV Scheme in Maharashtra and its functional aspect is briefly explained below:

TABLE 2.3: Community TV Sets* as on April 1986

Centre	Location			Total
	School	Panchayat Ghars	Others	
1. Delhi	318	—	136	454
2. Bombay	225	1,617	272	2,114
3. Calcutta	23	3	263	289
4. Madras	140	578	20	738
5. Jalandur	4	187	9	200
6. Amritsar	125			125
7. Lucknow	248	—	571	819
8. Srinagar	236	205	138	579
9. Ahmedabad	740	—	—	740
10. Jaipur	649	—	385	1,034
11. Raipur	240			240
12. Muzaffarpur	193	24	31	248
13. Gorakhpur	816	—	—	816
14. Cuttack	614	—	3	617
15. Hyderabad	540	365	—	905
16. Gulbarga	240	—	—	240
17. Nagpur	867	—	—	867
18. Rajkot	500	—	—	500
19. Ranchi	639	—	—	639
Total				12,164

* Provisional.

Doordarshan

(a) Production and transmission of programmes,
(b) Limited supply of TV sets on behalf of Government of India under the Centrally-sponsored scheme.

Directorate General of Information and Public Relations

This controls the Directorate of Rural Broadcasting which is the executing department.

Directorate of Rural Broadcasting

Technical department is administering the hard-ware aspects of both

Community TV and Community Radio schemes. The department purchases receiver sets, as per the allocation by the District Development and Planning Councils. These sets are handed over to the Divisional Office for installation and maintenance.

The District Development and Planning Council

The District Planning and Development Council is concerned with the flow of funds. It decides the priorities in the activity-wise allocation of funds within the overall ceiling set by the Government for the particular district.

Ownership of Sets

A sum of Rs. 750 towards initial purchase and Rs. 200 towards annual maintenance costs is realised from the Gram Panchayats (Village Councils) receiving the Community Television set. The rest is subsidised by the State Government. It is the responsibility of the Gram Panchayat to arrange for the operation of the set and pay towards the electricity charges. Normally, the Panchayat Peons are deputed for the operation of the set and no additional amount is paid to them for the service.

The State Government appears to be satisfied with progress of the scheme, in terms of physical achievements, for the reason that it started with the installation of 25 sets in 1972 and the distribution of the sets as on 31-12-1983 is as under :

Pune Region : 721
Bombay Region : 369

It is gathered that approximately 80-85 sets are located in urban areas and the rest in rural areas. The contribution of Doordarshan was about 250 sets (free of cost) to promote the scheme.

Linking of LPTs in Maharashtra

Very recently a major development was achieved by linking all low power transmitters with Bombay TV (9-8-1986). This achievement has helped in bringing the TV audience nearer to programmers. Nineteen LPTs in Maharashtra linked with Delhi TV through INSAT

1B Satellite. In the premises of Bombay TV Centre remote track terminal has been installed and programmes originated from Bombay TV Studio is uplinked to satellite and via 'C' Band TVRC equipments installed at different LPTs can receive it. The programmes of Bombay TV can be seen by each LPT under its jurisdiction. Moreover LPTs will have a choice of selecting a programme either from Bombay or Delhi. A special facility of switching over Delhi and Bombay whenever LPT requires is provided. This has resulted in the feasibility of network TV Programmes from 8.40 p.m. onwards. The time from 6 to 8.40 p.m. is now devoted to Bombay TV programmes. This has given scope for transmission of regional programmes. Naturally Area Specific Programmes (ASP) could be covered for cultural enhancement. The audience of Bombay TV in Maharashtra has increased, and State had come closer for communication messages. This also has increased demands of people regarding programmes talents, subjects covered etc. Major achievement in the area of rural development can be significant because latest useful agricultural information can reach rural audience through the LPTs in Maharashtra.

This experiment will be adopted in other States also.

The month of September would always evoke fond memories in the annals of Indian history as they witnessed the emergence of television in the country with very modest beginning of one hour experimental service twice a week. It has made significant strides, both qualitative and quantitative-wise. The sage thoughts and principles underlying *Satyam, Shivam, Sundaram*, (The truth, the good, the beauty) have been the propelling force of Doordarshan, Indian acronym for television. It would not be an exaggeration to maintain that Indian television has grown as one of the biggest networks in the world in just three decades of its evolution. Through 183 transmitters the TV in India today reaches and estimated population of 70 per cent. There are 11 full-fledged centres, 5 SITE continuity centres and six INSAT stations. The remaining 157 centres are Delhi linked low power transmitters. From 9th August, 1986, all LPTs in Maharashtra have been linked with Bombay for relaying programmes through C, B and Transponder and INSAT 1B. Indeed this phenomenal expansion backed by indigenous technology is a commendable achievement and a matter to be proud of . Hence it is of prime importance to study the communication process dealing with rural development which is attempted in this thesis.

Conclusion

The increase in TV sets during the 24 years has shown a phenomenal rise showing the popularity of it in India. This increase in TV receivers is not uniform in the sense that there is a marked differentiation in different States. The States, wherein metropolitan cities are located have shown considerable number of TV receivers, for example, Delhi with 441,462 receiver sets, while Maharashtra with 901,749 sets which had four major industrially developed cities like Bombay, Pune, Nagpur and Aurangabad. In States where there is industrial development followed by urbanisation more number of TV receivers are found. The access to television to rural people is a recent innovation in majority of the states. In 1983, the LPTs were installed in different parts of India.

Starting with one experimental station at Delhi in 1958, TV broadcasting increased to 11 main Doordarshan Kendras, 5 relay centres and 183 broadcasting centres. Majority (157) of LPTs relay only network programmes telecaste from Delhi. Total population covered by Doordarshan is 43.85 crores (64%). 24.02 crores of urban population which is 85 per cent of the total urban population and 29.83 crores (56%) of the total rural population are covered by TV broadcasting.

Second channels are introduced at Delhi and Bombay to cater to the varied language and cultural groups living in these cities.

The school telecasts which were in existence since the inception of TV has further boosted by the satellite communication system for wider coverage. Recently Educational Television on all All India basis was also introduced for distance learning in higher education to bring about an improvement in the quality of education. Four educational Media Research Centres (EMRC) at Jamia Millia, Pune University, University of Gujarat and Osmania University were established to produce educational programmes for country-wide class-room telecast.

Sponsored programmes were introduced in 1984 in the All India Net-work. These programmes augmented the revenue of the Doordarshan. The gross revenue increased from Rs. 77.18 lakhs in 1976-77 to Rs. 6227.92 lakhs in 1985-86 which is phenomenal.

At the risk of over simplification it may be stated that the contents of TV has an urban stamp. Consumerism and individualism are the dominant value thrusts in our mass media fare. And entertainment is the major gratification the people seek from the radio, TV and film media. Even newspapers besides giving hard news along with radio and TV news generally serve entertainment function as would be obvious from the popularity of glossy film and gossip magazines over the serious informative ones.

India has made substantial progress since independence. The development and communication infrastructures have been enormously expanded with the result the communication and development processes have been strengthened and supporting each other taking the country forward. At the same time it is also a fact on which not many would disagree, that both development and communication processes have not been equitable and participatory enough resulting in increase of disparities.

TV though commenced with the aim of promoting the objective of socio-economic development of the rural people by disseminating of knowledge, through education and information. But during the course of expansion Doordarshan fulfilled the three widely accepted principals, namely, entertainment first, information second, and education last. The entertainment element went on increasing at the cost of education and information disseminating through their programmes. This has been amply revealed in a study of Delhi TV Centre conducted by Jha (1978) in which content analysis of one month TV programmes (May) for the years 1972 to 1978 were documented. He reported that "the consumption of transmission time by entertainment programmes ranged between 36.24 per cent and 38.40 per cent of the total transmission time followed by information programmes with time consumption ranging between 15.4 per cent and 27.8 per cent, where as the time consumption of educational programmes ranged between 7 per cent and 15.1 per cent only".

A similar finding has been reported by Raghavan (1983). According to him a content analysis of 14 days of Delhi Doordarshan offerings from 25th March, 1983 to April, 1983 showed that "feature films and film related programmes occupied the largest single chunk of telecast time, i.e., 21.1 per cent. This was followed by news and current affairs 18.9 per cent and programmes which were related to development including civic affairs, consumer prices and alike added up to less than 14 per cent.

In 1986 the analysis of one week's programmes revealed that education, information and entertainment is the order in terms of time given by TV to those programmes.

3

METHODOLOGY

In this chapter the procedures and strategies of data collection and analysis adopted for this study are discussed.

Most of the earlier studies undertaken so far on communication, in general, and on TV, in particular, deal with statistical information rather than analysing the social components involved in the context of TV communication. A few of those studies have attempted to analyse the impact of TV communication among the people. A couple of experimental studies undertaken elsewhere are, Foster (1962), Inayatullah (1967), Singh (1971), Swaroopanand (1978), F.T.I.I. (1978), Joshi, and others (1984) etc.

It would be appropriate at this juncture to acquaint ourselves with different types of methodologies that have been adopted by the earlier researchers in the field of development communication and particularly in the field of television as a medium for rural development. We get a general impression that in the past there have been mosaic studies of only three or four types. We may recollect that in his famous studies Evert Rogers (1981) attempted to evaluate the impact of Radio and Television Programmes on the viewers. He had adopted an experimental model, in order to critically evaluate the impact of a few instructional or educational programmes on the controlled and experimental samples. However, there is another type of methodology usually found in the typical impact studies. Here an attempt is made to collect informants' responses to a few selected programmes in order to judge the extent to which a particular programme has had its desired impact on the viewers. This also is a kind of experimental model only with a difference that there is no particular control group envisaged in the research design.

The SITE continuity centres have also accomplished a few studies on these lines. These studies could be termed as the 'Studies on Message System'. The method that was generally adopted is a type of content analysis. However, the researcher felt that what was lacking in these studies was the viewers' own analysis of the differential messages that were being passed on to them through various programmes.

On the more practical level a recent development in the field of research was undertaken by Doordarshan wherein the viewers are expected to send their impressions about the programmes and a careful analysis of these responses to the minor internal adjustments or modifications of particular programmes. Another method adopted by Doordarshan is a kind of formative research. Here different surveys are undertaken in order to reconstruct, 'Audience Profiles' and also the 'Need Assessment'- for the Area Specific Programmes. However, it was felt that such researches though they were invaluable for the operationality of Doordarshan, yet they lacked the Sociological relevance. Lastly, the Audience Research Wing of Doordarshan has been putting more efforts in the field of man-power utilisation, programme scheduling etc. However it is felt that they would be relevant only in so far as the perfection of the television as a mass media institution.

With this background of the different trends and methodologies in the field of research recently observed, let us now turn to the methodology adopted in this present work.

The present study focuses on the role and functioning of television on the community level. It is an attempt, therefore, to understand how rural viewer as part of the community perceives different programmes in TV in the context of his own socio-cultural mileau. This is certainly a kind of feedback study, but with a difference. The difference being that the background of the viewer is considered prominent for the presentation of the programmes. In other words, this aspect of the study makes it more sociological than mere policy-oriented research.

Keeping in view the objectives of this study it has been attempted to comprehend the position of television as a social institution *vis-a-vis* the rural people and their problems. It is further envisaged to understand the potentialities and problems of the rural masses who constitute more than 78 per cent of the Indian population. It is not more the aim of the present study, therefore, to analyse or to estimate the contribution system has provided for the people.

While the present study has been undertaken by the researcher after a considerable review and scanning of the earlier methodologies, a methodology was evolved which enabled him to contact the masses rather than treating them as just mere subjects for the study. The researcher has undertaken extensive in-depth interviews to understand their human problems which hinder their active participation with the medium.

Design of the Study

The Context

The present study has been conducted in the State of Maharashtra. In all, three districts – Pune, Satara, Ahmednagar, have been chosen for the study. These three administrative districts fell in the Western Maharashtra, which is considered as a distinct cultural region in Maharashtra.

The basic reasons for conducting this study in these three districts are the following :

(a) During the period of this study the above three districts were covered under the Poona Division for the transmission of Bombay TV Programmes.
(b) A maximum number of rural villages were covered through the Poona Relay Centre while Bombay area catered to the urban masses.
(c) A maximum number of community sets were installed by Rural Broadcasting Department in this area.
(d) Absence of scientific studies to understand this new medium of communication to be bridged.
(e) Being Poona-based, the researcher was familiar with the area and the situation which helped him a great deal in establishing rapport and data collection.

Selection of Units of Study

Having decided to concentrate in these three districts it was thought appropriate to select an adequate number of talukas from each district. The criteria for choosing the talukas was based on the transmission area coverage. Accordingly, 11 talukas from Pune and five talukas from Ahmednagar and four talukas from Satara were included in the study on random sampling basis.

FIG. 3.1: Maharashtra: Television Coverage.

The next step was to select a representative number of villages from the selected talukas. For selecting the villages it was decided that only those villages having adequate number of working television receivers were included. It was also planned not to include those villages having a higher concentration of tribal population and those areas with urban population. Thus the villages within 10 to 12 km radius from Pune city in Haveli taluka and also a couple of tribal villages from Ambegaon taluka have been left out from the study. A few villages, though covered under transmission could not be included in the study mainly because of the following reasons :

(a) Sets were out of order for a long time,
(b) Poor reception and thus less viewing,
(c) Far away from approachable roads,
(d) Minor political disturbances and non-cooperation from the viewers.

Considering the above factors in all, 304 villages were finally selected for the study (Table 3.1).

TABLE 3.1: Districtwise Villages covered under Study

District	No. of Villages
Pune	160
Ahmednagar	49
Satara	95
Total	304

Rapport Establishment

For the final selection of the villages a number of visits were initially made to the taluka headquarters for discussion and to take help from Block Development Officers (BDOs) and later to the village Sarpanchas and Gram Sevaks or Village Level Workers (VLWs). The study started in the month of September 1982. During the preliminary visits the researcher stayed in few selected villages to get acquainted with the people and officials of the villages. Although no attempts were made during these visits to fill in the schedule, a set of questions in the form of pilot survey were administered to gather adequate information. These visits proved useful to the researcher to strengthen his contacts with the villagers in an informal way.

Research Hypothesis

Although no specific theoretical orientation or conceptualisation has been envisaged for this study, certain broad research hypothesis have been adopted so as to give the study a direction and momentum. Following are the major hypothesis formulated for this study, namely, whether

(1) the extension of TV coverage would meet the basic communication needs of the masses in these rural villages.
(2) the conventional media system and the traditional media systems would not clash with the TV communication.
(3) the television media in rural areas is more popular as an entertainment medium rather than as an instructional medium.
(4) illiteracy is a barrier to understand and appreciate TV communication or not.
(5) the community TV in the village acts as a boon to the masses who do not have other medium of communication.
(6) community TV bridges the gap between the "media haves" and "media have-nots".
(7) television helps in the process of political socialisation of the illiterates.
(8) it is beneficial for transferring the technical know-how of agriculture to the rural population.
(9) it adds to the knowledge and awareness of the people.
(10) educational programmes help in rural development.

Pretesting of Schedule

Before finalising the interview schedule a pretesting of the interview schedule was conducted in a couple of selected villages. In all five villages were administered and the schedule reconstructed on the basis of the responses. The pretesting had helped the researcher in clarifying certain operational definitions for certain items such as :

Regularity in paper reading, movie going, radio listening etc., which were later on classified as 'regular', 'partly regular' and 'irregular'.

While selecting the respondents the researcher did not have many options for employing any specific sampling techniques. The custodian(s) who kept the community sets were hardly one or two officials in the village. Thus the sampling procedure adopted here may be termed as 'purposive sampling'. However, for contacting the respondents for the 160 schedules care has been taken to cover 10 to 12 individuals from each village at random. It may be mentioned in this context that a discrepancy in the form of more weightage for the male respondents has creeped into the data. The proportion between male and female respondents works out to be 84 per cent and 16 per cent respectively. This imbalance may be justified considering the less number of adult females, who were among the custodians. Secondly, field situations we also not convenient for the researcher to collect the required information at ease from the female respondents.

The age of the respondents ranged between 18 and 50 years.

Tools of Study

Interview Schedule

The researcher used three different schedules for data collection. After a considerable efforts on rapport establishment an interview schedule was constructed. The first schedule contained structured, semi-structured as well as open ended questions. This schedule at its initial part gathered information pertaining to the village as a whole. Questions on communication facilities, basic census, landuse and cropping patterns, education, health-care facilities etc., were included in the schedule.

The second schedule dealt with the information regarding community TV sets.

The third interview schedule elucidated information from the respondents, from the villages surveyed. In all 464 viewers were interviewed in the above 304 villages. Out of these 464 respondents, 304 were also handling the responsibility as a custodians. The data regarding the functioning of community TV sets has been gathered form these custodians. The data pertaining to general information about the villages was also collected from these custodians. This section contained both quantitative as well as qualitative information. The schedule in general was aimed to collect data on specific aspects like media participation, interaction with urban area or extension workers, utilisation of TV, educational level, political awareness, informational needs and respondents' occupation. It also tried to cover questions regarding their knowledge or awareness of various programmes, their preferences for programmes viewing, their convenience and suggestions for improvement in the quality of the programmes. This part of the schedule also contained many open ended questions inviting their critical comments and attitudes towards various programmes. Thus in all 464 respondents have been included for the study. For the convenience of statistical deductions the total sample of 464 has been taken together for the Part III of the schedule, while only 304 respondents have been included for the first and second part of the schedule. The reason for merging 304 schedules with the 160 for the Part III may be explained on the basis of many factors commonly shared by the respondents. Excepting the official status the custodians of all these community TV sets could be treated at par with many other common viewers.

Case Studies

A few case studies were also conducted among the respondents with a view to analyse their specific communication needs and information seeking behaviour. They were based on indepth interviews and participant observation. This data mostly qualitative was guided with the help of an unstructured open-ended interview guide. The case studies were found to be quite useful in understanding peoples' perception like patterns, aspirations and communication needs with reference to the TV programmes.

The method of observation adopted by the researcher, as a participant helped him to comprehend the peoples' reaction, comments and facial expressions while viewing TV.

An Experiment with Programme Feedback

In addition to the above-mentioned tools employed for the data collection the researcher has also experimented in some villages on playback of certain video programmes with the help of port-a-pak video equipment. These programmes were mainly rural-oriented with a theme and message. Indepth interviews were conducted with the viewers soon after the playback. Their reactions on the content presentation as well as their perception and comprehension were recorded. A couple of such experiments have also been given in this thesis.

Analysis of Data

After completion of the entire field-work which occupied the researcher nearly for two years, the schedules were arranged and the responses were coded for easy handling of the data. A master table was constructed systematically entering the recorded data. The entire data, then was transferred into a floppy for further computer processing. Initially a set of 160 schedules at random were processed for the frequency distribution of the various parameters. This exercise enabled the researcher to check the variables and the responses for their accuracy. Further, after necessary corrections and adjustments the distribution tables for all the important variables were obtained.

A selected number of independent and dependent variables were cross-tabulated with a view to test various research hypotheses mentioned in this chapter. Chi-square (χ^2) test has been employed to verify the association between any two variables considered in the contingency tables. The formula employed is given as under :

$$\chi^2 = \frac{(O-E)^2}{E}$$

where, O is the observed values and E the expected values, depending on the degree of Freedom (d.f.) calculated the χ^2 values were checked against the Yates tables for the distribution of significance level and the χ^2 values were considered significant only when they showed the level of significance beyond 5 per cent level. In the contingency tables the percentage for both column tables and the row totals have also been given. The entire data processing has been done on IBM Compatible C19.

4

MEDIA FACILITIES IN VILLAGES

The present chapter aims at presenting some of the basic data about the villages that have been surveyed for our research. As it was made clear in Chapter 3 on Methodology the researcher canvassed an interview schedule in order to gather some objective information regarding the geographical, demographic and socio-cultural details about the villagers under study. They are detailed as follows:

(1) Total population of the village
(2) Total number of households in the village
(3) Different types of land available in the village
(4) Physical distance from the nearest TV Centre, City, Railway Station, Bus Stop etc.
(5) Condition of the access road to the village
(6) Information related to Community Radio sets in the village
(7) Various formal and informal groupings in the village, e.g., Bhajan Mandals, Mahila Mandals etc.
(8) Different facilities such as schools, dairy, poultry, public health centre etc.

Since the information could not be obtained in its most reliable form from about six villages, out of the total sample of 310 villages, only 304 villages, were considered for the analysis of the data in the work. It is to be further clarified at this juncture that certain minute details have been omitted for convenience from the tabulation, which are not relevant to the study.

The population of Maharashtra as obtained from 1981 Census report is given in Table 4.1.

Table 4.2 depicts the district-wise distribution of 304 villages covered in the study. The table also indicates the higher percentage (52.63%) from Pune district. This is obvious as the installation of Community TV sets had been looked after by Rural Broadcasting

Department (RBD) of Government of Maharashtra. They had distributed a majority (80%) of these Community sets in Pune District. Moreover, the Pune transmitter at Sinhagarh covers a major part of Pune District. Hence, the number of sets depended on the area covered under Sinhagarh transmission. Therefore, the sample of CTVs in villages are selected in proportion to the number of villages under transmission area covered by RBD of Maharashtra.

TABLE 4.1: Number of Villages and Population of Maharashtra

State/District	Number of Villages in Maharashtra			Population	
	Inhabited	Uninhabited	Total	Rural	Urban
Maharashtra	39,354	2,479	41,833	4,07,90,572	21,99,594
Pune	1,468	13	1,481	21,92,245	19,70,039
Ahmednagar	1,301	11	1,312	23,59,283	351,933
Satara	1,417	20	1,437	98,97,220	10,49,555

Source: 1981 Census Report.

TABLE 4.2: Districtwise Distribution of the Villages

District	Number of Villages	
Pune	160	(52.63%)
Ahmednagar	85	(31.25%)
Satara	49	(16.12%)
Total	304	(100.00%)

Table 4.3 describes the talukawise distribution of the villages covered in the study. It is to be noted that the highest number of villages are in the talukas of Phaltan, Kharmala, Baramati, Shirur and Parner. Whether a village should have a Community TV set or not is decided by the Government. The installation of community TV was of politico-administrative in nature rather than option indicated by the villagers in the villages. They are not supposed to contribute any of their efforts in the procurement of community TV sets. A village in order to receive the broadcasts should fall within the area of the relay centre then only they are in a position to view the TV programmes.

TABLE 4.3: Talukawise Distribution of the Villages

Taluka	Number of Villages	
Purandhar	10	(3.29)
Mulshi	9	(2.96)
Bhor	5	(1.64)
Baramati	35	(11.51)
Ambegaon	23	(7.57)
Daund	4	(1.32)
Shirur	32	(10.53)
Junnar	14	(4.61)
Khed	14	(4.61)
Indapur	9	(2.96)
Haveli	5	(1.64)
Kharmala	35	(11.51)
Phaltan	48	(15.79)
Wai	2	(0.66)
Mahabaleshwar	2	(0.66)
Satara	8	(2.63)
Srigonda	15	(4.93)
Ahmednagar	3	(0.99)
Akola	3	(0.99)
Parner	28	(9.21)

Table 4.4 deals with the population of villages. In two villages, population data could not be obtained. Majority of the villages (71.7%) included in the present study have population between 1001 to 5000. Nearly 16 per cent of the villages are actually been townships or semi-urbanised centres according to the accepted definition of urban areas, with a population of more than 5,000. However, there are 26 (8.55%) of villages with a population of 501 to 1000 which can be classified as a small village.

Looking at the population size of the villages, we observed majority of the villages (71.7%) have only one community TV set in the village, irrespective of the population. The probability of the responsibility's exposure to TV was less in high population villages compared to low population ones. Furthermore, it was felt that as the high population villages may have higher infrastructure. These factors influenced TV viewing behaviour of the people in these villages. This could be justified that tendency of getting CTV in these villages has more chance because of the overall development of village. The respondents informed the researcher that they took active lead and approached the Government for CTV installation in their village.

TABLE 4.4: Population of Villages under Survey

Population Range	Number of Villages	
Up to100	3	(0.99%)
101 to 500	6	(1.97%)
501 to 1000	26	(8.55%)
1001 to 5000	218	(71.71%)
5001 to 10,000	43	(14.14%)
10001 to 15,000	6	(1.97%)
15,000 and above	2	(0.66%)
Total	304	(100.00%)

It is also observed from Table 4.4 that in majority of the villages 218 (71.71%) the population is in the range of 1000 to 5000. In 2.63 per cent of the villages the population is more than 10,000. This means that villages are mostly scattered in population range of 1,000 to 10,000. This also indicates that for this population one community TV set is not enough.

TABLE 4.5: Population in Agricultural Occupation *Vs.* Number of Villages

Number of Persons	Number of Villages	
Up to 50	3	(0.99%)
51 to 100	9	(2.96%)
101 to 500	183	(60.19%)
501 to 1,000	72	(23.68%)
1001 to 1,500	21	(6.90%)
1501 to 2,000	10	(3.29%)
2001 to 3,000	6	(1.97%)
Total	304	(100.00%)

It is seen from the above table that in 255 (83.87%) of the villages, majority are engaged in agricultural occupation. The population range of these villages varies from 100 to 1000. This indicates that agriculture is the main occupation.

Table 4.6 highlights that in 129 (42.43%) of the villages with population up to 500 have dominated by agricultural labourers. Even villages with higher population range of 501 to 5,000 have indicated griculture labour population.

TABLE 4.6: Population of Agricultural Labourers

Population	Number of Villages	
Up to 50	45	(24.67%)
51 to 100	62	(20.39%)
100 to 500	129	(42.43%)
501 to 1,000	23	(7.56%)
1,001 to 1,500	6	(1.97%)
1,501 to 2,000	1	(0.33%)
2,001 to 3,000	8	(2.63%)
Total	304	(100.00%)

It is observed that in majority of villages they do not have irrigated water supply, hence they depend on rainwater for cultivation. Consequently we find that majority of the farmers grow *Jawar* and *Bajari*, while in villages which have irrigated water or underground water, which is tapped by borewells and the farmers grow sugarcane as a cash crop.

TABLE 4.7: Cash Crops in Villages *Vs*. Number of Villages

Cash Crops	Number of Villages			Total
	Pune	Ahmednagar	Satara	
Rice	23	—	7	25
Rice, Sugarcane	5	—	—	5
Rice, Potato, Onions	23	—	—	23
Sugarcane	41	46	88	175
Potatoes, Onions	14	—	—	14
Onions, Jawar	30	—	—	30
Sugarcane, Tobacco	—	3	—	3
Sugarcane, Ginger	—	—	5	5
Vegetables	15	—	—	15
Sugarcane, Jawar	9	—	—	9
Total	160	49	95	304

In Maharashtra the Sugar Co-operative Societies have been established in a big way. Farmers joined the Sugar Cooperatives and agreed to grow sugarcane and supply the same to the sugar factories. This movement is very strong in Maharashtra and we find that in 175 villages in all the three districts sugarcane is grown as the only cash crop. Besides this a few villages grow sugarcane along with other cash crops.

TABLE 4.8: Major Crops

Major Crops	Number of Villages			Total
	Pune	Ahmednagar	Satara	
Jawar, Bajra	115	32	50	197
Jawar, Wheat	—	2	24	26
Jawar, Rice	25	—	—	25
Jawar	1	14	—	15
Jawar, Bajari, Rice	6	—	—	6
Jawar, Bajari, Wheat	4	1	—	5
Bajari, Wheat	3	—	—	3
Rice Nachani	—	—	2	2
Rice, Ragi	5	—	—	5
Total	160	49	95	304

It is observed from the above table that *Jawar* and *Bajra* are the major crops of 197 villages, while *Jawar* and Wheat and rice are grown in 26 villages. Only in 25 villages of Pune District, *Jawar* and Rice are grown as major crops.

TABLE 4.9: Crop Protection Society Markets and Co-operative Banks in Villages

Type of Facilities	Yes	No
Crop Protection Society	121 (39.80)	183 (60.20)
Markets	69 (22.70)	235 (77.30)
Co-operative Banks	90 (29.61)	214 (70.39)

In all the villages dominant occupation of the majority of the people is agriculture. Facilities like Crop Protection Society, Market, Cooperative Bank are essential for protection of crops, marketing of their produce and Bank loan facilities. It is observed that these are essential amenities and are not available to more than 60 per cent of the villages. From the development point of view only 22.70 per cent of the villages have market of their own, while 29.61 per cent of the villages have Cooperative Banks in the village itself.

TABLE 4.10: Population *Vs.* Number of TV sets (CTV and Private TVs)

District	No. of Villages under study	Total Population of Villages under study	No. of CTV sets in Villages	Total No. of Private TV sets in Villages
Pune	160	4,92,252	389	720
Ahmednagar	49	1,61,420	73	60
Satara	95	2,62,347	146	175
Total	304	9,16,019	608	955

Ratio of Population to CTV sets 916019/608 = 1506.42
i.e., One Community TV set caters to 1506.42 viewers, which is far below UNESCO Standard.

Though there are 955 private TV sets, in the villages, they cater only to their family members.

Table 4.10 indicates the inadequacy of community TV sets in villages as compared to the population size of villages. It is also observed that one CTV caters to 1506.42 viewers which is far below the UNESCO standard. This also helps us to foresee problems of comprehension, appeal, credibility of TV programmes in addition to physical arrangement of CTV.

TABLE 4.11: Number of CTVs provided by R.B., Pune during the period from 1980–86

District	1980-81	1981-82	1982-83	1983–86 (Up to 31-10-86)
Pune	343	386	466	806
Satara	144	161	169	219
Ahmednagar	69	79	86	178
Total	556	626	721	1203

It is observed from the above table that 106 villages had no private TV sets, while 133 villages had 3 TV sets per village. In the largely populated villages (65) had 4 to 11 private TV sets. It was also noticed that private TV sets are available only to the family members.

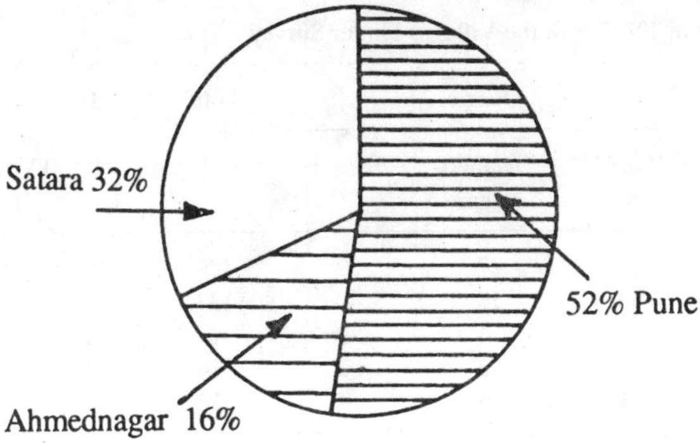

No. of private and community sets in villages Pune, Ahmedangar, Satara under study

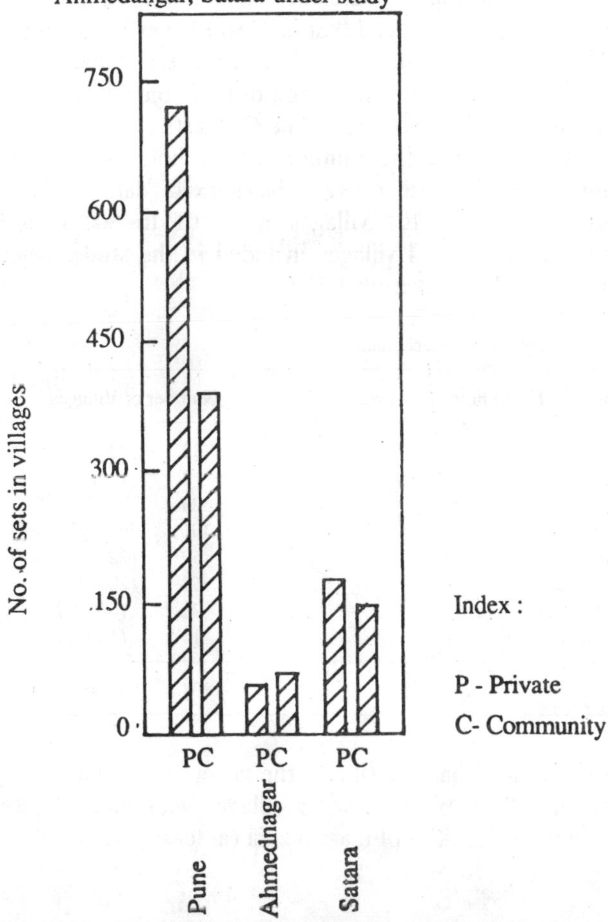

FIG. 4.1: Number of Villages Under Study (in percentage).

TABLE 4.12: Private TV Sets in the Villages Under Survey

No. of sets	District			Total No. of Villages	Total No. of Pvt. TV sets
	Pune	Ahmed-Nagar	Satara		
Nil	40	27	39	106	—
1 to 3	80	13	40	133	399
4 to 6	16	4	9	29	174
7 to 10	9	2	3	14	140
7 to 10	15	3	4	22	242
Total	160	49	95	304	955

It is understood that Maharashtra Government supplies CTVs in a phased manner. We noticed that in 1980-81 they installed only 556 sets, while in 1983–86 only 1203 CTV sets are installed. We found that out of 4,230 villages in the three districts only 3,106 have CTV sets while in 1,124 villages there are no CTVs still.

Table 4.13 describes the number of households in the villages of our sample. In the case of 12 villages exact data could not be obtained. There are 101 villages with 101 to 300 households. However, there were 14 villages included in the study, where the number of households exceeds 1,500.

TABLE 4.13: Number of Households

Number of Households	Number of Villages	
Don't know	12	(3.95%)
Up to 50	2	(0.66%)
51 to 100	24	(7.89%)
101 to 300	101	(33.22%)
301 to 500	69	(22.70%)
501 to 1000	61	(20.07%)
1001 to 1500	21	(6.91%)
1501 and above	14	(4.61%)
Total	304	(100.00%)

It was thought that the size of the village was related to media participation. Probably the larger villages with more households could have more facilities of mass media (at least in terms of number of radio sets, newspapers and TV) than smaller villagers. This could result in higher levels of participation. In this sense the larger villages were more open to outside influences than smaller villages.

It is seen from Table 4.14 that in majority of villages from our sample 290 have two CTVs while a few big villages had three CTVs, while a lone village with a population of 15,000 had five Community Television Sets.

TABLE 4.14: Number of CTVs Available in the Villages

No. of Villages	No. of CTVs Available	Total
8	1	8
290	2	580
5	3	15
1	5	5
304	11	608

Communication, although an essential ingredient of change, is nevertheless dependent on other inputs from other sectors including such things as roads, buildings, and other environmental conveniences, educational facilities, technological development and ancillary services, supply etc. The success of communication depends on joint and cooperative action and calls for the needed coordinating machinery and for policy planning, which takes such needs and such interdependence into consideration (Lakshman Rao, 1972, p.25).

Proper communication networks are important for development of a village. New ideals, innovations and modernisation can percolate into village life and society when adequate modern communication systems are available to the villagers. The geographical location of a village and its nearness to urban centres and their proximity to the railway station, and bus stand, will provide opportunities for the individuals to commuate and interact with other communities, thereby dissemination of ideas and knowledge takes place. This in turn, provides basic framework for development. The network of roads leading to urban centres is also an important factor contributing to modernisation and development. Let us now turn to these infrastructural facilities available to our villagers under our sample.

In earlier days radio was thought to be an innovative

breakthrough in the field of development communication. The government had installed community radio sets in large number of villages. We are now trying to understand the level of people's being used to the mass media.

TABLE 4.15: Distance from TV Centre

Distance from TV Centre	Number of Villages	
Up to 3 km	5	(1.64%)
Up to 10 km	4	(1.32%)
11 km and above	295	(97.04%)
Total	304	(100.00%)

The above table indicates the physical distance between the villages and the nearest TV relay centre. It is to be noted that in case of 97.04 per cent villages the distance has been more than 11 km and above still are within the area of relay centre. So all the villages in the sample are in a position to view the TV programmes.

To communicate with people from outside the village depends on the infrastructural facilities available in the villages. If the villages want to have interpersonal communications with others from other areas transport facilities are essential. The transport system connecting the village to other areas is discussed below.

Distance from urban centres is an important factor of communication, because modern ideas, values and knowledge can be obtained by interaction with urbanites.

Table 4.16 indicate that in majority of cases the nearest urban centre is at a distance of 12 km or more. Further the provision of CTV can play a very important role since it is the only available medium and it is the main place of interaction, for the villagers. Naturally the communication through television programmes could have a direct impact on the development of the village. If communicators fail to reach this potential target audience it is likely that Government will find it difficult in achieving the aims of rural development. It is essential to capture the attention of the rural audience in prime time to give the messages of rural development for achieving rural development.

It is essential to reconstruct the profiles of the villages in terms of their nearness to the city, bus station, railway station etc., in order to throw light on the extent of the urban way of life to which these villages have been subjected to.

TABLE 4.16: Distance from the Nearest City

Distance	Number of Villages	
Less than 1 km	3	(0.99%)
Up to 3 km	8	(2.63%)
4 to 6 km	13	(4.28%)
7 to 11 km	37	(12.17%)
12 and more	243	(79.93%)
Total	304	

TABLE 4.17: Distance from Railway Station

Distance	Number of Villages	
In village	5	(1.64%)
Up to 3 km	13	(4.28%)
3 to 5 km	9	(2.96%)
6 to 10 km	43	(14.14%)
11 and more	234	(76.97%)
Total	304	

Tablc 4.17 shows the distance of villages from the nearest railway station. It has been found that 5 (1.64%) of the villages have a railway station right in the village itself. While 234 (76.97%) villages are located at a distance of 11 km and above. The need for collecting such data are to assess accessibility of the important factors in the study related to our communication.

Table 4.17 explains the contact and communication facilities available for the majority of the villages under study. As seen from the data in the table that Railway Station, which are considered as the economic and quick mode of communication, is at a distance of 11 km and more for majority 234 (76.97%) of the villages. This naturally indicates the dependence on road transport. In case the CTV set goes out of order, majority of villages have no option other than informing the RBD or bring mechanic from city by road. This also indicates that only two per cent of villages could take benefit of Railway for the repair of their TV sets.

A few studies (Jesudason, 1977) have shown that urban contact and participation in mass media are essential and are associated with TV viewing behaviour (SITE, 1977). Perhaps all these are the indicators of modern outlook. It may be recalled here that the villages selected under study were within Bombay TV Kendra served by Sinhagarh transmitter at Pune. These villages were approachable by jeep.

Table 4.18 indicates the distance of village from the nearest bus stop. It is observed that more than one-fourth of the villages are located in a comparatively remote geographical areas wherefrom the nearest bus stop is more than 10 km (25.33%) away. For these villages both train and bus transportation is far away and inaccessible.

TABLE 4.18: Distance from Bus-stop

Distance	Number of Villages	
In village	97	(31.91%)
Up to 3 km	38	(12.50%)
4 to 5 km	22	(7.24%)
6 to 10 km	70	(23.33%)
11 and more	77	(25.33%)
Total	304	

Nearly 31.91 per cent of the villages have bus stop in the village itself. Out of the remaining nearly 42.77 per cent of the villages have to travel a distance of 3 to 10 km to reach the nearest bus-stop. It is noticed that villagers often prefer the bus transportation for going to nearby urban areas than by the train, because of infrequent trains and odd timings of the trains. It is also noticed that villagers for all their major necessities have to communicate by bus to city. This might help us to conclude that for contact with the city, bus is the only effective mode of communication. It is also to be considered essential that maintenance of CTV could be done effectively without delay provided the information regarding the faults in CTV is conveyed to Rural Broadcasting Office to enable the authorities to take prompt action to depute TV technician.

It is very important to know the basic transportation facilities that are present in these villages and the infrastructural facilities that are available to the villagers.

TABLE 4.19: Condition of Roads

Condition of Roads	No. of Villages	
Kutcha	6	(1.18%)
Motorable	140	(46.05%)
Metal	3	(0.99%)
Brick	1	(0.33%)
Murum	(17)	(5.59%)
All Seasons	112	(36.84%)
Not operational in rainy seasons	25	(8.22%)
Total	304	

Table 4.19 depicts the condition of the access road to the villages under study. While nearly 46 per cent of the villages have been connected by motorable roads, nearly 15 per cent of the villages have very poor seasonal access facilities. However, it is seen that 144 (47.37%) of the villages are connected by motorable metal or brick roads. All 118 (38.02%) of the villages can be approached without much difficulty during all seasons.

It is also seen that 8.22 per cent of the villages are inaccessible during rainy season as the existing roads are submerged under water and makes it very difficult to use these roads. This also helps us to think that participation in CTV viewing could have factors like demographic characteristics along with socio-economic factors. In real sense contact with urban areas could influence on TV viewing behaviour.

Earlier studies have indicated that in almost all development-oriented activities including communication, a higher percentage of the people from socio-economic status (i.e., the 'haves') participated than the people of lower socio-economic status (i.e., the 'have not'). For example, in a village study aimed to determine the importance of communication in the adoption process of utilising the high yielding varieties of seeds, it was shown that the size of land holding was an important factor. The greater the size, the greater was the exposure to publicity material over radio, newspapers etc. (IIMC, 1968).

The above table deals with the information about availability of community radio sets in the village. These data are important insofar as these show the number of villages already prepared with the mass media being shared at the level of the community itself while a majority (267 – 87.83%) of the villages have been making use of the community radio sets: only in 37 villages (12.17%) do not enjoy the facility.

TABLE 4.20: Community Radio Sets

Reply	Number of Villages	
Yes	267	(87.83%)
No	37	(12.17%)
Total	304	

Installation of community radio sets as a part of village self-government (Panchayati Raj) has been in operation for quite a few years. The farm market information programmes of AIR have been popular with farmers. The commercial film songs programmes have been popular with young people. The majority of the sample villages had electricity, so they are used to radios. Transistors were found in at least in few houses in most of the villages. Further a few of the villages that were on the main road served by buses often had tea shops which also owned radio sets. So respondents in our study were exposed to and familiar with radio broadcasts.

It is also assumed that the participation in mass media is an acquired habit. So it can be expected that people who were familiar with listening to radio broadcasts i.e., they acquired the habit and would also view TV frequently.

TABLE 4.21: Number of Private Radio Sets Available in the Villages

No. of Radio sets	No. of Villages	
1 to 10	30	(9.87%)
11 to 25	38	(12.50%)
26 to 50	56	(18.42%)
51 to 100	30	(9.87%)
101 and more	92	(30.26%)
Don't know the number	58	(19.08%)
Total	304	

Table 4.21 gives the data about the number of private radio sets available in the villages. Exact number could not be ascertained in

the case of 58 villages. Nearly 30.26 per cent of the villages have more than 100 radio sets in each one of them. This indicates the fact that the villagers are not only aware of the importance of the mass media and are educated enough to make use of it for personal benefit.

The data from Table 4.22 shows the community radio tuning time. It is to be noted that in 103 (33.88%) of the villages where the community radio set is out of order for a long time. This may be due to the fact that as the number of privately owned radio sets increased the importance and care of community sets decreased. However, it is also observed that in 116 (38.16%) villages, the community radio is put to work during noons, afternoons and evenings.

We find negligence in maintenance of community radio sets, surprisingly the villages which had community radio sets working they utilised it throughout the day. The villages where radio sets were out of order due to apathy the people have not reported the matter to government, Department of Rural Broadcasting, which was responsible for maintenance of these sets. It is understood from the Rural Broadcasting Department that due to heavy workload of maintenance of community TV sets, radio sets, repair work could not be attended to promptly. Moreover, the majority of old community radio sets were valve sets and their spares were not available. In addition, the trend of using private transistors is increasingly seen in these villages, hence neglect of community radio sets.

TABLE 4.22: Community Radio Tuning Time

Tuning Time	Number of Villages	
No Community Radio	14	(1.32%)
Morning	17	(5.59%)
Noon	1	(0.33%)
Evening	14	(4.61%)
Not Working	103	(33.88%)
Daily	5	(1.64%)
Noon and Evening	116	(38.16%)
Don't tune	35	(11.51%)
Don't listen	9	(2.96%)
Total	304	

Table 4.23 clearly indicates that radio is heard in villages for programmes like News, Agriculture, Film songs, crop information

and other programmes also. In spite of the fact that radio sets were available in villages, apparently participation in the mass medium was still a prerogative of a few (8%). Perhaps the combination of audio with video in TV medium was able to attract people, who rarely listened to radios. Similar trend was established in SITE studies. A higher proportion of people who reported frequent radio listening habit in the pre-SITE survey also reported frequent TV viewing (Agrawal Pre-SITE, 1975).

TABLE 4.23: Hearing of Radio Programmes

Type of Programmes	No. of villages	
News	9	(2.96%)
•Agriculture	9	(2.96%)
Film Music	3	(0.99%)
News and Crops	5	(1.64%)
News and Agriculture	4	(1.32%)
News, Agriculture and Bhavgeet	3	(0.99%)
News, Agriculturc, Film Music, Climate	3	(0.99%)
All Programmes	24	(7.89%)
News/Agriculture/Film Songs	6	(1.97%)
News/Film Music	12	(3.95%)
News/Agriculture/Film Music/Mahila Mandal	4	(1.32%)
Don't listen to Community Radio Programmes	148	(48.68%)
Total	304	

It is to noted that nearly 148 (48.68%) villages, as far as the community sets are concerned, do not listen to any programmes whatsoever. In the case of 24 villages (7.89%), however, it is observed that the community set is put on for all the programmes such as news, agriculture, film music and classical music etc. However, it is noted that in the case of nine villages (2.96%) the villagers preferred to listen to only agriculture programmes and news.

In villages generally, schools, libraries and Panchayat Offices serve as disseminators of knowledge and information. Dissemination of knowledge is a prerequisite for modernisation. Adoption of modern techniques and methods particularly in agriculture and other occupations will bring forth economic development in villages. Social activities contribute to interaction with knowledge to people and provides per dissemination of information.

TABLE 4.24: Other Facilities Available in the Villages

Other facilities	Reply			
	Yes		No	
Library	136	(44.74%)	168	(55.26%)
Panchayat Office	279	(71.78%)	25	(8.22%)
Place for Social Activity	257	(84.54%)	47	(15.46%)
School	289	(95.07%)	15	(4.93%)
High School	145	(47.70%)	159	(52.30%)
College	38	(12.50%)	266	(87.50%)

While assessing the availability of these facilities in the villages of our sample we notice that in large number of villages Panchayat Offices, (71.78%), places for Social Activities (84.54%) and Primary Schools are available (95.07%). Public library facilities, however, are not available in majority (55.26%) of the villages. Even though most of the villages have primary schools, only in 47.70 per cent of the villages had high schools and 12.50 per cent had colleges. Maharashtra Government has introduced compulsory Primary Education in the State. To facilitate and implement this scheme there are government established primary schools which are available in almost all villages. However, high schools and colleges should have some minimum number of students, so high schools and colleges are expected to cater to a number of villages. Students can have primary education at their door step while for high school and for college education they have to shift to nearby Taluka or District Headquarters. This eventually would lead to dropping out of school in the case of a number of children.

Normally in villages private doctors are scarce. Even when there are private clinics, the majority of the rural population cannot afford to go to the doctors due to economic reasons. So for the maintenance of health and hygiene of the rural people, primary health centre is essential. Similarly, veterinary hospitals are also needed in the villages since the villagers normally keep life stock with them.

It is seen from Table 4.25, that in 61.19 per cent of the villages there are dairy facilities, while in 81.58 per cent of villages there are no poultry maintained. Equally there is inadequate facilities of primary health centre and veterinary hospital i.e. 71.71 per cent of villages have no health centre and 66.45 per cent of them have no veterinary hospitals.

TABLE 4.25: Availability of Health Centre, Poultry, Dairy Facilities

Facilities	Reply			
	Yes		No	
Primary Health Centre	86	(28.29%)	218	(71.71%)
Veterinary Hospital	102	(33.55%)	202	(66.45%)
Poultry	56	(18.39%)	248	(81.58%)
Dairy	186	(61.19%)	118	(38.42%)

The inadequacy of the above-mentioned facilities can be considered as negative developmental indices of the villages.

It is seen from Table 4.26 that private medical facilities like dispensary, doctor or nurse are not available in more than 54 per cent of the villages. Hence dependence on Primary Health Centre is obvious.

TABLE 4.26: Availability of Medical and Other Facilities in Villages

Facilities	Reply			
	Yes		No	
Private Dispensary	138	(45.40%)	166	(54.61%)
Doctor	139	(45.72%)	165	(54.28%)
Nurse	121	(39.80%)	183	(60.20%)
Vaidu	270	(69.08%)	94	(30.92%)
Police Station	258	(84.87%)	46	(15.13%)

When the researcher tried to examine the relationships of indicators of socio-economic status and health parameters with TV viewing behaviour, it can be seen that except dairy, other economic facilities like PHC, Veterinary Hospital, Poultry are lacking in majority of the villages. In this area it can be stated that differential exposure to CTV could result in different levels of change. In areas of health, education etc., rural people are making use of the inputs from the mass media TV.

At this juncture it is essential to know whether the traditional institutions of entertainment are present or absent in the villages. The information relating to these entertainment institutions would be valuable in so far as it would help us to understand whether television can act as a substitute to the traditional entertainment. It was also attempted to understand the background of the villages in terms of their awareness and use of the earlier dominant mediums of communications.

TABLE 4.27: Other Entertainments

Other Entertainments	Reply	
	Yes	No
Village Play Mandals	87 (28.62)	217 (71.38)
Mahila Mandals	112 (36.84)	192 (63.16)
Gymnasium	97 (31.91)	207 (68.09)
Mobile Cinema House	20 (6.58)	284 (93.42)
Bhajani Mandals	263 (86.51)	41 (13.49)
Tamasha	56 (8.55)	278 (91.45)

Table 4.27 and Fig. 4.2 show about the presence of various classical/traditional channels of entertainment in the Indian Rural Society. It has been a part and parcel of the rural India that the institutions considered here would make up for traditional patterns of entertainment.

Primary and Secondary or formalised type of social groupings would be facilitated under the name of the above institutions to make the village society self-sufficient even in its entertainment or leisure time activities. In villages some of the classical entertainment mediums such as *Tamasha* and village play mandals are withering away. Once popular Mobile Cinema Houses are becoming extinct. As regards *Bhajani Mandal*, however, it is to be noted that they are not only have survived in the present era but have also grown in strength (86.51%).

Other entertainments were found to be popular entertainment among the villages under study. As cinema theatres are established in urban areas and small towns, often villagers combine their visit to an urban centre with a visit to cinema theatre. Some studies carried out in USA have shown that when commercial TV was introduced a

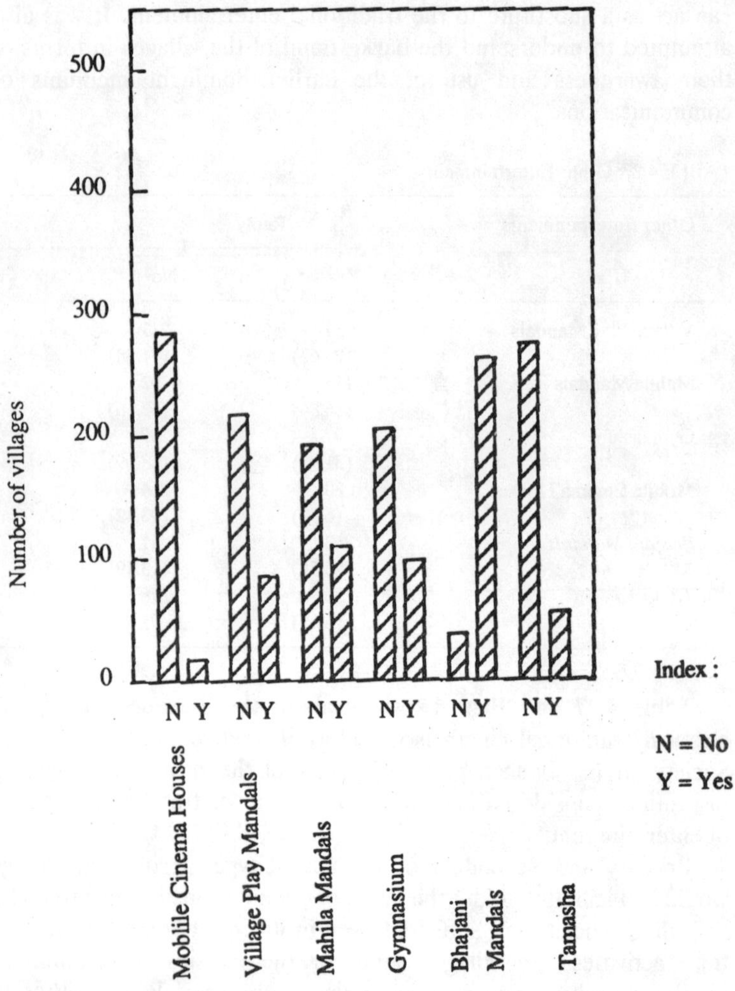

FIG. 4.2: Other Entertainments.

higher proportion of the people who had the habit of going to movies were the first ones to purchase it (Himmelvvet et al., 1950). So it can be expected that the people who visit cinema frequently would shift to watching CTV more frequently than others, who do not have that habit.

TABLE 4.28: Postal Services Available in Villages

Facilities	Reply			
	Yes		No	
Post Office	235	(77.30%)	69	(22.70%)
Telegraph Office	46	(15.13%)	258	(85.87%)
Telephone Office	74	(24.35%)	230	(75.66%)

It is observed from the above table that majority of the villages (77.30%) have Post Offices but do not have telegraph offices (85.87%) and telephone offices (75.66%) in their villages. This clearly shows that the villagers do not possess the modern speedy communications such as telegraph or telephone facilities. This clearly indicates the backwardness of these villages as far as communications are concerned.

Conclusions

Poverty, population growth and unemployment are crucial problems in our society. The population growth is 24.8 per cent in the last decade as evident from recent Census figures (676.2 million persons – Census, 1981). During the earlier four decades there is an explosion of population in India. The population of the 304 villages is 24,79,300.

The development of villages takes place with the inception of new ideas, innovations and modernisation. Development can percolate into village life and society only when adequate modern communication systems are available to the villagers. Raising economic productivity and living standards of millions of farmers in our developing India calls for dissemination of technical expertise and useful knowledge among the rural masses. Indian Government wished to accomplish this task of rural development in a few years what advanced countries took centuries to accomplish. The conventional means of communication proved inadequate. When mass media entered the calculus of development, it offered the greatest possibilities for effective action. Amongst the various mass media available for rural population television seems to be the most potent media by virtue of its unique features. Television attracts the attention and captures the imagination of the people because of the compelling combination of sight, sound, motion and emotion, brings depth and dimension of life and intimacy of the events telecast through it. It extends the rich experience of specialists and experts to a large number of people simultaneously. Television has a great potential in the field of education and dissemination of information to rural masses for overall development.

With the introduction of LPT in 1983, the television coverage exceeded 64 per cent of the population in India. Against the national scenario TV has had phenomenal growth both in urban and rural areas in the last decade. Television in India is meant to aid the socio-economic development of the country and to impart special education and information about various topics which are useful for our people.

There is a difference in urban rural audiences. As it stands today urban TV is conceived by viewers primarily as a medium of entertainment and to some extent for educational purposes. In urban areas TV receivers are owned by middle, upper middle and higher classes of people who can spend money for purchase of TVs. TV is viewed by the entire family members in the evenings, week-end movies, no doubt, sometimes attract a few friends or relatives who watch TV along with the family members. TV in urban areas is a family entertainment.

While in rural villages TV is a new innovation. Majority of rural population cannot afford the heavy expenditure to purchase TV sets independently for family viewing due to poverty. Responsibility of introducing developmental programmes rested with the government. The major burden of bringing about the desirable changes in rural life for development is attempted by Government through provision of CTVs in villages. These CTVs are meant for community viewing. Policy planners, policy-makers and administrators have considered seriously since majority of the population in India live in the rural areas, the dissemination of knowledge can be attempted by community viewing.

Of late, the realisation that rural development is not just

economic development but has to be the integrated development of health, hygiene, proper water supply and improved agriculture. It was found that television is a potent medium to educate the rural masses in India.

The United Nations advocated that every country should provide at least the following media facilities for 1000 people : 100 copies of daily news papers, 50 radio receivers, 20 cinema seats and 20 TV receivers. We have tried to compare the demographic factors like population, number of households in the village correlated with mass media factors.

In the 304 villages surveyed we found 608 community television sets for the use of 9,16,019, population which works out to one TV set for 1507 people. This shows the gross inadequacy for community television sets in villages. Even if it is estimated that at least one member views the programmes they can spread it to other members in the family. There are only 5 villages which had 3 CTV sets with 1,500 households and over 15,000 population. Even in these villages also community TV sets are grossly inadequate according to UNESCO standards.

When we examined the provision of Community Radio sets the position is still worse, that is only 267 radio sets are found in 304 villages. It is surprising to note that 37 villages do not have a single community set. It was also noticed that 148 village people do not hear the radio programmes. The participation in mass media was only 8 per cent. Even though the radio hardware coverage is near 100 per cent in India, the radio hearing is only 8 per cent of the population. Transistors have become quite popular in India, however we find that hearing of agriculture programmes and integrated rural programmes has not become very widespread in India. Most of the community radio sets are old, so they require constant repair, non-availability of spare parts, frequent failure of electric supply are some of the factors responsible for non-listening of community radio.

When we reconstructed the profiles of villages in terms of their nearness to the city, bus stand and railway station, which bring the villagers nearer to urban areas and modernisation we found a mixed picture.

Majority of villages had railway station which is more than 11 km distant from the village and it was also noticed that only one or two trains stop at these railway stations. So commuting by train is rather difficult. Only 1/3rd of the villages had Bus Stop in their villages, but majority had to commute more than 4 km to reach the bus stand and wait for the infrequent buses to commute to urban areas.

Schools, libraries and Panchayat Offices serve as disseminators of knowledge and information which are the prerequisites for modernisation and rural development. In majority (55.24%) of the villages, there is no library and literacy rate in rural is 35 per cent for males and 23 per cent for females. The use of library books in minimal. However, school and Panchayat Offices are available in 94 per cent and 71.78 per cent of villages respectively. Nearly 35 per cent of the schools are single teacher schools. Even the school buildings are in dilapidated condition, except only a few villages, which had pucca school buildings. In Maharashtra, it was found that children who enter the school, nearly 63 per cent drop out of school in five years, when they are supposed to complete their primary education. Only 18 per cent of boys and 12 per cent of girls complete their secondary education in ten years time. It was also noticed that absenteeism is the highest in rural schools. Less than one per cent of the rural students get their first degree. There is clear cut evidence to show that the proportion of school drop-outs (or wastage) between Classes I to V and Classes I – VIII is very high (about 60 per cent and 75 per cent respectively) and has remained unchanged during the past 38 years. This shows the non-utilisation of educational facilities in rural areas. It was also found that the provision for all children between the ages of 6 to 11 years in villages is inadequate. When we are on the threshold of entering the 21st Century, we find still some villages without schools and Panchayat Offices. Adequate health and hygiene facilities and pure drinking water in villages are still distant goals. Rural people are always interested in community activities, but here also we noticed that 84.54 per cent of the villages had a common place for social activities. The size of the community place is very inadequate.

We considered recreational and other facilities and their utilisations we found that facilities for dairying are adequate. The other facilities like public health centre, veterinary hospital and poultry are not enough in most of the villages. Proper dairy collection of milk and its transportation would have improved economic status to some extent but this aspect is also very inadequate in many of the villages.

As regards entertainment facilities, we noticed a greater inadequacy in Play Mandals, Mahila Mandals, gymnasiums, cinema houses and *Tamasha* shows. We found that the essential features of communication conducive to rural development are inadequate. They are far below the UNESCO specification of communication media.

Considering the above facts, we may conclude as under :

- media facilities are not available in adequate number in rural areas.
- the existing facilities are not utilised properly.
- due to population explosion available media facilities are inadequate. Hence 'media coverage' though it is more for CTV 'media reach' is not sufficient.
- recreational and other facilities in rural Maharashtra are not adequate.

5

COMMUNITY TELEVISION

An attempt has been made in this chapter to present the data about functioning of the community television sets in the villages. The Rural Broadcasting Department of the Ministry of Rural Development of the Maharashtra State had undertaken to install a community television set in each village. For the past 10–12 years the Government of Maharashtra started installing a few sets in villages every year. In the light of the aims and objectives of the present research programme it was found appropriate to have data on the community television. In addition to these it was also found desirable to survey some details about the custodians of the community television set in every village.

With a view to assess the impact of CTVs on rural masses, factors such as the: (1) TV sets and duration of installation, (2) Physical placement of the CTVs, (3) Structural arrangements for viewing, (4) The role of CTV custodian, (5) Availability of infrastructural facilities, and (6) lastly, the existence of videos in villages, were analysed in this chapter.

Constraints Experienced by Rural Audiences with Reference to CTV Viewing

The constraints of the rural population can broadly be classified under two categories:

(1) Human constraints, and
(2) Physical constraints.

Human Constraints

(a) The human blocks in the distribution system, the operation of gate keepers (CTV Care-takers), the seepage in communication, involvement of the leadership and viewers.

(b) Production variables such as operational problems, skills of producers, their knowledge and perception of rural scene, their involvement in projecting the rural progress. These aspects are not in the preview of this book.

Physical Constraints

(a) Place of location of sets,
(b) Physical arrangements for viewing,
(c) Breakdown in sets,
(d) Maintenance problems,
(e) Power failures,
(f) Seasonal fluctuation in attendance.

The above factors influence the CTV viewing in villages and are studied in this book.

TV Sets and Duration of its Installation

Table 5.1 describes the number of privately owned television sets in the villages under study. Nearly 46.4 per cent of villages do not possess any privately owned TV sets. This signifies that the community TV sets at the villages is the only available source of facility for viewing. There are, however, nearly 7.24 per cent villages where more than 11 privately owned TV sets are present. Also the number of villages where 1 to 3 TV sets are available is very high (106 villages – 34.96%).

TABLE 5.1: Number of Private TV Sets

No. of Private TV sets	Number of Villages	
No private TV Sets (only CTV is available)	141	(46.38%)
1 – 3 sets	106	(34.86%)
4 – 6	22	(7.24%)
7 – 10	13	(4.28%)
11+	22	(7.24%)
Total	304	(100.00%)

Television is an electronic gadget which like any other equipment is prone to develop defects after prolonged use. Also the earlier TV sets which were installed in the villages are old models with valves. Valves and tubes have a specific life span. After certain usage these parts have to be replaced. Thus the older the TV set, the breakdown will be more frequent. Let us examine the duration of Community TV installed in these villages.

Thus we can say that the provision of CTV sets in the villages is inadequate. CTVs are old and may develop frequent breakdowns and may require repairs. These involve considerable expenditure and are uneconomical to maintain.

The total number of community TV sets provided by the Rural Broadcasting Department (RBD) in the three districts of Maharashtra under study, are shown in Table 5.2.

TABLE 5.2: CTV Sets in Villages as on 30-10-1986 in the Three Districts

Districts	No. of villages	Black & White TV	Colour TV	Total
Pune	1,481	703	103	806
Satara	1,437	177	42	219
Ahmednagar	1,312	163	15	178
Total	4,230	1,043	160	1,203

Now let us look at the Community TV sets available in the villages under survey (Table 5.3).

TABLE 5.3: Number of CTVs in the Villages under Survey

Number of CTV sets	No. of Villages	
Only one set	8	(2.66%)
Two sets	290	(95.39%)
Three sets	5	(1.64%)
4 or 5 sets	1	(0.33%)
Total	304	(100.00%)

Table 5.2 deals with the number of community TV sets in the villages. While a majority of villages (290 or 95.39%) have two TV sets per village, meaning thereby that the population of the village is covered by two television sets. There were some very big villages where 3 or sometimes up to 5 TV sets were installed to cover the population of the village which is considered infinitively small i.e. 6

(1.97%) villages had 3 or more sets where the population is more than 12,000.

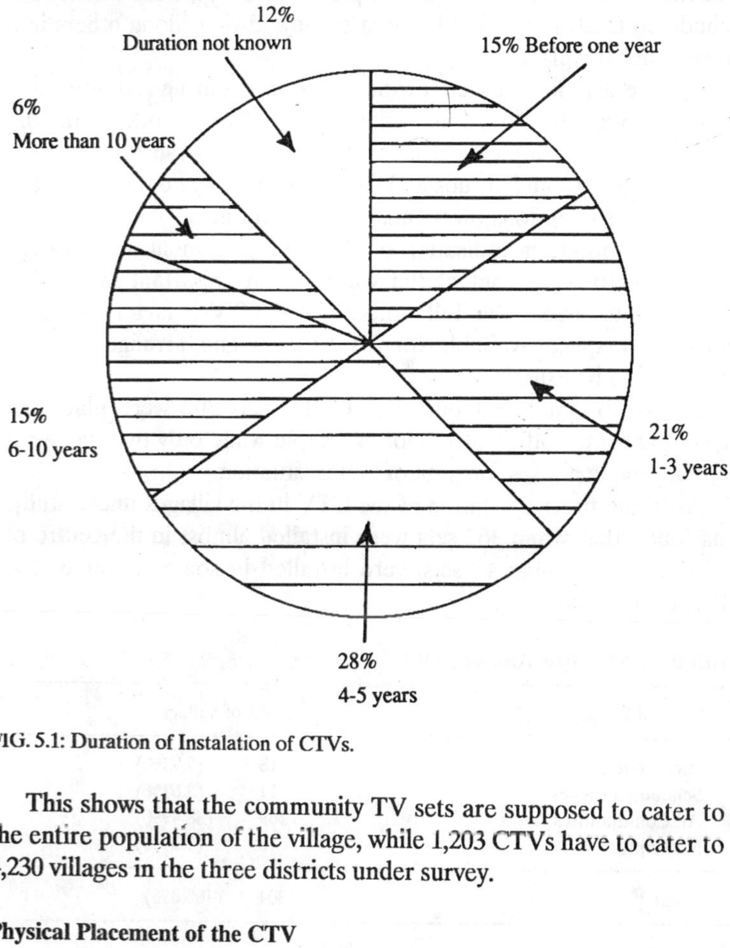

FIG. 5.1: Duration of Instalation of CTVs.

This shows that the community TV sets are supposed to cater to the entire population of the village, while 1,203 CTVs have to cater to 4,230 villages in the three districts under survey.

Physical Placement of the CTV

Location of CTV is an important factor. If the CTV sets are located at a central place and is easily approachable during all seasons, this type of placement of CTV is ideal. If on the other hand, it is located in the Harijan Basti, where Scheduled Castes live, the high caste audience will not visit it, or if it is placed in a high class locality the Scheduled Castes may feel hesitant to sit and view along others in a crowed viewing place.

If there are no facilities for indoor viewing during monsoon and winter months, the attendance will be scanty. If on the other hand the CTV is located in a public place with proper overhead covering and free from bushes and shrubs and free from snakes and scorpians, the viewers can sit comfortably without any constraints.

For the optimum utilisation of CTVs its placement and location in relation to the layout of the village is an important factor. To enable us to assess the full utilisation of CTVs, factors such as capacity of space available for TV viewers and arrangement for sitting are to be examined.

It was observed that out of 304 CTV sets 302 were placed in either panchayat office or school or temple while only two sets were kept in private houses for want of better situation.

As to the precise location of the CTV in the villages under study, was found that while 362 sets were installed almost in the centre of the village remaining 42 sets were installed in some corner or the other of the villages.

TABLE 5.4: Who Stays Around CTV

Type of People	No. of Villages	
Rich People	18	(5.92%)
Scheduled Castes	11	(3.62%)
All Communities	269	(88.49%)
No Reply	6	(1.97%)
Total	304	(100.0%)

Table 5.4 deals with the people living around the CTV. As was described in the previous table the CTV sets have been installed mostly in the central place of the village. The present table shows that a large number (88.49%) of CTV sets are surrounded by households of mixed population while only 3.62 per cent sets are installed in the settlement of Scheduled caste households.

Structural Arrangements for CTV Viewing

Let us now look at the structural arrangements made in the villages under survey and see what is the position regarding the viewing facilities available in Maharashtra.

Table 5.5 describes the capacity of the place to accommodate the viewers in an open space near the CTV. It is observed that in the case of nearly 200 (65.79%) CTV sets, the place could accommodate as many as 100 to 400 viewers and in the case of 25.33 per cent of the villages the capacity is more than 400 viewers.

TABLE 5.5: Number of Viewers (Outsiders)

No. of Viewers	No. of Villages	
Up to 50	4	(1.32%)
50 to 100	6	(1.97%)
101 to 300	118	(38.82%)
301 to 400	82	(26.97%)
401+	77	(25.33%)
Don't know	17	(5.59%)
Total	304	(100.00%)

The villages in majority had a population of 1000 to 5000, so the accommodation of 100 to 400 viewers does not even cater to 5 per cent of the population. It shows the inadequacy and the need for installation of more CTV sets if the benefits of rural welfare and educative programmes are to be disseminated to the entire rural population.

Provision of viewing facilities all through the year is essential if the viewers are to get reinforcement from TV maintained by constant viewing. To enable the rural population to get the fullest benefit of watching the TV programmes arrangements should be made in such a way that there is no break during any season due to the vagaries of the weather conditions. If there is any break in the viewing habits of individuals the interest will wane away after a lapse of time of non-viewing. For watching TV programmes uninterruptedly even in rainy season a closed accommodation is essential.

We now look at the arrangements made for viewing CTV in rainy season in the villages.

It was found that in 125 villages some alternative arrangement of viewing CTV was made whereas in case of 179 villages there was no such arrangement available.

TABLE 5.6: Rainy Season Accommodation

Accommodation	No. of Villages	
Shifted to Custodian's house	94	(30.92%)
Changed set Position	13	(4.28%)
No accommodation	2	(0.66%)
Shifted to Panchayat Office	1	(0.33%)
In the shade	1	(0.33%)
Don't know	15	(4.93%)
TV in the hall only	178	(58.35%)
Total	304	(100.0%)

It is seen from Table 5.6 that the information about the arrangements made for viewing the CTV during rainy season. It is observed that in the case of merely 109 (35.86%) villages some temporary or improvised arrangements were made during the rainy season to facilitate CTV viewing. This makes shift arrangements are not satisfactory for viewers. During rainy season the CTV from the open ground is usually shifted to rooms or closed halls of Panchayat Office, school or custodian's house.

In India, particularly in rural areas, segregation of sexes is a normal practice. A separate seating arrangements is essential if women are to reap the full benefit of TV viewing.

However it was found that while in 83 villages separate sitting arrangement for female viewers was deliberately made, in the rest of the villages necessity for such an arrangement was not felt.

It was also observed that the cast hierarchy does not prove to be a hindrance for watching the CTV for in almost in all villages' viewers from all cast groups were found watching the CTV together.

Custodian and His Role

The CTV sets are kept under the custody of some responsible members. These custodians can be called as, 'the gate-keepers' in rural TV viewing. They are the fulcrum on which the CTV viewing depends. If the custodian due to any of his personal reasons does not turn up, the CTVs cannot be operated. Considerable seepage in communication at these gates during the flow is because of the absence of the custodian who operates the TV.

It is observed that nearly 83.88 per cent have been grouped under the category of servicemen. It is to be inferred that this high percentage is only due to the custodians being an office bearer at the village administrative unit while he is also a true representative of the village community and is an agriculturist.

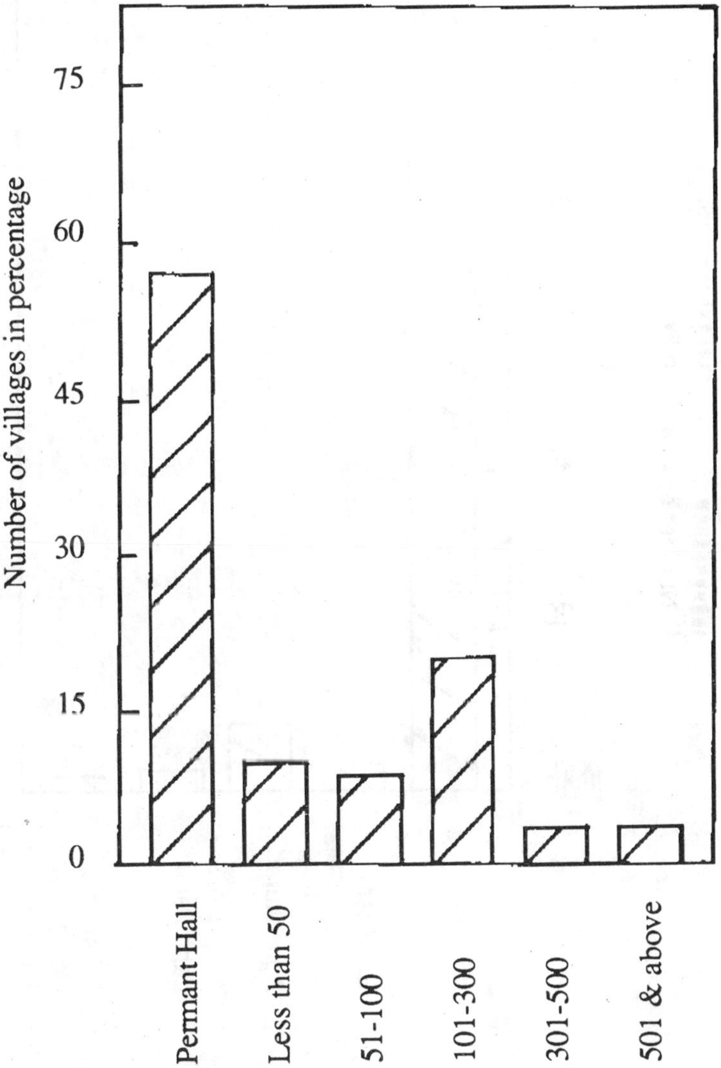

FIG. 5.2: Accommodation Capacity of the Viewing Hall in Rainy Season.

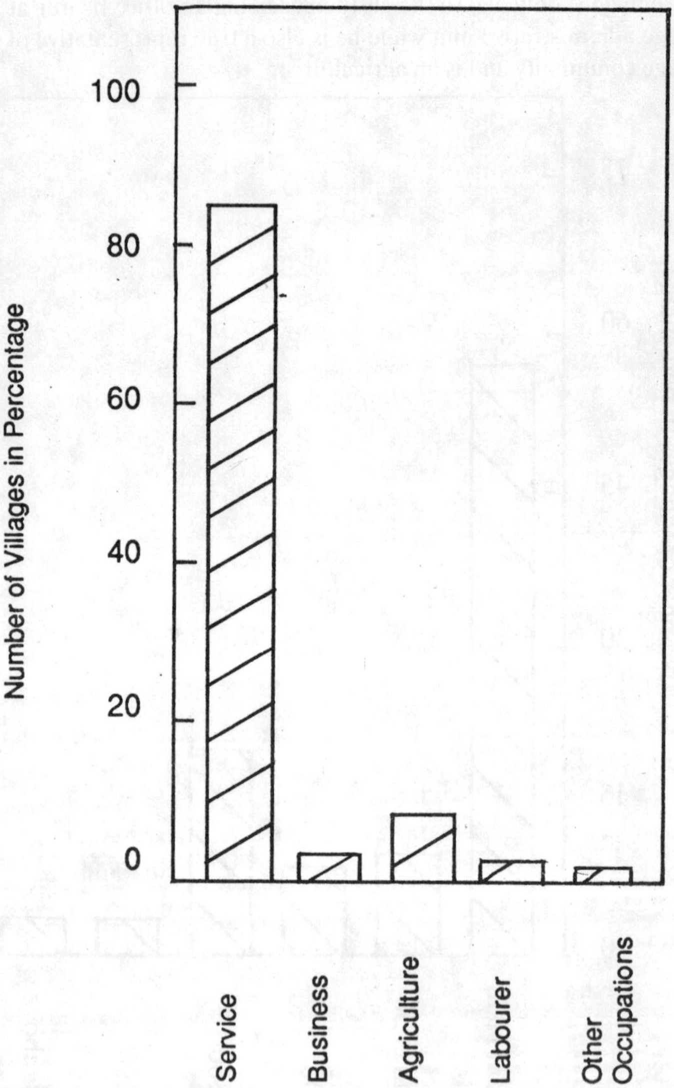

FIG. 5.3: Custodian Occupation.

TABLE 5.7: Custodian's Age

Age	No. of Villages	
18-19 years	6	(1.97%)
20-30 years	88	(28.95%)
31-40 years	101	(33.22%)
41 +	109	(35.86%)
Total	304	(100.00%)

Normally the government entrusts the CTVs to responsible mature individuals. This fact is corroborated by the data on the age of the custodians.

TABLE 5.8: Custodian's Education

Education	No. of Villages	
Illiterate	6	(1.98%)
Up to 4 standard	35	(11.51%)
Up to 10th standard	100	(32.89%)
College	152	(50.00%)
Technical Diploma	(11)	(3.62%)
Total	304	

Table 5.8 describes the custodian's education. The village community in Maharashtra is still largely illiterate or less educated. It is seen that 45.72 per cent of the custodians of CTV are educated upto 10th standard or less. Majority are either college educated, technical diploma holders. Thus we find RBD has entrusted the CTVs to educated persons. It is observed that the CTV set is put to work everyday in case of 230 villages whereas 74 villages reported choosed viewing.

The data in Table 5.9 show the frequency of the use of the CTV per week. It is to be noted that in 64.80 per cent of the villages the CTV was put on to use on all seven days. Also the number of villages making use of the CTV on three or more days per week is quite high (100-29.60%) villages. Though it is the government's intention that CTVs should be switched on daily for the benefit of the villagers still in 17 villages, they were not operated for periods ranging from all days in a week to 2 or 3 days a week. Thus the main purpose of installing the CTVs is not served at all on such days.

TABLE 5.9: Days on which CTV was on

Use of CTV in a Week	No. of Villages	
Not a single day	7	(2.30%)
Only one day	1	(0.33%)
2 days	9	(2.96%)
3 days	18	(5.92%)
4 days	16	(5.26%)
5 days	37	(12.17%)
6 days	29	(6.25%)
All days	187	(64.81%)
Total	304	(100.00%)

TABLE 5.10: Time Preferences for CTV Viewing

Time Preference	No. of Villages	
Morning	7	(2.30%)
Evening/Night	195	(64.16%)
Morning	5	(1.64%)
Morning/Evening/Night	97	(31.90%)
TV out of order	5	(1.64%)
Total	304	(100.00%)

Table 5.10 show the preference of the villagers as regards the time suitable to them for viewing the CTV. It is worth-noting that less than 2.3 per cent of villagers go for morning programmes. It is a known fact that most of the villagers found free time for viewing the TV programmes during evenings. It is also seen from the above table that in 195 villages they preferred to view the TV programmes during evening/night. The villagers from 97 (81.90%) villages showed preference for Noon/Evening/Night times.

Infrastructural Facilities

Infrastructural facilities include continuous supply of electricity without voltage fluctuations, proper maintenance of CTV sets without mechanical breakdown.

In the spot surveying the researcher found that out of 304 CTV sets 40 sets were out of order on the day of his visit to the respective villages.

TABLE 5.11: Period Since the CTVs were not Working

Period	No. of Villages	
Last week	2	(0.66%)
Fortnight	2	(0.66%)
Month	4	(1.32%)
Since three months	10	(3.29%)
Since six months	12	(3.95%)
Since one year	7	(2.30%)
More than one and half years	2	(0.66%)
Working	265	(87.16%)
Total	304	(100.00%)

The data in Table 5.11 show the period of breakdown of which the CTV sets which have ceased to function. As already stated the sets in 265 villages, out of a total sample of 304 villages were working satisfactorily at the time of the visit of the researcher. Nine sets have been out of order for one to one and half years, while 26 sets have stopped functioning for the duration ranging between one month to six months. Keeping the sets out of order for periods beyond fortnight is a serious lapse on the part of the R.B.D. when the villagers had paid Rs.200 and entered into service contract.

Let us assess the duration during which the complaints about non-functioning of CTV were kept pending in DDD's Office.

It is seen from Table 5.12 that in the case of six villages the complaint was made before six months or more, still it was not attended to. Equally alarming is the number of the cases (21 villages – 6.91%) where the complaint was not made at all by the custodians of the CTV.

It is seen from Table 5.13 that 265 sets were functioning at the time of interview. However, 39 sets were found not functioning. Let us examine how these complaints are attended to and action initiated by R.B.D. Provision exists in the contract entered into by the villagers with the R.B.D. according to which the TV service technician should villages and examine the functioning of CTV periodically.

TABLE 5.12: Complaints Made If Any

Period	No. of villages	
Complaint not made	21	(6.91%)
One week	2	(0.66%)
One month	4	(1.31%)
Three months	6	(1.97%)
Six months	2	(0.66%)
More than 6 months	4	(1.31%)
CTV working	265	(87.18%)
Total	304	

TABLE 5.13: Any Reply to Complaints Made

Action Taken	No. of Villages	
Repaired, still not working	9	(2.96%)
Acknowledgement received	6	(1.97)
Checked by Technician	4	(1.31)
No action taken	2	(0.66)
Spares awaited	1	(0.33)
Technical fault	1	(0.33)
TV repair not attended to	16	(5.26)
TV functioning	265	(87.18)
Total	304	(100.00%)

It is seen that in 16 of the villages where the service mechanic had not attended to the complaint, while in nine villages the sets were not working, through the repairs were executed. In 6 villages there was only a paper acknowledgement. This indicates the deplorable condition of TV maintenance.

TABLE 5.14: Number of Days in a Week the CTV was not on

No. of Days	No. of Villages	
TV was on, on all days	227	(74.66%)
5 days	20	(6.60%)
4 days in a week	9	(2.96%)
2 days in a week	8	(2.63%)
1 day in week	1	(0.33%)
Out of order	39	(12.83%)
Total	304	(100.00%)

The data in Table 5.14 point out the frequency of the use of the CTV set by the villagers. It is noticed that in the case of nearly 74.66 per cent of the villages the CTV was put on on all the week days. It is also interesting to note that in 17 villages however, the set works for two to four days a week.

TABLE 5.15: Reasons

Reasons	No. of Villages	
TV on	252	(82.89%)
Out of order	39	(12.83%)
No electricity supply	7	(2.31%)
No reason	6	(2.17%)
Total	304	(100.00%)

Table 5.15 describes the reasons as to why the CTV set is generally not put to use on the days of the week, the information given was that the set works only a few days per week. Most common reasons, given were that the TV set was out of order 12.83 per cent or there was no electric supply in the case of 7 (2.31%) of the villages.

TABLE 5.16: Arrangements for Repair

Arrangements made	No. of Villages	
TV is under warranty period	19	(6.25)
R.B.	156	(51.31)
To city	9	(2.96)
No arrangements made	107	(35.20)
City Mechanic was brought	11	(3.62)
Booster required	2	(0.66)
Total	304	(100.00)

The present table highlights the arrangements that the villagers have got to be done to get the CTV set repaired. In the case of 5.16 per cent villages, there has not so far been any cause to make any arrangements, because of warranty period of the set. A large number of the villages (156 – 51.32%) depended for repairs on Rural Broadcast Department. Equally worth-noting is that nearly 107 (35.20%) of the villages have not made any arrangements whatsoever for repair of the set.

Table 5.17 shows how long it takes for the villagers to get their TV set repaired. It is noted that in nearly 43.75 per cent instances, the villagers informed that the time taken for repairs is not known since the CTV has not developed any complaints. However, in the case of nearly 30 per cent of the villages, the set is repaired in less than 24 hours.

On inquiring about electric supply it was found that 235 villages had no complaints about the regularity of supply and 69 villages reported irregularity of electric supply as one of the main causes of non-functioning of CTV sets.

TABLE 5.17: Time Taken for Repair of CTV

Time Taken	No. of Villages	
Immediately	9	(2.96%)
1 day	83	(27.30%)
3 days	11	(3.62%)
1 week	12	(3.95%)
2 weeks	23	(7.57%)
3 weeks	1	(0.33%)
1 month	13	(4.27%)
More than a month	7	(2.30%)
Time not certain	12	(3.95%)
TV working, no complaints so far	133	(43.75%)
Total	304	(100.00%)

We critically evaluated the infrastructural facilities as well as deficiencies with reference to the functioning of the CTV sets. First of all the preliminary analysis showed that at the time of the data collection nearly 13 per cent sets were out of order. It is quite easy to imagine that this is only an average and at any time these sets would go out of order. If so, one may be able to grasp that the proportion of the number of sets out of order is quite high. Further in the analysis of the time period for which the sets have been out of order it has come to our notice that nearly 90 per cent of the sets have been disfunctional for more than a month up to even one year. This situation is extremely alarming and points again at the inefficiency of the custodians, who are supposed to maintain the sets in order. However, the administrative side alone is not to be blamed for in more than 53 per cent of the cases the complaints have not been made at all. To share their part of non-punctuality, the repairers have received complaints in nearly 42 per cent of the cases. These complaints have remained unattended for periods ranging from one month to more than six months due to the reasons best known to the users and repairers only. However, in case of nearly 46 per cent of the sets complaints have remained unattended and also in the case of 23 per cent cases the sets are not functioning even after repairs supposed to have been completed. With the result we see that in as many as 18 per cent of the cases the sets are functioning only part of the week. Apart from the usual reasons in case of 2.33 per cent sets failure of electricity supply is shown as a reason for its non-functioning. In the analysis of the arrangements made for repairing the set it was found that the Rural Broadcasting Department has taken this responsibility in nearly half of the villages. What is alarming is that in more than one-third of the sets no definitive arrangements have been fixed for repairing. The electricity supply is a precondition of proper function of the CTV was found to irregular in the case of nearly 22 per cent of the villages.

Existence of Video

When the investigation was carried out in the districts of Satara, Poona and Ahmednagar, only 23 villages have video sets. The recent information revealed the fact that number of the registered video houses in these three districts is more than 400 (Poona 253, Ahmednagar 57, and Satara 98). However, unregistered video clubs are estimated to range between 1000 to 1200 in the rural parts of these three districts. It is, therefore, quite understandable that there is a great boom in the popularity of the video programmes. The video facility is a selective entertainment and thus differs from the programmes of Doordarshan. Growing popularity of video programmes is of pertinent threat to the objectives of the development communication in an important way namely that the objective educational, informative as well as instructional programmes, is dispensed away by the selective entertainment programmes facilitated by the videos. However, another positive approach can be evolved regarding the present video book. A number of Area Specific programmes can be prepared and channalised through governmental as well as voluntary sources in the rural areas. Such programmes would help restoring the objectives assigned to the television.

The video mode of entertainment spontaneously developed had already become a factor to taken into account in the be spread of mass media in the country. It is estimated that in our country over 600 thousand VCRs are in use and out of which at least 100 thousand are already being used for commercial purposes. The number of VCRs being added every month is over 15,000. If we take into account the number of video mini-theatres which have sprung up all over the country and the video libraries already in existence, the videos will soon become in its own right an effective medium of communication.

It is possible to imagine that the VCR medium will infiltrate into distant and remote areas more speedily than either TV or cinema. The video is the most decentralised medium and it could cater to specific regions and sub-regions, social groups and sub-groups, more conveniently than it is possible either through TV or cinema. Video can be used effectively for social communication because it is less expensive, portable, convivial and easy to manage. The Kheda experiment (of Space Application Centre) is a demonstration that gives a hollistic conception of social communication not divided by 'hardware' and 'software' considerations can result in effective social communication.

From the rural development objectives a willingness to use video as a tool is essential. The important thing is to make the unheard voices heard, to exchange experiences across communities to bridge the gap between the administrators and the administered. Video can make it possible for the communicator to go about his business without being unnecessarily bothered with the tools.

The number of video libraries is 15,000 and of video bars and coaches 2,000 each. The informal theatres may be organising as many as three to four shows a day on 20" screen. Therefore, the number of persons exposed to VCRs showing a day may be in several lakhs.

The electronic revolution is here. It is a clear concept of its utilisation. The answer to questions like, can VCR be used as an aid? Why it cannot be used to make TV programmes available at the viewer's convenience or to enable the viewer to watch a single programme more than once? This possibility alone enables VCR to be used extensively to further the objectives of education. This technology can become a relevant factor at village level communication.

Conclusion

In the villages we found that 69 villages have CTV sets which were more than six years old. Consequently, these sets develop recurring repairs and on account of mechanical breakdowns, lead to lose of potential exposure time.

Majority of CTVs were installed in Panchayat Offices, which are accessible to all castes. However, only 40 per cent of the villages have facilities for viewing CTVs all the year round, while 57 per cent of the villages have no adequate and convenient places where the viewers can watch TV during rainy seasons. The reasons are due to shifting of CTVs to custodian's residences and inadequate seating arrangements. No special arrangements exist for female viewers. Consequently it inhibits female audience from optimum utilisation.

The role of custodian cannot be ignored and the custodian is one among the villagers though he is a petty officials. Custodians are found to be matured and are reasonably educated persons. Twenty-five per cent of the villages CTV sets are not switched on everyday due to the preoccupation of the custodian. Even though many viewers expressed interest to view during day time, they could not avail of the facility due to non-availability of custodian to operate the CTV. The custodians (gate-keepers) acted as human blocks in preventing the people from viewing the programmes at their leisure time. If the custodian did not like certain programmes the CTV is not put on. When there were clashes between the leaders in villages, the viewers were the losers in programme viewing.

We noticed various physical constraints due to the placement of sets, breakdown in sets, power failure and maintenance problems, which accounted for missing of rural development programmes in more than 30 per cent of the villages.

Infrastructural facilities showed inadequacy due to electricity failure, voltage fluctuations and improper maintenance of CTVs and mechanical failures of CTVs. We found that for 64.8 per cent of the villages CTV viewing is possible for all days, but in 35.2 per cent villages CTV is not put on for one to six days. If the custodian is busy he will not put 'on' the CTV in the evening wherein programmes meant for rural development are televised. This selectivity by the custodians in programme viewing emphasizing entertainment in preference to information dispersal and educative programmes lead to the failure of the aim of the government i.e., educating the rural masses for rural development.

Videos and Video Parlours, we find, are increasing in villages and these are attracting the rural population because of its entertainment value. The video screenings are throughout the day unlike the TV programmes, which are televised for a few hours in a day. Villagers flock to these parlours mainly because of their entertainment and convenience of time. In a way TV is loosing ground on this score. Instead of watching programmes, which are informative and educative and specially meant for rural development, people are prefering to watch cinemas on videos.

6

COMMUNITY TELEVISION AND RURAL VIEWERS

The understanding of the viewers' participation in the process of television communication is very important. Development communication is a two-way process and to substantiate this point the present chapter has been divided into three major sections:

Section I deals with the socio-economic factors relating to the identification data of the viewers.

Section II deals with the programmes preferences.

Section III deals with the superstition with vedio experiment.

SECTION I

Socio-economic Background of the Viewers

The socio-economic background of the viewers is very important as the class structure of the respondents will have a bearing on their programme preference. The sex of the respondents is ascertained in order to obtain male/female preferences of respondents. In India due to the division of labour women perform household duties and men perform out of the house work. Naturally the interests of men and women are different.

The researcher had interviewed in all 464 rural respondents – the CTV viewers. Of these were 391 men and 73 women.

Occupation

People of different occupations are interested in problems which pertain to their occupation. Programme preferences could be different. Occupation of the respondents is given in Table 6.1

It is seen from the data given in Table 6.1 that major groups are from the service (38.36%) category and Agriculturists form the next higher group (32.54%). As one would expect the majority of the respondents should be from farmers, however, since custodians were included in the sample they expressed themselves as in service, because they were the custodians and received some remuneration from government, through their occupation is mainly agriculture.

TABLE 6.1: Occupation of the Respondents

Occupation	No. of Respondents
Service and Agriculture	178 (38.36)
Agriculture	151 (32.54)
Artisans	13 (2.80)
Business	16 (3.45)
Students	47 (10.13)
Labourers	13 (2.80)
Household workers	28 (6.03)
Others	18 (3.89)
Total	464 (100.00)

Age

Age is an important factor for programme preferences. Younger people may be more interested in entertainment, while the middle aged may show preference for educational programmes. On the other hand the elder generation may show preference for religious programmes. The age of the respondents is given in Table 6.2.

The age composition of the respondents is characterised by a higher proportion of middle aged group, category 21-40 years and they form 58.84 per cent while 97 (20.90%) younger group and 94 (20.26%) of the elder generation are represented in our sample.

TABLE 6.2: Age of the Respondents

Age	No. of Respondents
16 to 20 years	97 (20.90)
21 to 30 years	157 (33.84)
31 to 40 years	116 (25.00)
41 to 50 years	72 (15.52)
51 and above	22 (4.74)
Total	464 (100.00)

Education

Education and family income determine the socio-economic status of the individual. Table 6.3 shows the educational level of the respondents.

TABLE 6.3: Education of the Respondents

Education	No. of Respondents
Illiterate	79 (17.03)
Primary	151 (32.54)
High School	167 (35.99)
College	52 (11.21)
Technical Diploma	11 (2.37)
Vocational Training	4 (0.86)
Total	464 (100.00)

Since the survey was conducted in villages, so it to be is expected the educational levels of the people is low. 17.03 per cent of the respondents were illiterates, while 32.54 per cent and 35.99 per cent had primary and secondary education respectively. These form a majority of the respondents i.e., 318 (68.53%), while the college educated were 11.21 per cent and Technical Diploma-holders were 2.37 per cent.

TABLE 6.4: Family Income of the Respondents

Monthly income	No. of Respondents
Up to Rs. 500	160 (34.48)
Rs. 501 – Rs. 1,000	175 (37.72)
Rs. 1,001 – Rs. 3,000	77 (16.59)
Rs. 3,001 – Rs.5,000	20 (4.31)
No income	32 (6.90)
Total :	464 (100.00)

Family Income of the Respondents

Among the respondents more than 70 per cent came under the two categories of income – up to Rs. 500 (34.48%) and Rs. 501 to 1000 (37.72%). Only very few people 97 (20.90%) had income ranging from Rs. 1,001 to Rs. 5,000. Thus it is evident from Table 6.4 that majority of the respondents belonged to poor income levels with reference to cost of living index. The small percentage (4.31%) of the respondents whose income is from Rs.3,001 to Rs.5,000 may be having more than one earning member in the family or might be having agricultural income besides their job.

Type of Family

From the total sample of 464 respondents 280 respondents were members of joint families, while 184 reported the membership of nuclear families (Table 6.5).

TABLE 6.5: Number of Persons in the Family

No. of Persons	No. of Respondents
Up to 5	132 (28.45)
6 to 10	8 (1.72)
11 to 15	133 (28.66)
16 to 20	141 (30.39)
21 to 25	35 (7.54)
26 to 30	10 (2.16)
30 and more	5 (1.08)
Total	464 (100.00)

Contrary to the conception of small family norms of the urbanites, it is noticed in the villages that there are families having 16 to 20 members in the family. In our sample majority 274 (59.05%) of the respondents had 11 to 20 members in their families. Cases where there are 30 or more members in the family are also not uncommon. Such cases exist in our survey where there are 5 (1.08%) who had 30 or more members in their families. However, we find 132 (29.05%) respondents who had a small family norm i.e., less than five members.

Frequency of Viewing

Though TV is a recent innovation, people from both urban and rural areas are getting used to watching the programmes. Figure 6.1 gives the frequency of watching the TV programmes.

It is seen from Figure 6.1 that although there are respondents who 'never' or 'very rarely' watched (1.72% and 15.52% respectively), a considerable number 224 (48.28%) of them watched the TV programmes from 3 days in a week to daily and 160 (34.48%) of the respondents watched the programmes from 1 to 2 days in a week.

However, a small number (13.15%) watched the programme daily. People are not fully utilising the medium but still are getting into the habit of viewing TV Programme as a leisure time, passtime.

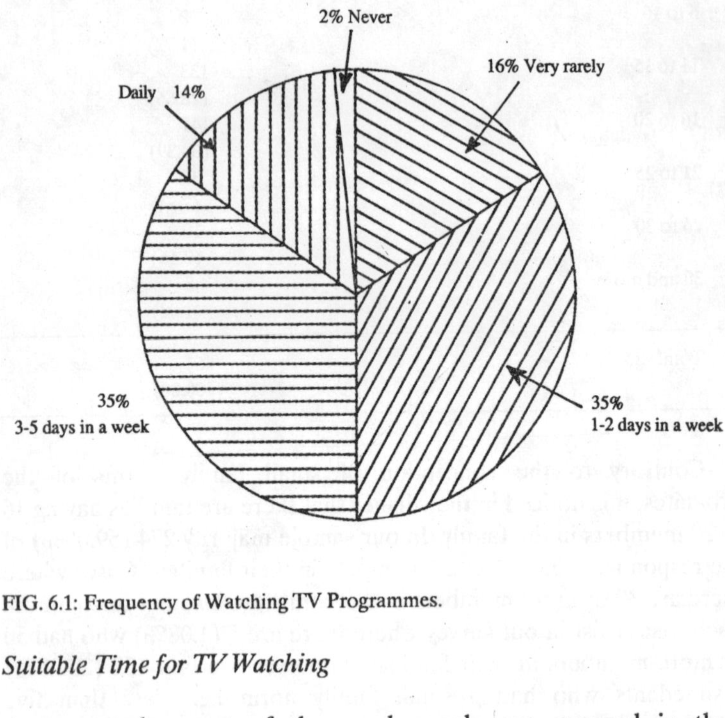

FIG. 6.1: Frequency of Watching TV Programmes.

Suitable Time for TV Watching

As expected, most of the rural people are engaged in their occupations during the morning time and they can hardly afford to spare any time for TV watching during that time. Generally most of them will be free in the evenings after a day's work outside.

After an early dinner they prefer to watch the TV Programmes for recreation and for gaining knowledge through these programmes. It is seen from Fig. 6.2 that a majority 367 (85.09%) of the respondents found evening-night time suitable for TV watching. It is surprising to see that there are 97 (20.91%) of the respondents who indicated their preference to afternoon watching. Some of these respondents may be house-wives who are free after finishing their lunch or others who are pursuing their occupation at home. None of the respondents wanted to watch any programmes during mornings.

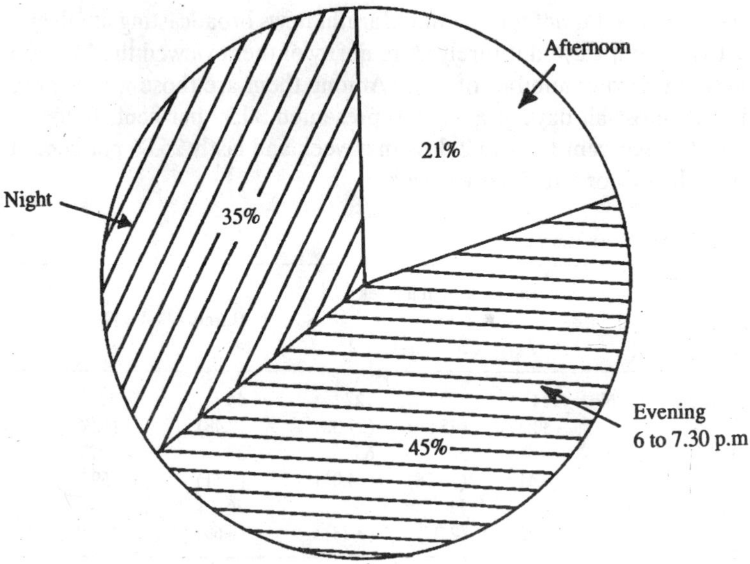

FIG. 6.2: Suitable Time for TV Watching.

SECTION II

Programme Preferences

The news viewing has an educative and informative value. Sitting at home watching the TV one can know the happenings in national and international scenes. Educated people can get detailed information from media such as newspaper, magazines and books. This media is not useful for rural-urban illiterates. The TV is an universal media which is not linked with education for comprehension. TV is the ideal communication media for dissemination of knowledge for development.

It is seen from Table 6.6 that a majority 83.63 per cent of the respondents listened to the Marathi TV news, while 33.2 per cent to Hindi and infinitesimally small number 9.48 per cent to English news ranging from once a week to all the seven days of the week. However, a considerable number of the respondents rarely or never viewed the Hindi and English news (66.81% and 90.5%, respectively) programmes. The reason can be attributed to the language difficulty in understanding. It is observed that only 6.96 per cent of the respondents did not viewed the Marathi news broadcasting at all, and 9.18 per cent viewed it rarely. A majority of them viewed the Marathi news in varying number of days. Among them are those who viewed it on almost all days in a week represented 30.39 per cent, followed by 27.38 per cent for 1 to 2 days in a week and lastly 25.86 per cent of them heard for 3 to 5 days a week.

TABLE 6.6: News Viewing

Language		No. of days in a week 6-7	3-5	1-2	Rarely	Never
Marathi	No.	141	120	127	44	32
		(30.39)	(25.86)	(27.38)	(9.48)	(6.96)
Hindi	No.	39	50	65	33	277
		(8.41)	(10.78)	(14.01)	(7.11)	(59.70)
English	No.	15	11	18	26	394
		(3.23)	(2.37)	(3.88)	(5.60)	(84.92)

The above pattern is completely reversed in the case of both Hindi and English news viewing. Majority (59.70%) of the respondents did not care to see the Hindi news programme at all as compared to a great majority (84.92%) of the respondents who did not view the English news. There is not much difference among those who hear rarely the news as far as all the three languages are concerned. It is conclusively proved that the rural people preferred to know about their regional specific news in their own mother tongue. Since in Maharashtra rural illiterate people can comprehend only Marathi language so Hindi and English are known by few educated people.

Reasons for not Viewing News

When the respondents who do not viewed the news items, the reasons given by them are shown in Table 6.7.

Majority of the respondents opined that the languages (Hindi and English) were not understood by them (23.06% for Hindi and 38.79% for English). Only infinitesimally small number (5 or 1.08%) of the respondents expressed a similar opinion about the Marathi news. Unsuitably of the time of news broadcast is the other major reason for not viewing news item. Only a small percentage of the respondents did not like the news in Marathi (1.08%), Hindi (1.29%) and English (2.80%). Similarly a small percentage of respondents gave other reasons for not viewing the news.

TABLE 6.7: Reasons for Non-viewing of News

Language	Reasons for not viewing			
	Don't like	Time not suitable	Language not understood	Other reasons
Marathi	5 (1.08)	23 (4.96)	5 (1.08)	10 (2.16)
Hindi	6 (1.29)	38 (8.19)	107 (23.06)	12 (2.59)
English	13 (2.80)	37 (7.97)	180 (38.79)	12 (2.59)

Entertainment Programmes and Viewing Behaviour of Respondents

It is essential that periodical assessment of the various programmes is required to be made, so that the programme planners can make necessary changes or improvements of the programmes. Opinions of the respondents regarding the various programmes were collected under a 5-point scale of like it, don't like it, don't see it, aware of it but do not see it to don't know. The items that have been included in Table 6.7 relate to Marathi language programmes and hence have a greater communicability as far as the rural viewers of Maharashtra are concerned.

The entertainment programmes are divided under three broad heads: (1) Very popular, (2) Popular, and (3) Accepted programmes. Even in the case of entertainment programmes audience preferences vary, based on their interest and liking.

Figure 6.3 depicts the responses of the viewers with regard to viewing of the very popular entertainment programmes. The programmes which were found to be very popular are:

(a) Marathi Feature Films,
(b) Chhaya Geet,
(c) Hindi Feature Films,
(d) Chitra Geet,

(e) Marathi Play (Long),
(f) Lok Sangeet.

These are placed in the order of their preferences.

Marathi feature films are liked by 84.05 per cent of the respondents, while the lowest under this category is the Lok Sangeet, which is liked by 60.52 per cent of the viewers. The number of people who intentionally avoided the programmes is very low. It has also been found that the number was very low as far as the ignorance about the programme (Don't know) is concerned.

Rural people are exposed to cinema medium of entertainment for a long time. These very popular entertainment programmes are cinema-based and so they are preferred by rural people.

Figure 6.4 indicates the responses of the viewers regarding some of the popular entertainment programmes. It has been found that Chitrahar and Marathi TV Play (short) topped the list as far as the viewers liking is concerned. The Balachitrapat (Marathi) and the Cricket Match were the lowest in this category (45.47% and 47.84% respectively). It is also observed that the viewers were generally aware of the programmes mentioned in Fig. 6.4.

A sizable number of respondents (43.75%) do not see the Cricket Match. The reasons given by the respondents during the course of interview were that:

(1) The cricket game is alien to them,
(2) The game is of prolonged duration,
(3) It does not have entertainment value for rural audiences, adults, in particular,
(4) Since the game stretches for many days the sustained tempo and interest is not found in the audience,
(5) Since most of the viewers are workers they do not want to waste their whole day on watching this programme.

Kridangan and *Phool Khile Hain*. . . . are not seen by 39.07 per cent and 38.58 per cent of the respondents respectively, because they are urban-based entertainments and alien to their life styles.

Table 6.8 clearly depicts the responses of the viewers regarding the accepted entertainment programmes, which are accepted. The most liked programmes under this category are Balachitrapat (Hindi) (38.79%) and the Samsar Ha Sukhacha (37.50%). The Yuva

Darshan (26.29%) and Hindi Play (23.06%) are some of the less liked programmes. It has also been found that on an average, more than 10 per cent of the people did not know about these programmes.

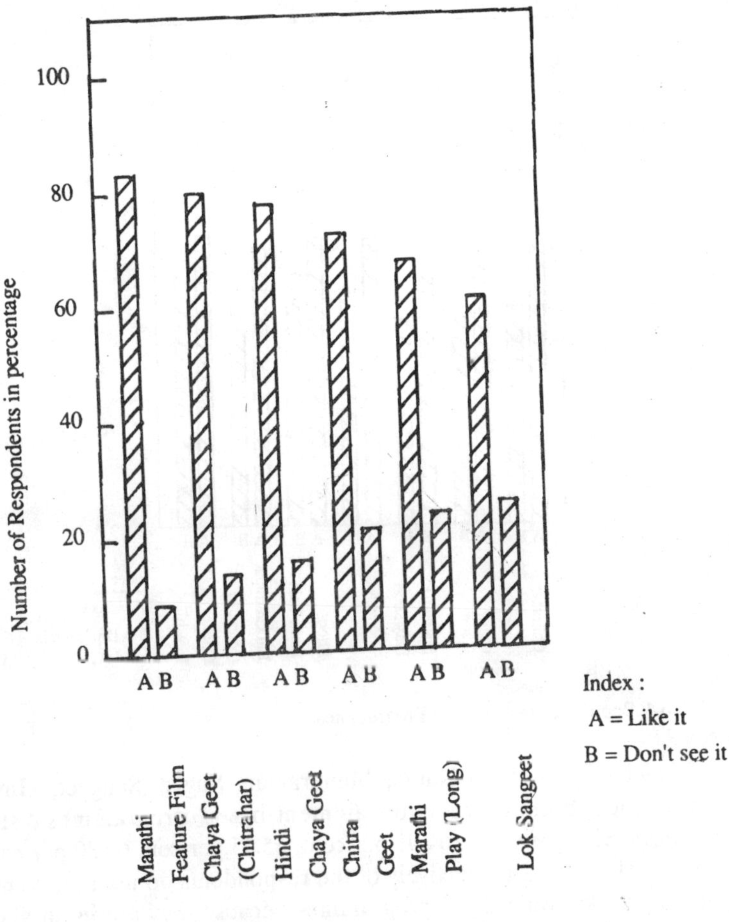

FIG. 6.3: Very popular entertainment programmes.

Since most of the programmes listed in the table are accepted entertainment programmes, the negative response is greater than the positive acceptance.

Programmes like Pratima and Prathibha and Yuva Darshan are in the format of discussion using high flown Marathi language. Even though these programmes are in Marathi, (the local language of the rural people), these programmes do not attract them.

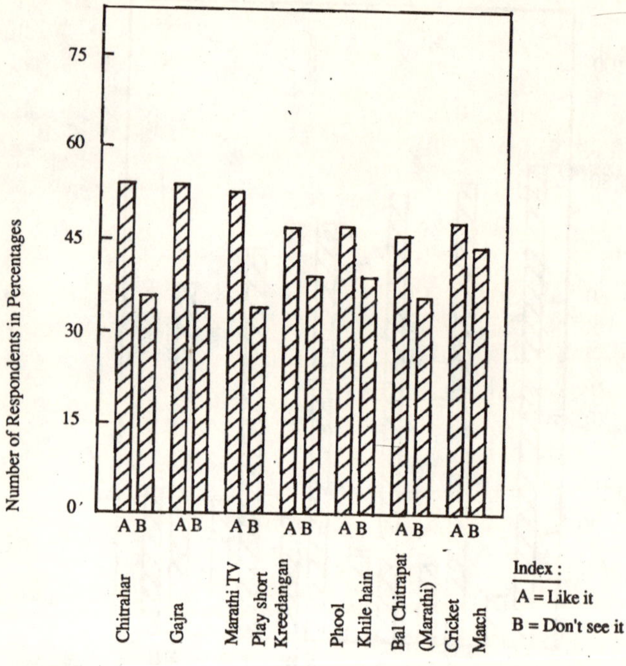

FIG. 6.4: Popular Entertainment Programmes.

Balchitrapat, Hindi Natak, Manoranjan, Sugam Sangeet, Hindi Play, though they are entertainment-based programmes, still majority, 61.21 per cent, 64.01 per cent, 65.95 per cent 69.30 per cent and 76.94 per cent respectively of the respondents do not see, do not like or not knowing these programmes because they are in an alien language. The rest of the programmes mentioned in the table visualised and planned as entertainment programmes by Doordarshan producers are not viewed by the rural respondents. For example, in the programme Sunder Majhe Ghar, deals mostly with making wall hangings, paper flowers and ornamental rengolis etc., do not attract the rural men and women. Women expressed that these are meant for the urban rich and can't be easily adopted by them.

Besides this as we have seen the respondents are poor and can't afford to waste money on unproductive activities.

TABLE 6.8: Accepted Entertainment Programmes

Programmes	RESPONSES				
	Like it	Don't likw it	Don't see	Know but not seen once	Don't know
Balachitrapat (Hindi)	180 (38.79)	9 (1.94)	211 (45.47)	38 (8.19)	22 (4.74)
Samsar Ha Sukhacha	174 (37.50)	26 (5.60)	166 (35.78)	25 (5.39)	67 (14.44)
Hindi Natak	167 (35.99)	25 (5.39)	202 (43.53)	34 (7.33)	32 (6.90)
Sundar Majhe Ghar	159 (34.27)	26 (5.60)	198 (42.67)	28 (6.03)	47 (10.30)
Manoranjan	158 (34.05)	14 (3.02)	201 (43.32)	24 (4.17)	62 (13.36)
Kilbil	151 (32.54)	21 (4.53)	208 (44.83)	42 (9.05)	37 (7.97)
Natya Sangeet	150 (32.33)	44 (9.48)	199 (42.89)	28 (6.03)	36 (7.76)
Sugam Sangeet (Marathi)	143 (30.82)	43 (9.27)	196 (42.24)	20 (4.31)	58 (12.50)
Sugam Sangeet (Hindi)	140 (30.80)	29 (6.25)	250 (46.34)	23 (4.96)	50 (10.78)
Khel Khilone	133 (28.66)	31 (6.68)	211 (45.47)	28 (6.03)	56 (12.07)
Pratima & Prathibha	126 (27.16)	19 (4.09)	226 (48.71)	34 (7.33)	54 (11.04)
Yuva Darsan	122 (26.29)	25 (5.39)	225 (48.49)	28 (6.03)	57 (12.28)
Hindi Play(Long)	107 (23.06)	37 (7.97)	223 (48.06)	30 (6.47)	63 (13.58)

Table 6.9 shows the responses of the viewers regarding the entertainment programmes in English language. It is obvious that though these programmes are entertaining in nature, the above listed

English programmes were very unpopular. The programmes like, Here is Lucy, Yes: Minister, Young World were liked by infinitesimally small (5%) of the viewers only. This observation could be a characteristic of rural viewers only. About 11 per cent to 15 per cent of the viewers did not know about these programmes. In general there is a dislike for English entertainment programmes among the viewers covered through the community television programme. The reason can be attributed to the obvious fact of their lack of understanding of these programmes, which are broadcaste in language other than their mother-tongue.

TABLE 6.9: English Entertainment Programmes

Programmes	RESPONSES				
	Like it	Don't like it	Don't see	Know but not seen once	Don't know
1	2	3	4	5	6
Young World	20 (4.31)	31 (8.84)	313 (67.46)	14 (3.02)	74 (15.95)
Magic Lamp	31 (6.68)	48 (10.34)	307 (66.16)	11 (2.37)	65 (14.01)
English Short film	40 (8.62)	51 (10.99)	304 (65.52)	8 (1.72)	58 (12.50)
English Feature film	63 (13.93)	41 (8.84)	287 (61.85)	16 (3.45)	55 (11.85)
Yes: Minister	25 (5.39)	45 (9.70)	313 (67.16)	17 (3.66)	62 (13.36)
Here is Lucy	27 (5.82)	43 (9.27)	312 (67.24)	12 (2.59)	68 (14.66)
The World of Sports	46 (9.91)	35 (7.54)	308 (66.38)	13 (2.80)	60 (12.93)

Though some of the programmes like 'Here is Lucy' is humorous still it has got caught the attention of rural viewers since the humour is of verbal format and depicts incidents of an alien culture. Since majority of rural audiences is illiterate or barely literate English programmes even though they are entertainment-based, failed to attract the rural audience.

Table 6.10 depicts the response of the viewers regarding the Gujarati entertainment programmes. These programmes are unpopular among the viewers. None of the programmes listed in the above table are liked by the viewers. It is also rated that nearly 13 per cent to 15 per cent of the viewers did not know about the programmes. The least liked among these programmes are: Gujarati Sugam Sangeet and Gujarati Yuva Darshan with only 2.16 per cent viewers liking them. It could be said that generally the Gujarati entertainment programmes are unpopular among the viewers due to the language barrier. Consequently the responses under the heading. 'Don't see' are quite considerable even though they are meant for entertainment.

Programmes in any language other than their mother tongue have no appeal to the respondents because of the language and cultural barriers. Rural folk in Maharashtra can appreciate 'Lavani'; or 'Powada' than 'Garba' dance. These folk media have verbal appeal in their language, which is lost if it were to be in other language.

Table 6.11 depicts the response of the viewers with reference to the entertainment programmes in other languages. It has been observed that Pradeshik Chitrapat has been one of the accepted programmes with 28.23 per cent viewers liking it. The Sindhi programme and the Urdu programme, Mahephil-E-Yara are not popular among the respondents 71.77 per cent and 15.26 per cent respectively. Thus the percentage of responses under the heading, 'Don't see', is substantial.

Pradeshik Chitrapat programmes though in other languages still are popular to some extent because they are cinema medium. They contain entertainment, music, humour and story. Also most of the tunes of the music, story have great similarity with the Marathi movies and treatment of the story plots are also similar. Another reason for viewing other language movies may be due to the curiosity, to know about other cultures and the way of life in other states.

Table 6.12 illustrates the responses of the viewers regarding the entertainment programmes which are very unpopular as far as the preferences of the respondents are concerned. It has been observed that Shabdanchya Palikadle, Vandanwar and Punarbhet are a few of the least liked programmes. Punarbhet which is appreciated by 12.73 per cent of the viewers seem to be the most unpopular of all the programmes among the respondents. It has also been observed that more than 20 per cent of the viewers did not know about the programmes like Saradache Chandane and Amrit Manthan. Except Amrit Manthan all the other programmes are in Marathi, the mother-tongue of the viewers. The non-appeal to these programmes may be because of the very difficult literary Marathi used in these programmes and the programmes are in the form of dialogues.

TABLE 6.10: Gujarati Entertainment Programme

Programmes	RESPONSES				
	Like it	Don't like it	Don't see	Know but not seen once	Don't know
1	2	3	4	5	6
Ghar Baitah	18 (3.88)	48 (10.34)	307 (66.16)	15 (3.23)	70 (15.09)
Aao-Mare Sathi	24 (5.17)	33 (11.42)	300 (64.66)	16 (3.45)	68 (14.66)
Parijat	(14 (3.02)	54 (11.64)	310 (66.81)	11 (2.37)	73 (15.73)
Gujarathi Sugam Sangeet	10 (2.16)	16 (13.15)	309 (66.59)	14 (3.02)	68 (14.66)
Gujarathi Short Play	17 (3.66)	57 (12.28)	309 (66.59)	14 (3.02)	65 (14.01)
Gujarathi Play (Long)	18 (3.88)	56 (12.07)	311 (67.03)	12 (2.59)	64 (13.79)
Dairo (Gujarati)	13 (2.80)	59 (12.72)	311 (67.03)	8 (1.72)	71 (15.30)
Santa Kukdi (Gujarati)	18 (3.88)	52 (11.21)	310 (66.81)	19 (4.09)	63 (13.58)
Gujarati Chitrageet	31 (6.68)	63 (13.58)	293 (63.15)	14 (3.02)	61 (13.50)
Gujarati Yuva Darshan	10 (2.16)	61 (13.15)	307 (66.16)	20 (4.31)	64 (13.79)

TABLE 6.11: Entertainment Programmes in Other Languages

Programmes	Responses				
	Like it	Don't like it	Don't see	Know but not seen once	Don't know
Pradeshik Chitrapat	131 (28.23)	25 (5.39)	231 (49.78)	15 (3.23)	59 (12.72)
Sindhi Programmes	27 (5.82)	64 (13.79)	287 (61.85)	17 (3.66)	67 (14.44)
Mahephil-E-Yara	22 (4.74)	49 (10.66)	307 (66.16)	19 (4.09)	64 (13.79)

TABLE 6.12: Unpopular Entertainment Programmes*

Programmes	RESPONSES				
	Like it	Don't like it	Don't see	Know but not seen once	Don't know
Varhadi Mansa	91 (19.61)	35 (7.54)	232 (50.00)	34 (7.33)	65 (14.01)
Natyavalokan	89 (19.18)	33 (7.11)	252 (54.31)	31 (6.68)	54 (11.64)
Saradache Chandana	78 (16.81)	37 (7.97)	220 (47.41)	28 (6.03)	97 (20.97)
Amrıt Manthan	78 (16.81)	23 (4.96)	229 (49.35)	37 (7.97)	93 (20.04)
Shabdanchaya Palikadale	70 (15.09)	44 (9.48)	240 (51.72)	30 (6.47)	70 (16.38)
Vandanwar	61 (13.50)	23 (4.96)	265 (57.11)	33 (7.11)	74 (15.95)
Punarbhet	60 (12.93)	25 (5.39)	252 (54.31)	45 (9.70)	77 (16.59)

Table 6.13 assesses the programme preferences of viewers to classical Music and Dance. Classical music is too scientific and is not appealing to the rural respondents. However, the classical dance programmes even though they are not like the folk dances, still attracted 22.84 per cent of the respondents because they are colourful with music and costumes.

Informative and Educative Programmes

The aim of introduction of television in India was to educate and inform the rural masses about the advances in science, technology, social change and modernisation taking place in the world in general and in India in particular. Since the majority of rural people are illiterate and cannot benefit from the written media such as newspapers, magazines etc. TV which is a powerful media has visual and audio was considered the ideal medium for the purpose of imparting education and information dissemination.

TABLE 6.13: Music Programmes

Programmes	RESPONSES				
	Like it	Don't like it	Don't see	Know but not seen once	Don't know
Classical Music (Vocal)	28 (6.03)	59 (12.72)	282 (60.78)	18 (3.88)	75 (16.16)
Classical Music (Instrumental)	31 (6.68)	65 (14.01)	274 (59.05)	18 (3.88)	74 (15.98)
Dance	106 (22.84)	38 (8.19)	247 (53.23)	13 (2.80)	57 (12.28)

Now let us examine whether this medium has made any inroads into the rural audiences in this direction. Amacha Mati programmes were generally related to high yielding variety of seeds, seed treatment, use of chemical fertilizers, pesticides, insecticides and other methods of plant protection. Soil testing, field preparation, irrigation, sowing, harvesting and storage methods were also covered in these programmes. Besides these vegetable growing, animal husbandry, cattle diseases, poultry farming, pig rearing are some of the topics covered in these programmes.

Figure 6.5 indicates the responses of the viewers with regard to some of the programmes which are considered as 'very popular' as well as 'popular' informative/educational programmes. It is observed that Batmya and Amchi Mati, Amchi Manase are very popular and these programmes are liked by 79-96 per cent and 71.12 per cent of the respondents respectively. Since the programme, Amchi Mati Amchi Manase, is rural based, the village folk can easily understand and appreciate it. Dyanadeep and Udyache Kryakram are popular with 50.43 per cent and 46.34 per cent of the viewers respectively and they liked them. The number of viewers who do not know about these programmes is very low. It appears then that the above listed information/educational programmes have become much appreciated by viewers.

Batmya is a new programme, which caters mostly to the regional news still left 20.04 per cent out of the purview because these respondents are too busy with their own problems and for them TV viewing is only for entertainment.

Amachi Mati Amachi Manase is specially meant for agriculturists and still 28.88 per cent of the respondents did not like these programmes. The reasons expressed by the non-viewers is as followers: One respondent said, "The programme is too scientific and technical. I can't understand it". Another opined that 'Whatever agricultural suggestions given are untimely, so they are not remembered by me when the need arises; so I don't care much for these programmes".

Regarding the Dyanadeep programme, still nearly half the respondents are not interested in it. These programmes are based on the activities of different mandals located in Maharashtra. Majority of the mandal programmes are with the mandals in urban areas, the rural viewers find limited appeal. They do not find any information nearer home shown in these programmes.

Rural respondents indicated that repetition of agricultural programmes will help in understanding. However, it is not adopted in the Amacha Mati programmes. However, some cultivators among TV viewers complained that the agricultural programmes did not follow the cultivation cycle, thereby making them untimely. According to the respondents some programmes are redundant as they were not related to crops grown in their villages.

A variety of programme formats – lectures, discussions with experts, fields demonstrators, documentaries were used frequently. Though demonstrations were favoured, documentaries, lectures and discussion were not appealing to the respondents.

Table 6.14 shows the responses of the viewers with regard to the informative/educational programmes, which are acceptable to them. Kamgar Vishwa, the National Programmes (English and Hindi) and *Saptahiki* (Hindi) topped the list of accepted programmes. *Baten Filmoki* (Hindi) and *Dainandin Vignan* are some of the less popular among the above liked programmes with only 23.49 per cent and 22.84 per cent of the viewers liking them. However, these programmes were not known to 18.53 per cent and 14.22 per cent of the viewers respectively.

Since these programmes are mostly informative and educative, they have less entertainment content in them. Consequently the number of respondents which are listed under the heading. 'Don't see' is fairly large.

Table 6.15 shows the responses of the viewers with reference to informative/educational programmes, which are unpopular among most of the respondents. The above listed programmes are least liked programmes with less than 16 per cent of the viewers liking the programmes. It has been observed that about 16 per cent to 22 per cent of the viewers did not even know about these programmes. As expected the responses under the heading, 'Don't see' are in majority. They are all informative programmes and discussion format is utilised. Except Chakravyuha all other programmes listed above are in Hindi. The unpopularity of these programmes is due to alien Hindi language and discussion format.

Table 6.16 indicates the responses of the viewers with reference to the informative/educational programmes from other languages. It is surprising to note that some programmes are liked by less than four per cent of the viewers, for example, 'Aapne Sambhodine' (Gujarati) and 'What is the Good Word' (English) are liked by 3.88 per cent and 2.16 per cent respectively. Even the programmes that topped the list under the heading, 'Like it', namely, TVNP is liked by only 18.97 per cent of the viewers. All the above programmes were not known to 11.85 per cent to 22.84 per cent of the viewers. It could then be said generally that these programmes are not popular among the viewers covered under the study. Since these programmes are mainly meant for educative and informative category, a minimum

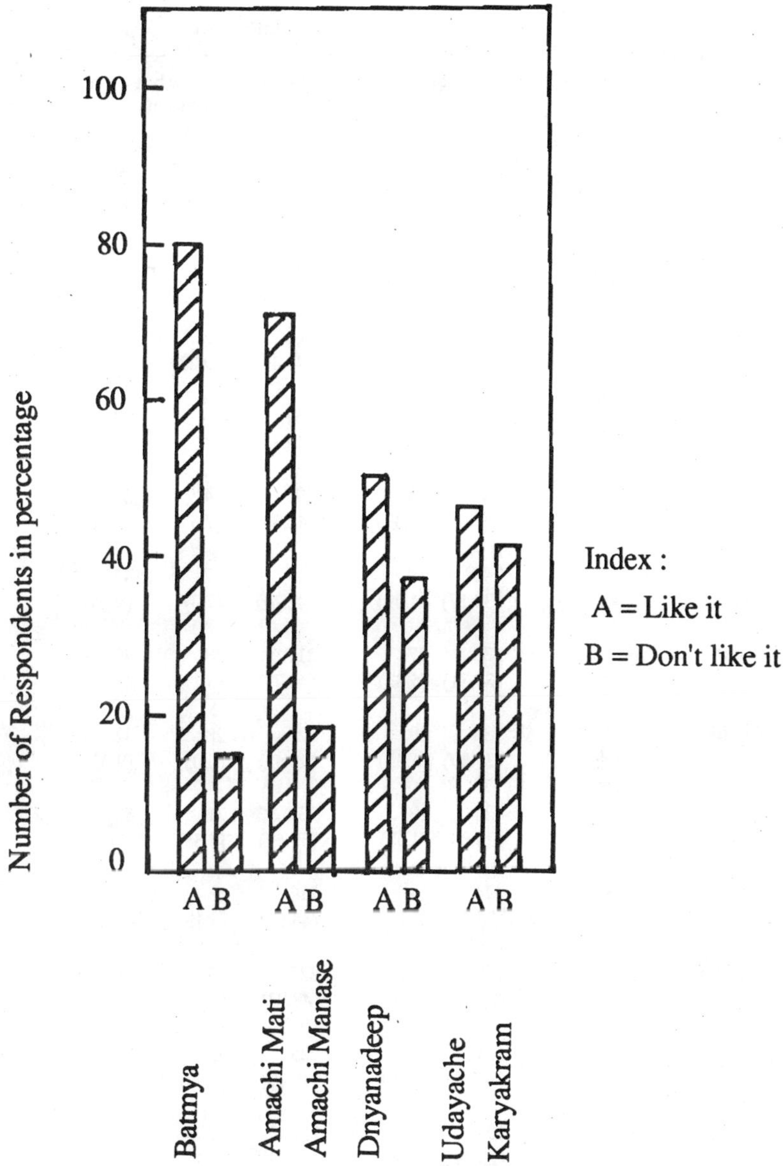

FIG. 6.5: Very Popular and Popular Information and Educative Programmes.

TABLE 6.14: Accepted Informative and Educational Programmes

Programmes	RESPONSES				
	Like it	Don't like it	Don't see	Know but not seen once	Don't know
Kamgar Vishwa	192 (41.38)	18 (3.88)	194 (41.81)	29 (6.25)	25 (5.39)
National Programme (English & Hindi)	177 (38.15)	31 (6.68)	228 (49.14)	12 (2.59)	14 (3.02)
Saptahiki(Hindi)	175 (37.72)	7 (1.51)	206 (44.40)	43 (9.27)	28 (6.83)
Kortachi Payari	163 (35.13)	13 (2.80)	187 (40.30)	33 (7.11)	64 (13.79)
Arogya Sampada	144 (31.03)	25 (5.39)	199 (42.89)	34 (7.33)	57 (12.28)
Mulkha Vagli Manase	140 (30.17)	19 (4.09)	219 (47.20)	37 (7.97)	42 (9.05)
Mukhawate Ani Chehara	136 (29.31)	27 (5.82)	217 (46.77)	38 (8.19)	40 (8.62)
Hoshiyar	135 (29.09)	29 (6.25)	225 (48.49)	28 (6.03)	42 (9.05)
Shaleeya Chitravani	134 (28.88)	19 (4.09)	235 (50.65)	21 (4.35)	53 (11.43)
Vrutha Chitra	124 (26.72)	26 (5.60)	212 (45.69)	38 (8.19)	57 (12.28)
Saprem Namaskar	115 (24.78)	36 (7.76)	227 (48.92)	23 (4.46)	55 (11.85)
Vartha Patra	115 (24.78)	29 (6.25)	225 (48.49)	32 (6.90)	57 (12.28)
Baten Filmonki (Hindi)	109 (23.49)	35 (7.54)	212 (45.69)	37 (7.97)	66 (14.22)
Dainandin Vignan	106 (22.84)	13 (2.80)	218 (46.98)	32 (6.90)	86 (18.53)

educational level is required to understand and appreciate these programmes. As our respondents are all rural people, who are least educated or illiterates, they showed no preference to watch these programmes. Hence the percentage of viewers under the head, 'Don't see', is considerable for most of these programmes.

TABLE 6.15: Unpopular Informative/Educational Programmes

Programmes	Responses				
	Like it	Don't like it	Don't see	Know but not seen once	Don't know
Chakravyuha	74 (15.95)	34 (7.33)	213 (46.77)	32 (6.90)	101 (21.77)
Aur Bhi Gam Hai (Hindi)	51 (10.99)	38 (8.19)	237 (51.08)	32 (6.90)	101 (21.77)
Rachana (Hindi)	43 (9.27)	47 (10.13)	255 (55.96)	36 (7.76)	78 (16.81)
Apaki Rai (Hindi)	46 (9.91)	44 (9.48)	258 (55.60)	28 (6.03)	82 (17.66)
Hindi Current Affairs	39 (4.81)	37 (7.11)	264 (56.90)	40 (8.62)	83 (17.89)

Rural Programmes and Audience Preferences

Rural programmes were aimed at bringing about awareness, imparting knowledge, adoption and use of Methods suggested by the experts. To achieve this objective the programmes telecast should be at a suitable time convenient to the viewers and duration of the programmes and the number of times the programmes are telecast. These are important parameters, so respondents' views covering these factors were assessed.

It is observed from Fig. 6.6 that most of the respondents often viewed the rural based programmes (71.77%). It is also observed those who could not view such programmes complained about the unsuitability of the timings (9.70%), or that their TV sets were out of order (7.97%). Those who do not like such programmes were very few (2.37%).

TABLE 6.16: Unpopular Information/Educational Programmes in Other Languages

Programmes	RESPONSES				
	Like it	Don't like it	Don't see	Know but not seen once	Don't know
TVNP	88 (18.97)	19 (4.09)	210 (45.26)	35 (7.54)	106 (22.84)
School Television (English)	52 (11.21)	30 (6.47)	295 (63.58)	29 (6.25)	55 (11.85)
Science Report (English)	44 (9.48)	37 (7.97)	301 (64.87)	12 (2.59)	67 (14.44)
Focus (English)	27 (5.82)	42 (9.05)	308 (66.38)	11 (2.37)	74 (15.95)
Aapne Sambhodine (Gujarati)	18 (3.88)	52 (11.21)	310 (66.81)	19 (4.09)	63 (13.58)
What's the Good Word (English)	10 (2.18)	44 (9.48)	321 (69.18)	16 (3.45)	71 (15.30)

Figure 6.7 is regarding the suitability of timing for viewing of the rural programmes, a majority of the respondents (48.28 %) preferred it to have the programme broadcast during the afternoon time. Those who wanted it in the morning (20.6%) or in the evening up to 6.30 p.m. were (19.96%) remained almost same. A few of them (about 10%) wanted the programmes at varying timings from 6.30 p.m. to 10.30 p.m. Since most of the people in the villages are engaged in agricultural activities, they have normally (except in harvest season) leisure time for rest during afternoon. Hence their preference to afternoon broadcasts.

Regarding the question as to whether three days in a week they would like to have the rural programmes telecast a majority of them answered positively (57.54%), while only a few (6.03%) were not satisfied with the proposed frequency. About 20 per cent of the respondents, however, wanted the programmes to be telecaste for more than four times a week although a few of them (7.33%) suggested even twice a week only.

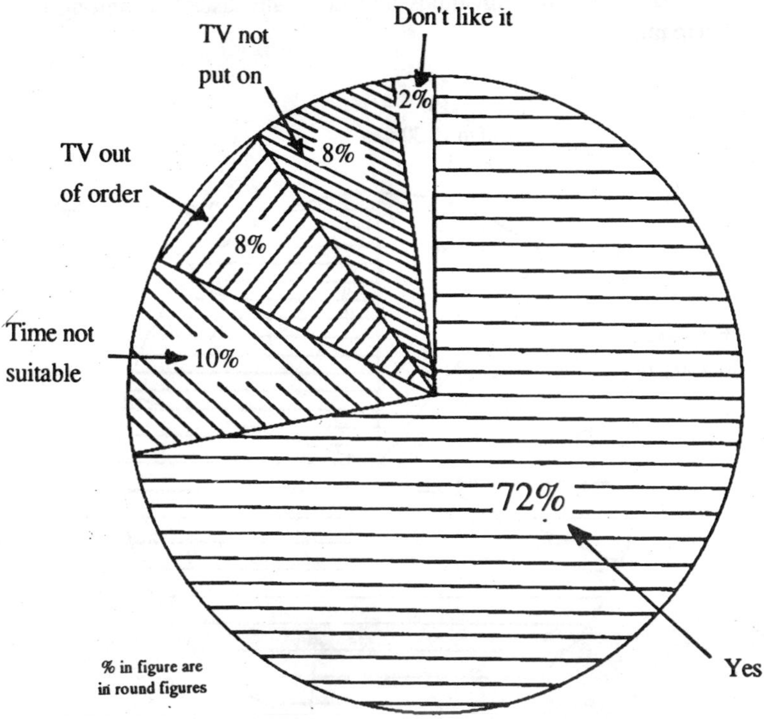

FIG. 6.6: Do You See Rural Programmes.

137

It is observed from Fig. 6.8 that quite a number of respondents (45.04%) liked to have the rural programmes for at least 30 minutes. Those who wanted it even for a longer duration represent about 27.00 per cent. In fact, 14.87 per cent of them wanted it to be only for 25 minutes. A few of the respondents 5.60 per cent were satisfied with the present duration of the programme as shown in Fig. 6.9. Almost an equal number of them 7.33 per cent could not express any opinion.

Varied Types of Programmes

In villages the children played some indigenous local games, such as *Kho Kho, Gulli Danda*, running and skill games. Sports build up competitive spirit in individuals and inculcate discipline among the participants.

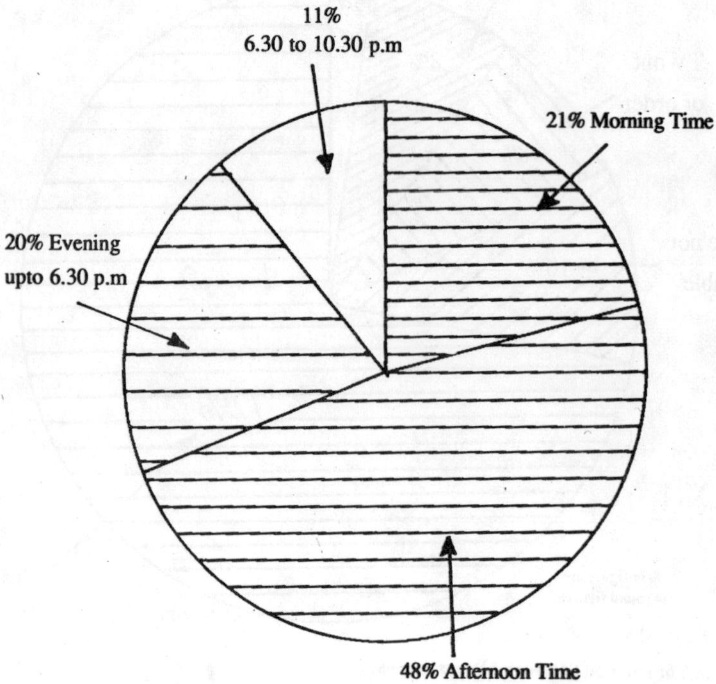

FIG. 6.7: Suitable Time for Rural Programmes.

Sports meet at international, national and regional levels are always being conducted and telecasted by Doordarshan. Modern games like, Cricket, Hockey, Football, Tennis, VolleyBall, sports like running, cycling, athletics, and aquatic races are telecasted in India to popularise these games among the rural masses. It is aimed that the viewing will bring forth national integration, unity and the spirit of nationalism among the people.

Let us examine the interest evinced by the respondents to various sports events telecasted.

It is seen from Table 6.17 that the rural masses are quite aware of regional sports and games. A sizeable portion of the respondents (66.81%) have been keenly watching the regional sports, whereas

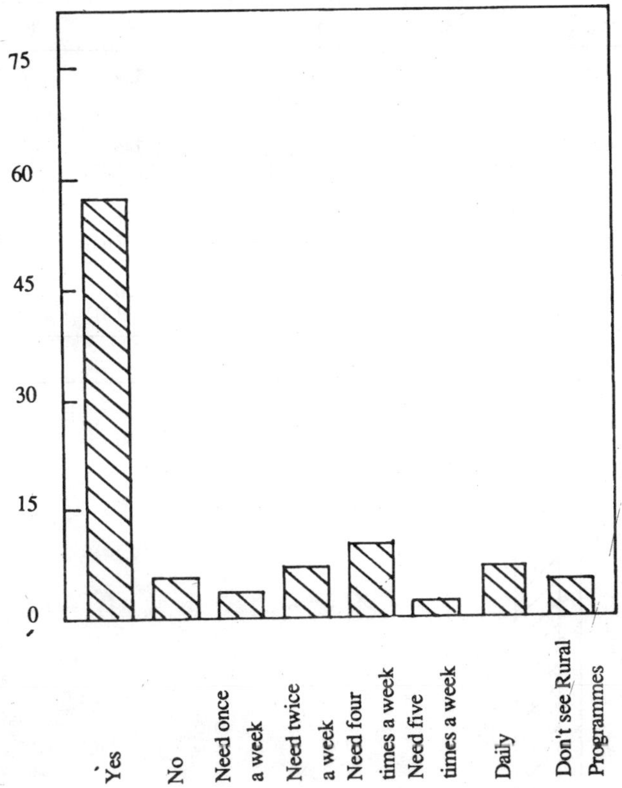

FIG. 6.8: Adequacy of Rural Programmes Thrice a Week is Enough.

about 33.19 per cent of the respondents were not keen on such programmes. A similar trend is also noticed in the case of sports competition programmes (68.53% liked and 31.47% did not like). However, it appears that quite a sizeable number (nearly 47.63%) did not seem to have much fascination for seeing the documentaries on how to learn games and sports, although 52.37 per cent were keen to see such instructive programmes. As it is in the cities, the rural folks are also equally enthusiastic about viewing the cricket matches and other games. 70.69 per cent of the respondents were in favour of such programmes. Majority of rural respondents showed liking for viewing sports events.

TABLE 6.17: Sports Programmes

Type of Programmes	Yes	No
Regional Sports	310 (66.81)	154 (33.19)
Sports Competition	318 (68.53)	146 (31.47)
Documentary on 'How to Learn Sports ?'	243 (52.37)	221 (47.63)
Cricket & Other Matches	328 (70.69)	136 (29.31)

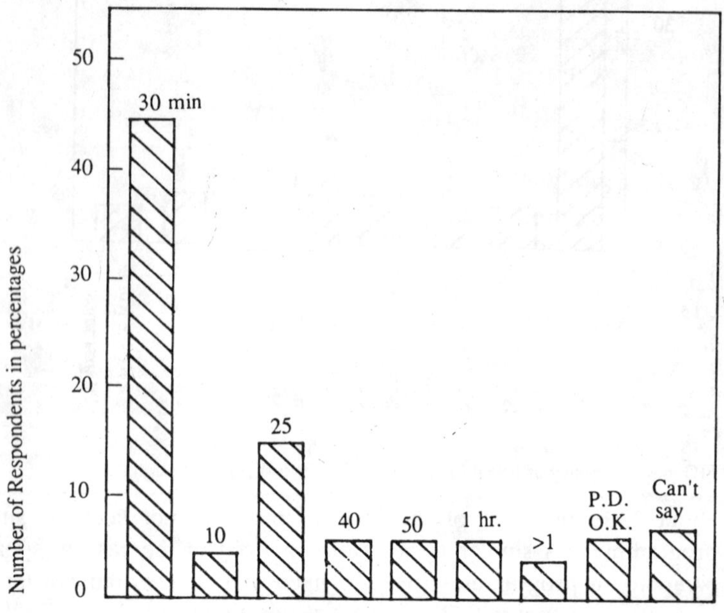

Fig. 6.9: Time duration for rural programmes.

Music is a part and parcel of village life and is a source of entertainment to the villagers in their otherwise drab existence. Folk music is popular in rural area. However, Doordarshan's musical programmes are enumerated in Table 6.18.

TABLE 6.18: Music – Regional Programmes

Type of Music Programmes	Yes	No
Indian Classical Music	145 (31.25)	319 (68.75)
Bhajan	329 (70.89)	135 (29.11)
Natyageet	212 (45.69)	252 (54.31)
Bhavgeet	350 (77.00)	114 (23.00)

Table 6.18 indicates the responses elucidated from the respondents with regard to their liking for the India classical music, Bhajan, Natyageet and Bhavageet. It is seen that a majority of the people (68.75%) do not like the Indian Classical music. Similarly, Natyageet also doesn't attract the attention of many people (54.31%). However, it is quite evident that Bhajan (70.89%) and Bhavgeet (77.00%) appear to be very much liked by the respondents since they are alien to the folk music.

It was observed that our respondents generally did not like Hindi music programmes – Gazals, or Hindi geet – nor did they appreciate Western music programmes. However, they seemed to be appreciating the National Dance and Music programmes to a remarkable extent.

SECTION III

Experimental Study on Superstitious Beliefs

One of the major objectives of TV communication on Indian context is to impart knowledge. The correct and scientific knowledge would no doubt improve the people's attitude towards many happenings in their day-to-day life. A vast country like India where most of the people are rural-based and illiterates, there is an urgent need to undertake such programmes which would orient the people towards their development.

Although most of the programmes telecasted through TV are

aimed at entertaining the masses there are few programmes which are instructional or educative in nature. However, programmes focusing certain aspects viz., superstitious beliefs and practices in the society are conspicious by their absence. Keeping the above situation in mind, an attempt has been made to produce a couple of programmes to highlight the futility of superstitions with a view to educate the rural audience. It was also decided to further undertake a study on the impact these programmes would have made on the audience with reference to their awareness attitude and practice of such superstitions. The details of such programme carried out are given below. The programme details an outline of the objectives, methodology, village selection feedback which are self-explanatory.

Superstitions – A Video Experiment

As a policy the primary objective assigned to television in India is dissemination of need-based information to rural folks in order to achieve socio-economic change in rural areas. However, there is ample evidence to show that there are some tasks which mass media can do and some they can't do and some they can do better than others. According to Klapper, "It has also been proved that mass communication is not very effective by itself in changing attitudes that are strongly held and deeply anchored. But it is quite possible through mass communication to have some effect on positions that are not strongly defended, or a new question concerning which there has been neither time nor information on to build up strong attitudes" (Klapper, 1960).

Specific information on the type of beliefs, attitudes and practices in Indian social life that respond to change, because of TV exposure is extremely meagre, with a view to gaining knowledge on what could be the influence or impact of series of TV programmes on commonly held beliefs, which are considered responsible for under-development, the researcher launched on an experiment.

Broad Goal of the Series

The series on superstition was on exercise mainly planned to study the consequent attitudinal and behavioural changes in superstitions commonly shared in Maharashtra villages.

Background Research

Preliminary research exercise conducted in one purposively selected village in Pune suggested that a variety of superstitious beliefs are shared by all communities in respect of :

(a) A new entrant into the family like a newly born baby, a daughter-in-law and a cow etc.
(b) The auspicious and inauspicious omens before starting any important work or launching a project.
(c) The influence of evil eye on children, teenage girls and crops etc., and
(d) Efficacy of a Bhagat/Mantrik in the cure of sickness, poisonous snake bites and spirits.

General Framework and the Series

The general framework adopted is outlined below:

Target Audience

All rural adults in the transmission zone without any specificity.

Format

Plays produced in the studio with six stock characters, representing a rural middle class family consisting:

- a semi-literate father with some beliefs in superstitions but receptive to modern ideas supported by reason and scientific evidence.
- illiterate orthodox mother with strong faith in superstitious beliefs
- a college educated grown up son, who thinks rationally.
- a grownup daughter educated up to high school.
- a school going son treated as kid.
- a daughter-in-law with urban contact who cannot oppose her in-laws but is not for, for superstitious beliefs and practices in the house.

Specific Goals

The series was produced in five programmes each dealing with specific object. The sub-goals identified for the individual programmes were:

(1) Superstitious beliefs connected with the entry of daughter-in-law.
(2) Omens for undertaking journey on an important assignment.
(3) Bhagats treatment for snake-bite.
(4) Evil eye on an infant.

Five programmes have different goals to test the superstitious beliefs are given below:

Paigun (14 minutes)

This programme was aimed to show how superstitious people for no reason attribute any unfortunate event to the entry of the daughter-in-law.

Nakatichya Lagnala (18 minutes)

Aimed at to show how success in work is dependent on efforts instead of omens.

Bap-re-Sap Re (18 minutes)

It is aimed at showing that very few snakes are poisonous and in case if poisonous snake bites, the patient should be taken to a qualified doctor, instead of a Bhagat.

Sarpa Danshawar Upchar (18 minutes)

The programme was aimed to acquaint the viewers with different types of poisonous and non-poisonous snakes and also to demonstrate proper first-aid to be administered for snake-bite.

Ida Pida Tado

The last programme of the series was to indicate how sickness is attributed to effect of evil eye.

Methodology

Keeping in view the limitations such as resources available for data collection, the researcher decided to confine the experiment to two villages. The villages Velhe and Murti were selected purposively, representing backward and progressive regions respectively. The researcher adopted the experimental design.

To estimate knowledge gain and to assess the impact, the researcher decided to have pre-exposure and post-exposure surveys in the two selected villages. The objective of the pre-exposure survey was to collect data in terms of knowledge, attitude and practices in respect of the selected superstitions, beliefs projected in the series with post-exposure survey. The composition of the sample of 131 respondents was fixed from two villages. The pre-tested questionnaire for pre-test exposure survey was used.

Brief on Villages

Velhe

Velhe village is the taluka headquarters of Velhe taluka and is 70 km from Pune. It can be reached by link route of Nasrapur on Pune-Satara route.

Murti

The village is situated in the prosperous Baramati taluka of Pune District. It can be reached from Pune by going on Saswad road to Jejury and from there a diversion route via Morgoan.

For the pre-exposure survey a total sample of 131 respondents of both the sexes and from different age groups was chosen, while for the post-exposure survey only 100 of them had presented themselves.

Programme Telecast

After the pre-exposure survey the telecast of the five programmes in the series was scheduled on a fortnightly basis. Researcher worked out the criteria for summative evaluation, which was to be done after the exposure of 5 programmes.

Post-Exposure Survey

Researcher had interviewed a total sample of 131 persons in the two villages for the pre-exposure survey. But 31 out of them could not be contacted for the post-exposure survey conducted after the telecast of the five programmes in the series.

Responses to the Programmes

The distribution of the respondents who had seen the programmes in the series is given in Table 6.19.

TABLE 6.19: Exposure to the Five Programmes in the Superstition Series

Exposure	No. of Respondents
None of the programmes	63
Only one programme	26
Two programmes	15
Three programmes	17
Four programmes	7
All the five	3

In both the selected villages, generally the community TV sets are kept open on only 3 days in a week for film-based entertainment programmes. However, because researcher was visiting regularly for feedback on the programmes in this series, the sets were kept open by the Gram Panchayat. Nevertheless, the data indicated that it is difficult to anticipate high exposure to the rural programmes. There are very few villagers who can regularly watched the telecast. There is frequent change in the composition of audience with the viewers of the rotating constantly. The extent of viewing of the individual programmes telecasted in the series are given in Table 6.20.

TABLE 6.20: Extent of Exposure to the Programmes in the Superstition Series

Programme	No. of Respondents
Paigun	39
Naktichaya Lagnala	45
Bapre Sapre	28
Sarpa Dhanshavar Upchar	25
Ida Pida Tado	12

Impact

Despite the limited exposure, the results of the post-exposure survey indicated marginal increase in awareness. The data showed that the information given on TV has had some effect with a slight improvement in knowledge in almost all the areas that have been covered in the series.

Beliefs in Respect of the Entry of a New Daughter-in-law

Before the exposure there were as many as 50 per cent of the respondents who entertained the belief that the entry of a new daughter-in-law has definite relation with anything good or bad that happens in the family afterwards. But, after the exposure, the percentage of this category has come down to 27 per cent. Simultaneously, the proportion of respondents who were of the opinion that such an occurrence is a mere coincidence had gone up from 21 per cent to 42 per cent after the exposure. However, those who believed in fate did not appear to have been convinced because both in the pre- and post-exposure surveys their proportion remained at 42 per cent.

TABLE 6.21: Beliefs in Respect of Entry of New Daughter-in-law

Belief	Pre-Exposure	Post-Exposure
	N=131	N=100
It is true that some bring good/bad luck with them	50%	27%
It is fate	42%	41%
It is coincidence	21%	42%
No belief at all	12%	8%

Beliefs in Respect of Evil Eye

The percentage of believers in 'evil eye' also marginally dropped down from 73 per cent to 63 per cent after the exposure. But, the pattern of response in respect of beliefs regarding the people who cast evil eye, the effect of evil eye, or the remedies for evil eye remained same both before and after the exposure.

TABLE 6.22: Beliefs in Respect of Evil Eye

	Pre-Exposure	Post-Exposure
	N=95	N=63
(a) People who cast Evil Eye:		
Barren women	69%	63%
Persons with evil eye	47%	41%
People practising witch-craft	46%	32%
Persons who are dissatisfied with life	45%	37%
Any body	35%	16%
(b) Victims of Evil Eye:		
Small children	92%	95%
Teenage boys/girls	84%	75%
Cattle	68%	78%
Crops	45%	62%
Eatables	34%	25%
(c) Effects of Evil Eye:		
Children fall sick	89%	83%
Cattle fall sick	82%	76%
Food gets spoiled	26%	29%
Poverty strikes the family	22%	38%
(d) Remedies:		
Household remedy	80%	82%
Mantrik's treatment	34%	43%

Beliefs in Respect of Omens

There was a marginal shift in the beliefs regarding omens after the exposure, as can be seen from Table 6.23.

Beliefs in Respect of Bhagats/Mantriks

An attempt was made in two programmes to highlight the beliefs regarding Mantriks and their role in curing major and minor ailments. The message seems to have been conveyed that for calamities like snake bites etc., it is futile to approach a Mantrik/Bhagat. However, the feeling that a Bhagat or Mantrik could be consulted for simple ailments seems to persist without much change. Since researcher did not have enough evidence to disprove, it may be difficult to convince the rural audience that whatever Bhagats do is ineffective and utter nonsense. The response in the pre- and post-exposure surveys in this regard is given in Table 6.24.

TABLE 6.23: Distribution of Believers in Omens

Category	Pre-exposure (N=131)	Post-exposure (N=100)
Has belief in omens	78%	66%
No belief in omens	22%	34%
Good Omens:	(N = 102)	(N = 66)
Person with pot of water	80%	58%
Married women	64%	61%
Eyes flickering	63%	59%
Corpse going	43%	44%
Others	11%	14%
Bad Omens:		
Cat crossing	85%	92%
Widow's face	51%	77%
Barber's face	49%	77%
Dog's cry	47%	52%
Donkey's bray	36%	61%

TABLE 6.24: Purpose of Consultation with Bhagats

Responses	Pre-exposure	Post-exposure
(a) Consultation with Bhagats:		
Consults Bhagats	60%	37%
Never consults Bhagats	40%	63%
(b) Purpose of Consulting Bhagats:		
For cure simple ailments	79%	87%
Neutralising effects of evil eye	47%	73%
Curing poisonous bites of insects	37%	35%
Helping in having children	37%	42%
To get fortune	19%	24%
To take revenge	13%	11%

Beliefs in Respect of Snake and Snake Bites

The programme on this subject attempted to convey the message that there are very few poisonous snakes, but a person bitten by a snake should be given first-aid and taken to a qualified doctor for immediate treatment. Before the exposure, there were as many as 22 per cent who shared the belief that all the snake bites are fatal. But, after the exposure their proportion dropped down to 3 per cent among the respondents. Similarly, before the exposure even though 55 per cent of the respondents have boasted that they could identify a poisonous snake, most of them were found to be under the wrong impression that it is possible to find out by hood, colour, length etc. After the exposure there seemed to be a little increase in the awareness that colour and length are not the criteria for judging whether a snake is poisonous or not. However, there has not been any perceptible change in the proportion of respondents who shared the knowledge that the incision/fang marks of snake are the correct indicators to find out if the snake is poisonous or not. While the percentage of such respondents was 39 before the exposure, after the exposure it marginally increased to 42 per cent. Perhaps the visual presentation and explanation of this aspect was not very clear and informative in the programme. Similar was the case with regard to first-aid. They seem to need more education on this aspect.

TABLE 6.25: Extent of Awareness and Identification of Poisonous Snakes

Responses	Pre-exposure (N=131)	Post-exposure (N=100)
(a) Extent of Awareness about poisonous snakes:		
All snakes are fatal	22%	3%
Only a few poisonous snakes are harmful	64%	87%
No snake bite is fatal	9%	13%
No knowledge	5%	4%
(b) Identification of poisonous snakes:		
(I) Can identify	55%	48%
(II) Can't identify	45%	52%
	(N = 71)	(N = 48)
Can identify by food	74%	38%
Snake turns after biting	47%	21%
From fang marks	38%	42%

Recall

More than three-fourths (48) of the respondents could recall without aid that the programme was regarding snake bites and first aid. Five more respondents replied that it was about superstitions on snake bite. Fifty out of 61 could recall Aba's conversation with doctor and the purpose of visiting the person who collected snakes.

Comprehension

More than three-fourths of the respondents could recall correctly how to make out from the incision whether the snake is poisonous one or not. As many as 53 out of 61 could recall correctly the information regarding how to prevent circulation of poison in blood and, how to clean the injury. Similarly, 38 out of 61 expressed satisfaction regarding medical facilities available in their villages.

Flash-backs

The first flash-back sequence from the last programme 'Bap-re-Sap-re', was understood correctly by 47 respondents and 14 could not comprehend the sequence and its purpose. This could be because most of them have seen the earlier programme. The second flash-back introduced in this programme which was an actuality coverage from a village, could also be properly linked up by 47 respondents. Perhaps, the dialogue support helped in explaining the position clearly.

Credibility

Characters and sequences of the programme were considered appropriate and realistic. However, the following comments are worth-noting :

(a) more time should be allotted for such formative programmes (8);
(b) close up of poisonous snakes for some more time should have been given (6);
(c) in Velhe though medical aid is available, Government dispensary does not have enough medicine for snake bite cases (3).

Languages of the Programme

No difficulty was faced in following the programme as the language was simple with rural accent.

Comments of the Researcher

Technical quality of the programme appeared to be poor as some of the visuals were not clear, in the community viewing situation.

The experiments proved that if the programmes were properly made with good visual effects it will improve the perception of the audience. Some of the deep-rooted beliefs even though could not be changed, even the slight impact proves that the TV can work as an effective media for bringing about change among rural people so for superstitions are concerned. Programmes on similar themes if taken and shown they will go a long way to dispel the age-old superstitious beliefs of the villagers.

Conclusion

The viewers in our sample are preponderantly males in the younger age group, having agriculture as their main occupation. Majority of the respondents belonged to low income big joint families. Their educational level is low and much to be desired. Because of their poverty the respondents cannot afford to purchase personal TV sets, so they depended on CTV for their entertainment, information and education, since they have no alternative media for this purpose. As they are barely literate written media is not useful to them.

Most of these rural respondents are ill-educated and can only comprehend and appreciate mother-tongue-based programmes.

The curiosity and interest to know the current affairs in their state, attracts viewers to intermittent viewing of Marathi news. The medium of cinema has already made great inroads in rural population. Cinema-based programmes in TV are very popular among the rural folk as they involve no expenditure and at the same time provide entertainment. Marathi feature films top the list of their preferences.

Any type of programme in Marathi with entertainment value has a great appeal over informative and educative programmes.

If the entertainment programmes are in English, Hindi and Gujarati they do not have much appeal to rural audiences because they cannot understand much and also they deal with alien culture. However, cinema in any language even in other regional languages are preferred by the viewers. This categorically proves that rural people have great attraction for feature films and cinema-based programmes.

Even the Marathi programmes such as Varhadi Manse, Natyovalokan, Shebdanchi Palekadale, Vandanvar and Punarbhet which were planned by Doordarshan as entertainment programmes have not been well received by rural audiences, because of their difficult Marathi and the discussion format utilised therein.

Classical music requires cultivated taste for appreciation and rural audience in majority seem to be lacking in this.

Television's main aim is to impart information and educate the rural population through their programmes. 'Batmya', which is a news programme is as popular as Marathi cinema in Doordarshan. It dispels the misconception that rural people are not interested in what is going on around the world. Rural people are interested in the happenings in the world in general and Maharashtra in popular.

'Amachi Mate Amachi Manas' which is a well received programme is agricultural based and shows the discussion by rural folk which the audience identify themselves as participating in it. These programmes are in dramatic discussion format using mostly rural Marathi language. 'Dynanadeep' is about voluntary organisations and villagers showed interest because they also like to organise themselves socially.

Informative programmes such as Kamgar Vishwa, Kortachi Payari, Arogya Sampada, Mulkha Vegla Manas, Hoshiyar, Vrutha Chitra, Saprem Namaskar, Vartha Patra and Dainandan Vignan have not been as well received as expected. Though they are very educative and informative, they lack entertainment value. Some of these programmes are too much technical, tending to infuse concentrated information in very short time. Since recall and use are limited, rural audiences have not shown much interest in viewing these programmes. Similarly educational programmes in Hindi are received by infinitesimally small number of respondents. Mostly these programmes adopt discussion format or lecture type which is least appreciated. The villagers after a heavy work the whole day want to relax and want entertainment. However, the programmes specially broadcasted for Krishidarshan etc., are devoid of this factor. Hence the villages are not interested in them.

According to Ramanamma (1986), "The morning programmes for schools the less said the better. The programmes are monotonous and uninteresting. The school children even if they see all the programmes televised for them, only 3 or 4 programmes televised for them. Only 3 or 4 programmes are related to their syllabus and class. Even subject-wise also there is no communication of the topics in the programmes. The timings 10.30 and 2 p.m. when the programmes are relayed invariably the children are busy in schools.

The UGC programme, 'Country-wide Class Room' one does not understand whether it is for urban or rural students. Most of the rural students study in colleges in their mother tongue and TV programmes for college students are in English. They are either very scientific or of high standard and also very general in nature. They have no relation with the syllabus in the college. If the programme is meant to reinforce the lectures in the classes, the short time heterogeneous programmes mean nothing to the students. If a student watches all the programmes in a week one or two may be marginally useful for their examinations".

Science Report, Focus and What is the Good word, though very educative, unfortunately are not well received because the medium of telecast is in English.

Majority of the rural respondents saw rural programmes showed heterogeneity of suitable timings because of their preoccupation. Most of the respondents are engaged in agricultural activities and have some leisure time in the afternoon wanted to have these programmes during that time. The respondents felt that twice a week is enough for rural programmes and time duration is expected is 25 to 30 minutes and felt that if the programmes extended beyond this time it will not sustain their interest.

Sports programmes are liked by the respondents in majority as they like outdoor life and also enjoy the competitive spirit involved in sports.

One can conclude that the rural people after their hard day's work want entertainment and make belief tinsel world programmes to forget their hardships. If the rural development is to be achieved the programmes must be of an entertainment format with song, dance and melodrama. If it is possible to include messages, and give information and education within the framework then only the programmes become popular among the rural population.

7

CORRELATIONAL ANALYSIS OF PROGRAMME PREFERENCES

In the earlier chapters an attempt was made to present some of the quantifiable data in the tabulated form. This chapter aimed not at the complex analysis of the raw data for it might have been prone to the error of over simplification and also to the error of making it appear that the present thesis depended more or less on sheer quantitative data. It was, therefore, decided that in this chapter, we would attempt to the reconstruction of the context through analysis of data and present the viewers' preferences and their avoidances of particular programmes, in a correlational matrix.

The present chapter aims at fulfilling the task of discussing some of the salient trends arising from the analysis of data partly accomplished in earlier chapter. It is hoped that the researcher would be able to interpret the relevant data – both the quantitative and qualitative types in the light of the aims and objectives already mentioned in the introductory chapter. It is found desirable to make use of some secondary data, references from other relevant researches etc., for this purpose. In order to arrive at an understanding of the scope and limitations of the television as a mass medium, the viewers' socio-cultural background is determining their perception of the television are correlated. In other words, here we devoted mainly on the analytical comments on how the television has been accommodated in the socio-cultural setting of the villages, how the rural viewers view the television programmes and what are the gaps between the viewers' and the policy makers' points of reference about the programmes. It has further been considered essential to discuss here, to what extent our television produces the effects that could be called desirable conditions for making itself on par with the competent medium of development communication. In the preceding chapter introduction of television in India, the definition and scope of developmental communication were examined. We have also given a lengthy note on the placement and advances of this audio-visual medium in the framework of their socio-cultural and economic conditions. A brief mention was made to the ongoing debate whether the television is basically entertainment-oriented or it could be considered as functional for the development of a society. In the light of the above perspectives and the lines of thought, the present chapter hopes to highlight the various trends brought out in the study.

In this chapter too, cross-tabulations have been presented in order to examine whether there exists any statistically meaningful association between the different variables. In doing so, proper care has been taken to maintain a certain format for the tables. The χ^2 values have been given wherever it was considered appropriate.

The chapter is divided into two parts. First part deals with the presentation of important cross-tabulations with their extensive interpretations highlighting the association between the variables and their statistical significance. The second part treats consolidated inferences drawn from the data in the light of the aims and objectives of the book.

PART I

This part is divided into four major sub-sections:

(1) Exposure to the media and change in viewing habits.
(2) Programme Preferences based on personal identification data and socio-economic factors.
(3) Frequency of viewing the CTV and preferences of different types of programmes.
(4) Comparison between different types of programmes. They cover areas such as :

(a) Own language programmes vs other language programme,
(b) Entertainment programmes vs Instructional Programmes,
(c) Personal Identification data vs time and programme preferences.

Exposure to the Media and Change in Viewing Habits

In the present section all those cross-tabulations have been included which have direct or indirect bearing upon villagers' acquaintance with the mass media.

Table 7.1 indicates the statistical significance between the condition of the access road and the duration for which the CTV has been installed in the villages. It is observed that while maximum CTV sets have been installed in the villages having a motorable road and the maximum number of CTV sets have been installed in the villages which are not accessible during the rainy season. It is also observed that the maximum number of sets have been given to the villages having a motorable access road. However, the χ^2 value (χ^2 =48.839) obtained from Table 7.1 indicates that there seems to be a correlation between the two variables.

The Government's main aim in installing the CTVs in remote and inaccessible areas is with the intention of dissemination of information to places where there is no other means of communication. The concept that developed villages with motorable roads will have more CTVs is a misnomer.

It is seen from Table 7.2 that those who possessed only one or two sets at the village have put on the TV more frequently (63.45% and 62.50% respectively) than those villages where there more than three sets (50.0%) viewed the CTV regularly. It is thus seen that there is a gradual decrease in the use where there are more number of sets in the village. A similar trend emerges when this variable (number of sets) is compared with the regularity of news viewing. Among those who have regular news viewers, in the villages, there were only two sets available and the viewers were much more regular at news viewing (95.83%), while in those villages having 3 to 5 sets the number decreases (1.57%). The obtained χ^2 value (χ^2=0.4584258 and d.f. =2) for this table though not significant at 5 per cent level, it still indicates the trend involved in the pattern of news viewing. As has been commented in the earlier chapter, irrespective of the number of sets available the regular viewers are more when compared to the irregular viewers.

Table 7.3 illustrates the comparison between the number of years of the installation of the CTV and the frequency of the habit of news viewing. It is observed that people have a tendency to switch on their sets more often when it is recently installed in their village (35.94%). This trend, however, shows a decline when sets were installed for 1 to 3 years back (26.56%). The number decreased to 14.58 per cent when the sets were older than 6 or more years, although it registers a small betterment in case of those sets which have been installed for more than 4 years but less than 5 years (22.92%). The probable reason for a very low percentage (14.58%) is due to the fact that people loose interest as they become familiar with the pattern of the programme, which they find it uninteresting or simply that the sets are rarely put on due some recurrent technical faults.

TABLE 7.1: Road Condition Vs Year of Installation

Road Condition	Year of Installation							
	Before 1 years	%	1 to 3 years	%	4 to 5 years	%	6 & more %	Total
Motorable	42 (26.09)	(43.00)	36 (22.36)	(54.54)	68 (40.37)	(76.47)	18 (11.18)	161 (52.56)
All seasons Kutcha	37 (31.36)	(44.04)	24 (20.34)	(36.36)	11 (9.32)	(38.98)	46	118 (38.02)
Not operational in rainy season	5 (20.0)	(5.95)	6 (24.0)	(9.10)	9 (36.0)	(10.59)	5 (20.0)	25 (8.22)
Total	84 (22.96)		66 (21.71)		85 (27.63)		69 (22.70)	304

$\chi^2 = 48.839$ df : 6.

TABLE 7.2: Number of CTV Sets Vs Availability of CTV for News

No. of CTV sets	News viewing					
	Regular	%	Irregular	%	Total	%
Only 1 set	5 (62.50)	(2.60)	3 (37.50)	(2.68)	8	(2.97)
2 sets	184 (63.45)	(95.83)	106 (36.55)	(94.64)	290	(95.39)
3 to 5 sets	3 (50.00)	(1.57)	3 (50.00)	(2.68)	6	(1.33)
Total	192	(63.15)	112	(36.85)	304	(100.00)

$\chi^2 = 0.4584258$ d.f. : 2.

Similarly, considering the time of TV installation with the regularity of news viewing, the new sets attract more regular news viewers (63.15%) because of its novelty, however, the novelty fades away as time advances.

This explains the fact that in general, there is a steady decline among the regular news viewers as their sets grow older. This trend is statistically significant as revealed by the χ^2 value computed for the table which is $\chi^2 = 38.52082$, d.f.=3.

Table 7.4 attempted to find out whether there exists any association between the 'duration for which the CTV has been installed' and 'frequency of viewers' watching the typically rural programmes'. It has been a general assumption that longer the duration of the CTV in a village, the more regular would be the villagers in viewing the programmes. We observed that irrespective of the years of installation of the CTV, respondents in majority (74.00%) viewed the rural programmes.

TABLE 7.3: Year of installation Vs. availability of CTV for news

	Availability of CTV					
How many years ago CTV was installed	Regular	%	Irregular	%	Total	%
Less than 1 year	69 (82.14)	(35.94)	16 (17.86)	(13.39)	84	(22.63)
1 to 3 years	51 (77.27)	(26.56)	15 (22.73)	(13.39)	66	(21.71)
4 to 5 years	44 (51.89)	(22.92)	41 (48.11)	(36.61)	85	(27.96)
6 and more years	28 (40.58)	(14.58)	41 (59.42)	(36.61)	69	(22.70)
Total	192	(63.15)	112	(36.85)	304	(100.00)

$\chi^2 = 38.52082$ d.f. : 3

We may, therefore, infer that it is definitely not the duration of the CTV in the village that determines the popularity of rural programmes. We may further say that the telecasting of the rural programmes has been quite successful in receiving a large proportion of rural viewers. However, the variables considered for the above cross-tabulation do seem to represent a statistically meaningful association ($\chi^2 = 34.66882$, d.f. = 3) between them. It could further be stated that there is quite a possibility of arising of the observed trend due to the 'non-availability of other alternatives'. Since the viewers have some leisure time for viewing and that there are no other TV programmes or traditional entertainment during that time, they viewed the rural programmes. However, such a possibility cannot be given much importance since the respondents have further qualified their response to question – they liked to watch the rural programmes. We may, therefore, conclude that the rural programmes as presented by the Doordarshan have successfully posed themselves as an alternative to the traditional entertainment programmes as well as some of them have proved their education/informative value.

TABLE 7.4: Year of Installation Vs. Rural Programme Viewing

Year of Installation	Rural Programme Viewing					
	Yes	%	No	%	Total	%
Only 1 year before	75 (89.28)	(33.33)	9 (10.72)	(11.39)	84	(27.63)
1 to 3 years	57 (86.36)	(25.33)	9 (13.34)	(11.39)	66	(21.71)
4 to 5 years	57 (67.05)	(25.33)	28 (32.95)	(35.44)	85	(27.96)
More than 6 years	36 (52.17)	(16.01)	33 (47.85)	(41.77)	69	(22.70)
Total	225	(74.00)	79	(26.00)	304	(100.00)

$\chi^2 = 34.66882$ d.f. : 3.

Programme Preferences based on Personal Identification Data and Socio-Economic Factors

Human nature is different from individual of individual. One man's liking may not necessarily be liked by others. Individual preferences are the spice of life. TV viewing is an independent phenomenon based on individual preferences and tastes. Sex, Age, Occupation and Education of the respondents influence the programme preferences and viewing.

The present section deals with cross-tabulations which are based upon the viewers' personal identification data as well as certain socio-economic factors as against the audience's programme preferences.

Choice of Marathi Programmes

It was generally observed that the majority of respondents of both the sexes liked the Marathi telecast. A very few of them, however, reported their dislike of Marathi programmes very emphatically.

Similarly both male and female respondents mostly appreciated programmes from other languages but in this case the dislike also was more emphatic and in slightly larger proportions.

Sex and Entertainment Programmes

It is seen from Fig. 7.1 the association between sex and liking of entertainment programmes. About 71.23 per cent of the female liked the entertainment programmes, whereas only 54.48 per cent of the male favoured entertainment. It is surprising again that more than 30.44 per cent of the men do not like the entertainment programmes. Both the sexes differ significantly in their liking of entertainment programmes. The chi-square (χ^2 = 5.968, d.f. =3) value computed for the present table shows non-significant association between the two variables.

Females are more interested in viewing Marathi, other language and entertainment programmes. Women generally have a monotonous life hence doing out and viewing Community Television programmes is in itself a relaxing pasttime. When they go to view CTV programmes they view what is being shown and also happy about it. Males have other avenues of spending their leisure time so are more discriminatory in their programme preferences.

On the whole we noticed that only 265 (57.11%) of the respondents of either sexes like the entertainment programmes, while 28.66 per cent are not liking the entertainment programmes which shows the non-entertainment value of the so-called entertainment programmes and makes us to infer that there is scope for improvement.

Sex and Instructional Programmes

Figure 7.2 focuses on the type of association between the sex and the state of liking of instructional programmes. Majority of women 43

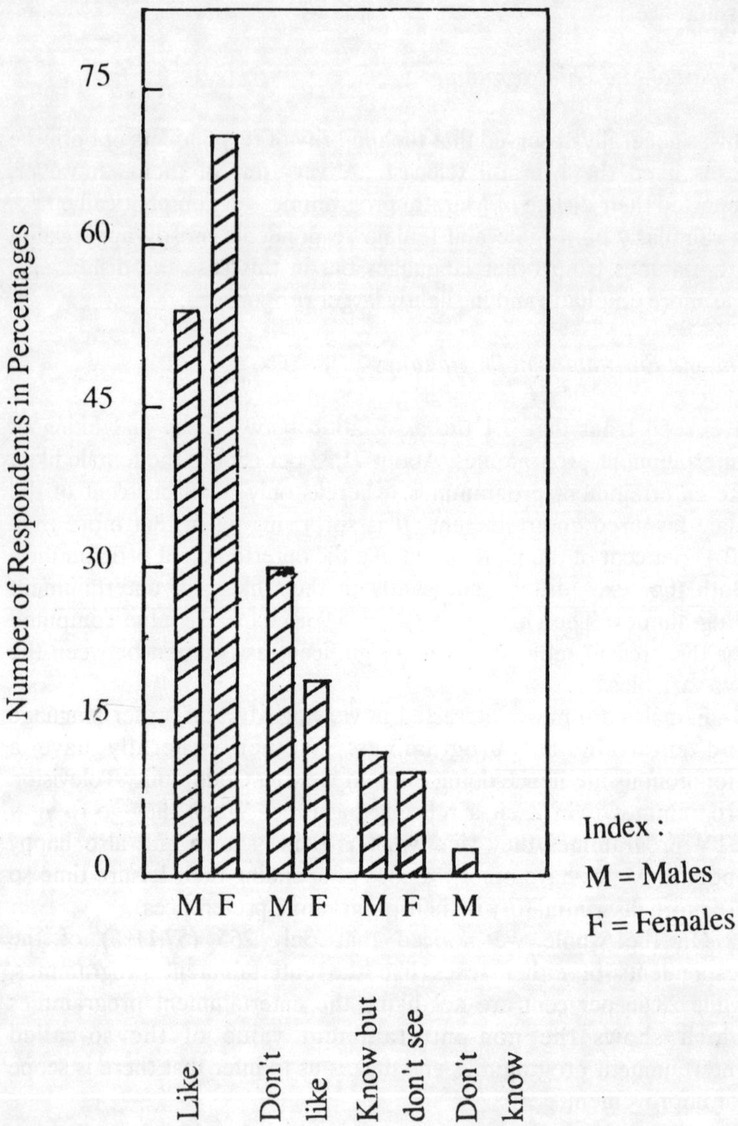

FIG. 7.1: Sex Vs. Entertainment Programmes.

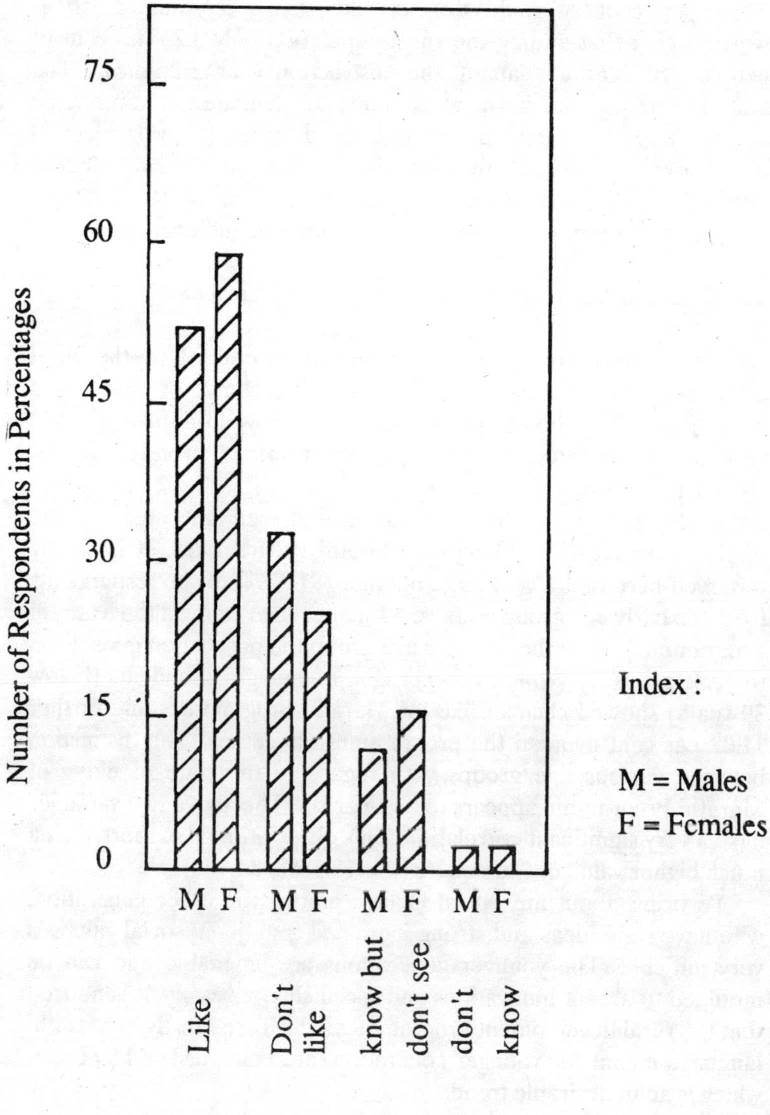

FIG. 7.2: Sex Vs. Instructional Programmes.

(58.90%) liked to see the instructional programmes, while 204 (52.18%) men liked instructional programmes. It is also noted that 32.99 per cent of male do not like such programmes. It is worth-noting that among the rural population only 3.23 per cent of people are ignorant about the instructional programmes. The scattered frequencies in the above table substantiate the lower value of Chi-square ($\chi^2 = 2.02$, d.f. =3) obtained for the two variables, do not show any significant association between them. These instructional programmes have captured the liking of 247 (53.23%) of the total respondents showing a big lacunae in audience liking.

Age Grades of Respondents and Programme Preferences

TV is an innovative mass media newly introduced to the rural audiences by the introduction of CTVs. Acceptance of innovations are influenced by the age grades of people. How different age grade respondents reacted to different programmes broadcasted by Doordarshan are examined.

Table 7.5 gives the association between the age of the respondents and their liking for Marathi Programmes. It is clearly observed here that a very large number (81.82%) of the respondents from the early age group – above 50 years of age enjoyed the Marathi Programmes. With the younger age group the proportion goes down to 52.36 per cent. While 31.50 per cent of young respondents (below 30 years) showed clear dislike for Marathi Programmes and further 11.02 per cent avoided the programmes altogether. The distinction between various age groups with regard to the state of liking of Marathi Programme appears to be clear cut. The above two variables have a very significant correlation. This observation is supported by a much higher value of Chi-square ($\chi^2 = 18.3268$, d.f. =6).

To bring about any social change among the older generation, who have rigid ideas and strong ingrained traditional social values is very difficult. The younger generations are amenable and can be moulded to accept innovations and social changes easily. It is noticed that the rural development programmes, which are mostly in Marathi language meant for younger generation, are being disliked by them, which is an undesirable trend.

Age and Other Programmes

It is observed that the respondents from middle age group (31 to 50 years) like the programmes (vide Table 7.6). The percentage of such individuals is 57.98, which is slightly higher than the other two age group categories. The older people disliked the programmes to the maximum (45.45%). The Chi-square value obtained indicated a highly significant correlation between the two variables of the study (χ^2=25.528, d.f.=6).

Age and Entertainment Programmes

Table 7.7 showed distinct responses for different age group categories. It could generally be said that the older people liked to see the entertainment programmes more often than the younger respondents. While 72.72 per cent of the individuals from the old age liked the programmes, 30.70 per cent of the young respondents have indicated a clear disapproval of the same. Additionally 16.93 per cent of them have shown deliberate avoidance. It is also observed that the respondents from the sample were aware of the telecasting of the entertainment programmes. The obvious differences among the respondents according to age groups indicated the significant association between the variables. This observation is further supplimented by the higher value of chi-square computed for the above table (χ^2 = 23.98, d.f. =6).

Age and Instructional Programmes

It is observed from Table 7.8 that the elderly age group respondents liked the programmes maximum (72.72%). While only 44.49 per cent from the younger age group liked the same. 35.82 per cent of the young respondents do not like the programmes and 14.17 per cent of the respondents avoided programmes. The above two variables do not have a significant association between them. The chi-square value obtained for the present table also suggests similar inference (χ^2= 1.16, d.f. = 6).

It is noticed while analysing the association between age Vs. Marathi language, other language, entertainment and instructional programmes, a uniform trend is observed i.e., that the younger generation showed less interest in these above programmes. Younger generation seems to have other media of communication available to them; hence they are not showing any preference for TV programmes. Newspapers, magazines, books and cinema attract the

TABLE 7.5: Age Vs. Marathi programmes

Age	Marathi Programmes								Total	%
	Like the Prog.	%	Don't like the Prog.	%	Know but not seen the Prog.	%	Don't know that the prog. is there	%		
Younger Age group (Up to 30 years)	133 (56.36)	(46.67)	80 (31.50)	(67.80)	31 (12.20)	(68.89)	10 (3.94)	(66.65)	254	(54.75)
Middle age group (31 to 50 yrs)	134 (71.28)	(47.02)	35 (18.62)	(29.66)	14 (7.45)	(31.11)	5 (2.65)	(33.35)	188	(40.51)
Elder age Group (51 and above)	18 (81.82)	(6.31)	3 (13.64)	(2.54)	1 (4.55)	(2.38)			22	(4.74)
Total	285	(61.42)	118	(25.43)	45	(9.05)	15	(3.23)	464	(100.00)

$\chi^2 = 18.3268$ d.f = 6.

TABLE 7.6: Age Vs. Other language programmes

Age	Other Language Programmes									
	Like the Prog.	%	Don't like the Prog.	%	Know but not seen the Prog.	%	Don't know that the prog. is there	%	Total	%
Younger Age Group (Up to 30 years)	114 (44.88)	(48.51)	88 (34.65)	(55.34)	17 (6.69)	(62.97)	35 – (13.78)	(81.40)	254	(54.75)
Middle Aged Group (31 to 50 years)	109 (57.98)	(46.38)	61 (32.45)	(38.36)	10 (5.32)	(37.03)	8 (4.25)	(18.60)	188	(40.51)
Elder Age Group (51 and above)	12 (54.55)	(5.11)	10 (45.45)	(6.20)	–		–		22	(4.74)
Total	235	(50.65)	159	(34.27)	27	(5.82)	43	(9.26)	464	(100.00)

$\chi^2 = 25.52803$ d.f. : 6.

TABLE 7.7: **Age** Vs. Entertainment Programmes

Age	Entertainment Programmes									
	Like the Prog.	%	Don't like the Prog.	%	Know but not seen the Prog.	%	Don't know that the prog. is there	%	Total	%
Younger Age group (Up to 30 yrs)	123 (48.43)	(46.95)	78 (30.70)	(58.65)	46 (18.11)	(79.31)	7 (2.76)	(63.64)	254	(54.75)
Middle Age group (31 to 50 yrs)	123 (65.43)	(46.95)	49 (26.06)	(36.84)	12 (6.38)	(20.69)	4 (2.13)	(36.36)	188	(40.51)
Elder Age Group (51 and above)	16 (72.72)	(6.10)	6 (27.28)	(4.51)					22	(4.74)
Ttotal	262	(56.46)	133	(28.66)	58	(12.50)	11	(2.37) 464	(100.00)	

χ^2 = 23.9772 d.f.: 6.

TABLE 7.8: Age Vs. Instructional Programmes

Age	Instructional Programmes									
	Like the Prog.	%	Don't like the Prog.	%	Know but not seen the Prog.	%	Don't know that the prog. is there	%	Total	%
Younger Age group (Up to 30 yrs)	113 (44.49)	(46.50)	91 (35.82)	(62.33)	39 (15.35)	(65.00)	11 (4.33)	(73.37)	254	(54.75)
Middle Age group (31 to 50 yrs.)	114 (60.63)	(46.91)	50 (26.60)	(34.25)	20 (10.64)	(33.33)	8 (2.13)	(26.63)	188	(40.51)
Elder Age (51 and above)	16	(6.58)	5	(3.42)	1	(1.78)			22	(4.74)
Total	243	(52.37)	146	(31.47)	60	(12.93)	15	(3.23)	464	(100.00)

$\chi^2 = 1.15705$ d.f. = 6

educated youth much more than the TV, which does not sustain their attention. It may be surmised that those who have no recourse to the other medias are attracted to TV.

Education of Respondents and Programme Preferences

In Tables 7.9 to 7.12 we are attempting to understand the relationship between the educational background of the respondents and their liking, preferences or avoidances of the Television Programmes in Marathi, other languages, entertainment and instructional types.

It is observed from Table 7.9 that among the illiterate informants nearly 72.15 per cent liked to view the Marathi Programmes. Liking for the Marathi programmes is also noticed among other categories : Primary Education 72.19 per cent, High School Education 50.90 per cent. It is clear that as the educational level increases, there appears a steady decline in liking of Marathi Programmes. As regards the deliberate avoidance of the Marathi Programmes, we find a similar trend – the lower the level of education, lesser is the deliberate avoidance of the Marathi Programmes while otherwise it is proved by high percentage (17.74%) of the respondents deliberately avoided the programmes. Lastly, as regards ignorance about the Marathi Programmes, it was found that illiterate respondents were more ignorant (12.73%) about some of the Marathi Programmes than the other categories.

Our observations make us to conclude that there exists a very strong correlation between the two variables. The χ^2 value (χ^2 =42.06, d.f. =9) computed for the above table also confirms our observation rather strongly and therefore, we could further infer that as a person educates himself more and becomes aware of the world at large, he develops a sort of dislike for the programmes from his own language.

Table 7.10 attempts to investigate the possibility of a statistically meaningful association between the viewers, educational background and representative profiles of their programme choices regarding the areas from the languages other than their own, i.e., Marathi. It is found that as we go from the illiterate category of respondents where the liking of the programmes from other languages is registered to be 64.56 per cent, the respondents who are educated into the college level or in the technical education, the level of liking of such

TABLE 7.9: Education Vs. Marathi programmes

Education	Marathi Programmes								Total	%
	Like the Prog.	%	Don't like the Prog.	%	Know but not seen the Prog.	%	Don't know that the prog. is there	%		
Illiterate	57 (72.15)	(20.00)	8 (10.13)	(6.78)	4 (5.06)	(8.70)	10 (12.66)	(66.65)	79	(17.03)
Primary Education	109 (72.19)	(38.25)	27 (17.88)	(22.88)	12 (7.95)	(26.08)	3 (1.99)	(20.01)	151	(32.54)
High School Education	85 (50.90)	(29.82)	60 (35.92)	(50.35)	20 (11.98)	(43.48)	2 (1.20)	(13.34)	167	(35.99)
Abcve High School Education	34 (50.75)	(11.93)	23 (34.33)	(19.49)	10 (14.92)	(21.74)	—	—	67	(14.44)
Total:	285	(61.42)	118	(25.43)	46	(9.92)	15	(3.23)	464	(100.00)

$\chi^2 = 42.0644$ d.f. = 9.

TABLE 7.10: Education Vs. Other Language Programme

Education	Other Language Programmes									
	Like the Prog.	%	Don't like the Prog.	%	Know but not seen the Prog.	%	Don't know that the prog. is there	%	Total	%
Illiterate	51 (64.56)	(21.70)	24 (30.38)	(15.09)	4 (5.06)	(13.79)			79	(17.03)
Primary Education	100 (66.23)	(42.56)	39 (25.83)	(24.52)	3 (1.99)	(10.34)	9 (5.96)	(21.95)	151	(32.54)
High School Education	66 (39.52)	(28.09)	65 (38.92)	(40.88)	14 (8.38)	(48.28)	22 (13.17)	(53.68)	167	(35.99)
Above High School Education	18 (26.87)	(7.66)	31 (46.27)	(19.50)	8 (11.94)	(27.59)	10 (14.92)	(24.39)	67	(14.44)
Total	235	(50.65)	159	(34.27)	29	(6.25)	41	(8.84)	464	(100.00)

χ^2 = 70.64353 d.f. =9.

programmes decreases i.e., nearly 26.86 per cent. These, higher educated respondents register their dislike of the programmes from other languages quite strongly nearly 46.22 per cent. As regards the educated respondents' deliberate avoidance of such programmes, it is noted that higher the education of a respondent, the more be tries to avoid other language programmes – illiterate 2.54 per cent as against above High School level 11.94 per cent. This represents a very strong association between the two variables considered above. The χ^2 value (χ^2 = 70.64, d.f.=9) also quite highly significant of such an association.

Table 7.11 aims at finding out whether there exists any meaningful association between the education of a viewer and his choice profiles regarding entertainment programmes. All the entertainment programmes have been put together to derive the association between the variables. It is observed that majority 67.31 per cent of the illiterate respondents liked the television as an entertainment media, in the case if primary educated category, the quantum of informants' liking the programmes is higher 70.86 per cent. However, as we go ahead towards more educated respondents we find that the level of liking of the entertainment programmes decreases, viz., from High School educated – 46.11 per cent to College educated 37.31 per cent. As regards the deliberate avoidance of entertainment programmes, we noticed that the less literate the respondents are, the less is their purposeful avoidance and the more the educated, their action becomes frequent and deliberate : illiterate 7.62 per cent, College Education : 20.90 per cent. Our observations definitely indicated that there exists a very strong association between the two variables. The χ^2 = 46.11, d.f. = 9) indicates a highly significant association between the variables under study.

Table 7.12 tries to understand the relationship between the viewers' education and their choice of the instructional/informative programmes broadcast by the Doordarshan. It is noticed that the illiterates and the primary school educated in majority opted for the instructional programmes, namely, 57.75 per cent and 62.91 per cent respectively, while there is a generally low liking for the programmes among the Secondary School educated respondents and college educated namely, 44.91 per cent and nearly 41.72 per cent respectively. As regards the ignorance about such programmes, we are led to believe that respondents from all the categories are quite aware of these programmes. However, as regards the purposeful,

TABLE 7.11: Education Vs. Entertainment Programmes

Education	Entertainment Programmes									
	Like the Prog.	%	Don't like the Prog.	%	Know but not seen the Prog.	%	Don't know that the prog. is there	%	Total	%
Illiterate	53 (67.08)	(20.14)	17 (21.52)	(13.26)	9 (11.39)	(15.52)	–		79	(17.03)
Primary Education	107 (70.87)	(40.66)	32 (21.19)	(24.00)	7 (4.64)	(12.07)	5 (3.31)	(45.45)	151	(32.54)
High School Education	77 (46.11)	(29.26)	58 (34.73)	(43.50)	28 (16.77)	(51.80)	4 (2.40)	(36.36)	167	(35.99)
College Education	25 (37.31)	(9.50)	26 (38.81)	(20.28)	14 (20.90)	(25.90)	2 (2.98)	(18.18)	67	(14.44)
Total	262	(56.46)	133	(28.66)	58	(12.50)	11	(2.37)	464	(100.00)

$\chi^2 = 46.11829$ d.f. : 9.

TABLE 7.12: Education Vs. Institutional Programmes

Education	Entertainment Programmes									
	Like the Prog.	%	Don't like the Prog.	%	Know but not seen the Prog.	%	Don't know that the prog. is there	%	Total	%
Illiterate	45 (56.96)	(18.52)	20 (25.32)	(13.70)	12 (15.19)	(20.00)	2 (2.53)	(13.34)	79	(17.03)
Primary Education	95 (62.91)	(39.09)	39 (25.83)	(26.71)	13 (8.61)	(21.67)	4 (2.65)	(26.68)	151	(32.54)
High School Education	75 (44.91)	(30.86)	62 (37.13)	(42.46)	24 (14.37)	(40.00)	6 (3.59)	(40.02)	167	(35.99)
College Education	28 (41.79)	(11.53)	25 (37.31)	(17.12)	11 (16.42)	(18.33)	3 (4.48)	(20.01)	67	(14.44)
Total	243	(52.37)	146	(31.46)	60	(12.93)	15	(3.23)	464	(100.00)

$\chi^2 = 39.94742$ d.f. = 9.

deliberate avoidance of these programmes we noticed that while the less liberate or Primary School Educated tend to be more attentive of the instructional programmes. The literate respondents in the community tend to avoid these programmes – Illiterate and Primary Educated – 10.43 per cent and 11.26 per cent respectively. Secondary Education of College – 14.37 per cent and 16.39 per cent respectively avoid these programmes. This indicates that there exists a very strong association between the two variables. The χ^2 value (χ^2 = 39.95, d.f=9) obtained for the table also supports our observation.

Occupational Categories of Respondents and Their Programme Preferences

The author also attempted to analyse if occupation of respondents had anything to do with their programme preferences. The data were accordingly analysed, tabulated and their chi square χ^2 values were derived, but it was concluded that at least in our sample and apart from slight variations occupation of the viewer does not have any influence on his preference or avoidance of specific programmes.

Frequency of Viewing CTV and Preferences of Different Types of Language Programmes

The present section involves presentation of these cross-tabulations (Table 7.13 to 7.18) which aim at exploring the association between the following :

(a) Frequency of watching and Marathi as well as other language programmes,
(b) Frequency of watching and entertainment programmes,
(c) Frequency of watching and preference and avoidance of instructional programmes,
(d) Timing felt suitable for watching Marathi programme, other language programmes, entertainment and instructional programmes.

It was found important to understand the relationship between the frequency of CTV viewing and the preferred and avoided programmes, because there is likelihood that those who may be watching the TV rarely may be doing so for a particular programme and also those who may be watching most frequently may be avoiding certain programmes. Also it was felt that an enquiry into the suitable timings for viewing the CTV may be useful because since there may be non-availability of time as a reason for avoiding a certain programme.

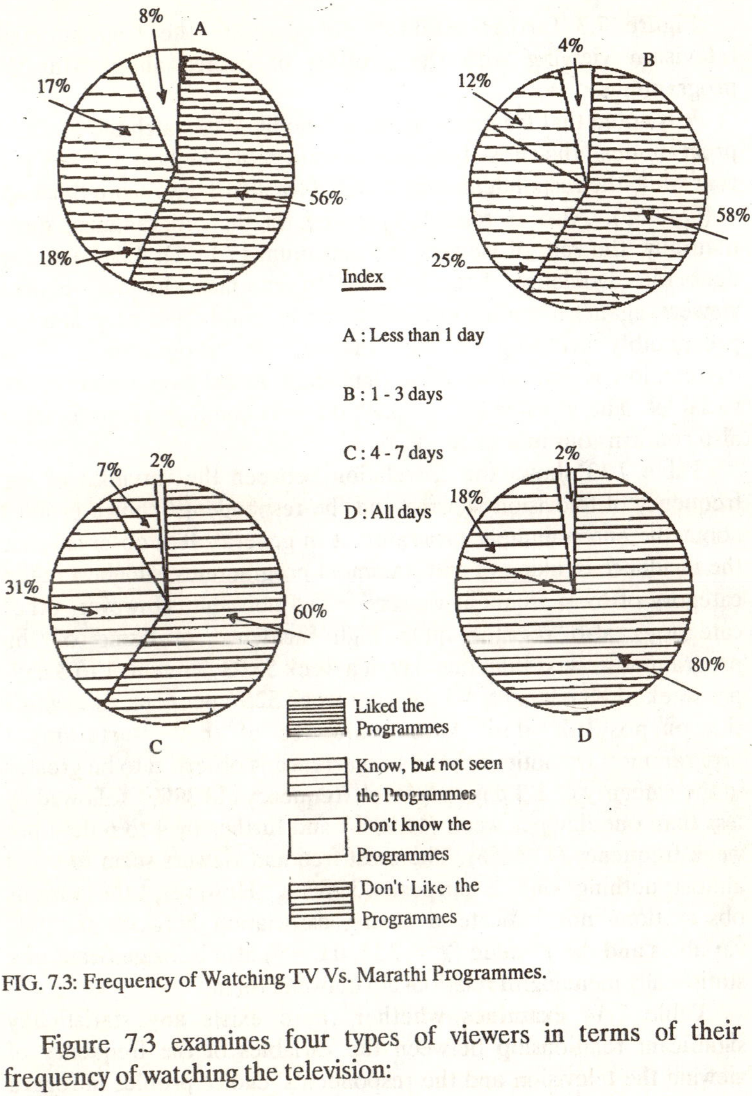

FIG. 7.3: Frequency of Watching TV Vs. Marathi Programmes.

Figure 7.3 examines four types of viewers in terms of their frequency of watching the television:

(a) those who watch on an average less than a day per week.
(b) those who watch for 1 to 3 days per week.
(c) those who watch for 4 to 7 days per week.
(d) those who watch it every day.

Figure 7.3 further attempts to correlate the frequency of television viewing with the profiles of choice about Marathi programmes.

It is noted that from among those who liked to watch the Marathi programmes, the most frequent viewers score highest – 80.33 per cent while the respondents who watch it for 1 to 3 days score the least – (58.12%). Also as regards ignorance of the programmes, quite naturally, the rate of viewers are maximum (7.14%). Likewise, the deliberate avoidance of the Marathi Programmes, the less frequent viewers, again quite naturally, are found to avoid these programmes, presumably avoiding for that matter, any programmes. This observation is indicative of a significant association between the variables. The χ^2 value (χ^2 = 20.79; d.f. =9) computed for this table also confirms our inference.

Table 7.13 shows the correlation between the variables of the frequency of television viewing and the respondents' choice profiles about the entertainment programmes in general. It is observed that the incidence of liking of entertainment programmes is highest in the category of most frequent viewers – 75.4 per cent. However, other categories also register quite high incidence of liking of the programmes – less than one day in a week 55.93 per cent, 1 to 3 days per week 51.88 per cent, 4-7 days per week 52.76 per cent. As regards the purposeful, deliberate avoidance of the entertainment programmes, we noticed that its occurrence is observed to be greater in the category of 1-3 days per week frequency (14.38%), followed by less than one day per week (11.90%) and further by 4 to 6 days per week frequency (11.66%). The most frequent viewers seem to avoid almost nothing with a purpose (3.28%). However, the various observations not indicate a strong association between the two variables and the χ^2 value (χ^2= 7.13, d.f. =9) also is insignificant of a statistically meaningful relationship between them.

Table 7.14 examines whether there exists any statistically significant relationship between the variables of the frequency of viewing the television and the respondents' choice profiles in regard to the instructional/educational programmes.

TABLE 7.13: Frequency of Watching TV Vs. Entertainment Programmes

Frequency	Entertainment Programmes									
	Like the Prog.	%	Don't like the Prog.	%	Know but not seen the Prog.	%	Don't know that the prog. is there	%	Total	%
Less than 1 day	47 (53.75)	(17.93)	18 (22.50)	(13.53)	14 (17.50)	(24.14)	1 (1.25)	(9.09)	80	(17.24)
1 to 3 days	83 (51.88)	(31.68)	47 (29 38)	(35.34)	23 (14.38)	(42.59)	7 (4.38)	(63.64)	160	(34.48)
4 to 7 days	86 (52.76)	(32.83)	55 (33.74)	(41.36)	19 (11.66)	(35.19)	3 (1.84)	(27.27)	163	(35.13)
All days	46 (75.41)	(17.55)	13 (21.31)	(9.77)	2 (3.28)	(3.70)			61	(13.15)
Total	262	(56.46)	133	(28.66)	58	(12.50)	11	(2.37)	464	(100.00)

$\chi^2 = 7.31314$ d.f. : 9.

It is observed that majority of respondents (78.68%) liked the instructional programmes and watched them daily. The respondents (49.69%) who watched the programmes for 4 to 6 days a week and 48.13 per cent who watched the programmes for 1 to 3 days expressed their dislike for the instructional programmes. Lastly, the deliberate avoidance of the programmes of instructional type is registered highest in the category of least frequent viewers – 16.23 per cent, followed by 1 to 3 days per week viewers – 15.00 per cent per cent, while the rest of the categories follow suit.

These observations indicate that there exists a strong inter-relationship between the two variables under study. The χ^2 value (χ^2 = 17.79, d.f. =9) obtained for this table is also quite highly significant of such an association.

Suitable Time and Marathi Programmes

Table 7.15 shows the association between the respondents' suitable time for community viewing and their preferences for Marathi Programmes. It is observed that for a large number (70.10%) of the respondents afternoon time is suitable to see the Marathi Programmes while 65.19 per cent preferred the night for watching the Marathi Programmes. Among the respondents who did not like to watch the Marathi Programmes the evening viewers were the highest (31.20%) number of respondents, while 12.90 per cent from this group deliberately avoided the Marathi Programmes. The above two variables indicated the significant association and had the higher value of Chi-square (χ^2 = 20.06, d.f. =6).

Suitable Time Vs. Other Programmes

Table 7.16 assesses the association between respondents' suitable time viewing and the state of liking for the programmes from other languages. The table shows that among those who liked the programmes from other languages the afternoon viewers topped the list (59.74%). Such programmes are liked by a comparatively less number of people (40.88%) by those who find evening time more suitable for TV viewing. However, the obvious dislike has been shown for the other programmes by 36.71 per cent of viewers for whom night time is best suitable as they will not be viewing. The two

TABLE 7.14: Frequency of Watching TV Vs. Instructional Programmes

Frequency	Instructional Programmes									
	Like the Prog.	%	Don't like the Prog.	%	Know but not seen the Prog.	%	Don't know that the prog. is there	%	Total	%
Less than 1 day	40 (50.00)	(16.40)	19 (23.75)	(13.11)	17 (21.25)	(28.33)	4 (5.00)	(26.68)	80	(17.24)
1 to 3 days	74 (46.25)	(30.34)	53 (33.13)	(36.57)	24 (15.00)	(46.96)	9 (5.63)	(60.03)	160	(34.48)
4 to 6 days	81 (49.69)	(33.21)	63 (38.65)	(43.47)	18 (11.04)	(32.22)	1 (0.62)	(6.67)	163	(35.13)
All days	48 (78.69)	(19.68)	11 (18.03)	(7.59)	1 (1.64)	(1.79)	1 (1.64)	(6.67)	61	(13.15)
Total	243	(52.37)	146	(31.46)	60	(12.93)	15	(3.23)	464	(100.00)

$\chi^2 = 17.97300$ d.f.: 9.

TABLE 7.15: Suitable Time for Watching TV Vs. Marathi Programmes

Suitable Time	Marathi Programmes									
	Like the Prog.	%	Don't like the Prog.	%	Know but not seen the Prog.	%	Don't know that the prog. is there	%	Total	%
Afternoon	68 (70.10)	(23.86)	23 (23.71)	(19.49)	5 (5.15)	(11.91)	1 (1.03)	(6.67)	97	(20.91)
Evening	114 (54.54)	(40.00)	65 (31.10)	(55.09)	27 (12.92)	(64.28)	3 (1.44)	(20.01)	209	(45.04)
Night	103 (65.19)	(36.14)	30 (18.99)	(25.42)	14 (8.86)	(30.43)	11 (6.96)	(73.37)	158	(30.05)
Total	285	(61.42)	118	(25.43)	46	(9.91)	15	(3.23)	464	(100.00)

$\chi^2 = 20.06253$ d.f.: =6.

TABLE 7.16: Suitable Time for Viewing TV Vs. Other Language Programmes

Suitable Time	Other Language Programmes									
	Like the Prog.	%	Don't like the Prog.	%	Know but not seen the Prog.	%	Don't know that the prog. is there	%	Total	%
Afternoon	58 (59.79)	(24.68)	29 (28.87)	(18.24)	5 (5.15)	(18.52)	5 (5.15)	(12.20)	97	(20.91)
Evening	87 (41.62)	(37.02)	72 (34.45)	(45.28)	19 (9.09)	(70.37)	31 (14.84)	(75.60)	209	(45.04)
Night	90 (56.96)	(38.30)	58 (36.71)	(35.48)	5 (3.16)	(17.24)	5 (3.16)	(12.20)	158	(30.05)
Total	235	(50.65)	159	(34.27)	29	(6.25)	41	(8.84)	464	(100.00)

$\chi^2 = 46.35792$ d.f. :6.

variables listed above do show very highly significant association which is indicated by a very high Chi-square value (χ^2 = 35.97; d.f. = 6) computed for the present table.

Suitable Time Vs. Entertainment Programmes

Table 7.17 examines the association between respondents' suitable time and the state of liking of the entertainment programmes. It is observed that the liking for the entertainment programme is maximum 63.92 per cent for whom afternoons are suitable while 62.09 per cent preferred the programmes in the night. A clear note of dislike has been indicated by 30.72 per cent of the viewers watching the CTV in the evening. Deliberate avoidance of the entertainment programme is observed in the case of 17.76 per cent of the evening viewers. It is also noted that the viewers are generally aware of the telecasting of entertainment programme. The Chi-square value obtained for the table is suggestive of a significant association between the variables studied here (χ^2 = 20.55; d.f. = 6).

Suitable Time and Instructional Programmes

Table 7.18 attempts to find out the association between respondents' suitable time and the state of liking of the instructional programmes. The respondents who find afternoon time more suitable do like to see to its maximum the instructional programmes, 69.01 per cent. The evening viewers are probably those who dislike the programme. This observation is further supplimented by yet another observation that while 32.64 per cent of them do not like the programme; 14.88 per cent of them deliberately avoid the instructional programmes which is a majority of viewers. The disapproval for the programmes has been indicated by a comparatively sizeable fraction of the respondents for 29.11 per cent to 32.96 per cent irrespective of the convenience of time for CTV Viewing. The Chi-square value obtained for the table however, indicates that there is no significant association between the variables that are studied here χ^2 (χ^2 = 14.94, d.f. =6).

Comparison Between Different Types of Programmes

It is worthwhile noting whether respondents who liked one type of

TABLE 7.17: Suitable Time for Viewing TV Vs. Entertainment Programmes

Suitable Time	Entertainment Programmes									
	Like the Prog.	%	Don't like the Prog.	%	Know but not seen the Prog.	%	Don't know that the prog. is there	%	Total	%
Afternoon	62 (63.92)	(23.67)	25 (25.27)	(18.80)	7 (7.22)	(12.92)	3 (3.09)	(27.27)	97	(20.90)
Evening	102 (48.81)	(38.93)	64 (30.62)	(48.12)	37 (17.70)	(68.52)	6 (2.87)	(54.55)	209	(45.04)
Night	98 (62.03)	(37.40)	44 (27.85)	(33.08)	14 (8.86)	(21.13)	2 (1.27)	(18.18)	158	(30.05)
Total	252	(56.46)	133	(28.66)	58	(12.50)	11	(2.37)	464	(100.00)

$\chi^2 = 20.55254$ d.f. : 6.

TABLE 7.18: Suitable Time for Viewing TV Vs. Instructional Programmes

Suitable Time	Instructional Programmes									
	Like the Prog.	%	Don't like the Prog.	%	Know but not seen the Prog.	%	Don't know that the prog. is there	%	Total	%
Afternoon	67 (69.07)	(27.57)	32 (32.99)	(21.92)	6 (6.18)	(10.71)	2 (2.06)	(13.32)	97	(20.10)
Evening	100 (47.85)	(41.35)	68 (32.64)	(46.57)	31 (14.83)	(55.36)	10 (4.78)	(66.67)	209	(45.04)
Night	86 (54.43)	(35.38)	46 (29.11)	(31.51)	23 (14.56)	(38.33)	3 (1.90)	(20.01)	158	(30.05)
Total	243	(52.37)	146	(31.47)	60	(12.93)	15	(3.23)	464	(100.00)

$\chi^2 = 14.93709$ d.f. : 6.

programmes showed similar liking for other programmes. The present section involves certain crucial cross-tabulations (Tables 7.19 to 7.25) aimed at exploring the inter-relations between the following:

Own Language Programmes Vs. Programmes From Other Languages

This enquiry would enable us to understand whether there is any meaningful association between habitual liking for Marathi Programmes and growing interest in the programmes from other languages. Here we hope to find out if different language programmes are complimentary to each other and whether or not do they ultimately contribute to the task of increasing the level of acceptability of television among our sample.

Entertainment Programmes Vs. Instructional Programmes

Similar to the above objective here also it is hoped that we may find certain interesting association between these two types of programmes as perceived by the people.

Certain Personal Identification Data and Socio-Economic Factors Vs. Suitability of Time and News Programmes

Here we hope to establish association between these factors as influencing the choice of the programmes through regulating the availability of time for TV watching. Also we hope to understand if there exists any relationship between the identification factors and news programmes in particular.

Table 7.19 attempts to understand whether there exists any correlation between the variables of profiles of choice of Marathi Programmes and the profiles of choice of the programmes from other languages. It is observed that the table firstly distinguishes five categories of viewers in terms of their choice regarding Marathi Programmes, namely:

(a) Those who do not see,
(b) Those who like,
(c) Those who don't like,
(d) Those who know about the programmes but avoid seeing them, and
(e) Those who don't know about the programmes.

TABLE 7.19 : Marathi Programmes Vs. Other Language Programmes

Other Language Programmes	Marathi Programmes									
	Like the Prog.	%	Don't like the Prog.	%	Know but not seen the Prog.	%	Don't know that the prog. is there	%	Total	%
Like the Programmes	219 (76.84)	(93.19)	62 (13.36)	(38.99)	3 (1.05)	(10.34)	1 (0.22)	(2.44)	285	(61.42)
Don't Like the Programmes	13 (2.80)	(5.53)	78 (16.81)	(49.05)	19 (16.10)	(65.52)	8 (6.78)	(19.51)	118	(25.43)
Know but not see the Programmes	—		9 (21.43)	(5.66)	4 (9.52)	(13.79)	29 (69.05)	(70.73)	42	(9.05)
Do not know that there is a prog.	1 (6.67)	(0.43)	10 (66.67)	(6.29)	1 (6.67)	(3.45)	3 (20.00)	(7.32)	15	(3.23)
Do not see	2 (50.00)	(0.85)		2 (50.00)	(6.90)				4	(0.86)
Total	235	(50.65)	159	(34.27)	29	(5.82)	41	(8.84)	464	(100.00)

$\chi^2 = 20.398946$ d.f.: 12.

These categories of viewers are further compared with the distinctive categories of choice of the programmes from other languages.

It is noticed that 76.84 per cent of the respondents liked both the language programmes. It is noteworthy that 13.36 per cent of the respondents who liked other language programmes did not liked the Marathi Programmes, while 16.81 per cent of them did not like both the Programmes.

These observations lead us to conclude that there could be strong association between the two variables. However, the χ^2 value (χ^2 = 20.398; d.f. = 12) also supports our observation.

Table 7.20 examines whether there exists any statistically meaningful association between the viewers' liking or disliking of the entertainment programmes and their liking of the instructional programmes. It is noticed that 84.35 per cent liked both instructional programmes and entertainment programmes, while only 15.27 per cent did not like both the programmes.

This means that there exists a very strong relationship between the two variables. The χ^2 value (χ^2 = 128.08; d.f. = 9) obtained for the table is also indicative of such a correlation.

Table 7.21 probes the possibility of a statistically meaningful association between the sex of the respondent and his or her spare time that the respondents feel suitable for TV viewing. It is to be noted that most of the men find evenings (45.59%) and nights (30.44%) suitable whereas among females night time is found to be commonly convenient. Considering the rural background of our respondents it is quite natural that their choice falls upon the given suitable times. The Chi-square value χ^2 (χ^2 = 34.13; d.f. = 2) computed for the table also indicates that the association between the variables is highly significant.

Table 7.22 attempts to establish the intensity of interdependence between the variables of occupational background of the viewer and time preferences for watching the television, while it is noted that there is no remarkable difference between the frequency of preferences of the evening timings of different categories of occupation. However, it is understandable that whatever minor differences are they may be due to respondents' particular occupation. The Chi-square value (χ^2 = 40.16678 d.f. = 10) obtained for the table also suggests that there is no particular association between the variables.

TABLE 7.20: Entertainment Programmes Vs. Instructional Programmes

Entertainment Programmes	Instructional Programmes									
	Like the Prog.	%	Don't like the Prog.	%	Know but not do seen the Prog.	%	Don't know that the prog. is there	%	Total	%
Like the Programmes	221 (84.35)	(90.95)	40 (15.27)	(27.40)	1 (0.38)	(1.79)			262	(56.46)
Don't like the Programmes	22 (16.54)	(9.05)	91 (68.42)	(62.33)	20 (15.04)	(35.71)			133	(28.66)
Know but do not see the programmes	—		15 (25.86)	(10.27)	35 (60.34)	(58.33)	8 (13.79)	(53.33)	58	(11.64)
Do not know that there is a Programme	—		—		4 (36.36)	(7.14)	7 (63.64)	(46.67)	11	(2.37)
Total	243	(52.37)	146	(31.46)	60	(12.93)	15	(3.23)	464	(100.00)

χ^2 = 128.08138 d.f. :9.

TABLE 7.21: Sex Vs. Suitable Time for Viewing TV

	Suitable Time						
Sex	Night	%	Evening	%	Afternoon	%	Total %
Male	119 (30.44)	(75.32)	190 (45.59)	(90.91)	82 (23.97)	(84.53)	391 (84.27)
Female	39 (53.43)	(24.68)	19 (26.02)	(9.09)	15 (20.55)	(15.47)	73 (15.73)
Total	158	34.05	209	(44.94)	97	(20.90)	464 (100.00)

χ^2 = 34.134945 d.f. : 2.

TABLE 7.22: Occupation Vs. Suitable Time for Viewing T.V.

	Suitable Time						
Occupation	Night	%	Evening	%	Afternoon	%	Total %
Service	52 (29.09)	(32.91)	78 (43.58)	(37.32)	49 (27.38)	(50.52)	179 (38.57)
Agri-culture	75 (47.22)	(50.60)	73 (40.55)	(34.93)	32 (12.22)	(25.29)	180 (38.79)
Industry/ Business	7 (24.14)	(4.43)	16 (55.17)	(7.66)	6 (20.69)	(6.19)	29 (6.25)
Educa-tion	11 (23.40)	(6.96)	32 (68.09)	(15.31)	4 (8.51)	(4.12)	47 (10.13)
Labour	5 (38.46)	(3.16)	5 (38.46)	(2.39)	3 (23.08)	(3.09)	13 (2.80)
Other Occupations	8 (50.00)	(5.06)	5 (31.25)	(2.39)	3 (18.75)	(3.09)	16 (3.45)
Total	158	(36.21)	209	(45.04)	97	(18.75)	464 (100.00)

χ^2 = 40.16678 d.f. : 10.

Table 7.23 aims at deriving the statistical association between the categories of age of the respondents and the timing that felt to be suitable by them for television. It is noted that for the three categories of age considered for tabulation. The respondents above 51 years opted for the night timing, while the evenings are generally preferable more to the respondents from younger age group. However, this is only a relative judgment and is not supported by the statistical exercises for the Chi-square value (χ^2 = 8.396622 d.f. =4) obtained for this table is not significant at all.

Figure 7.4 attempts to establish the association between the variables of frequency of television viewing and the choice of suitability of timing for viewing. It is noted that of those who watch TV for less than a day per week nearly 66 per cent prefer to watch it during the post-evening session. The evening choice is given by those who watched the TV for 4-7 days – 56.44 per cent, also by the ones who watched it for 1 to 3 days per week – 43.13 per cent. However,

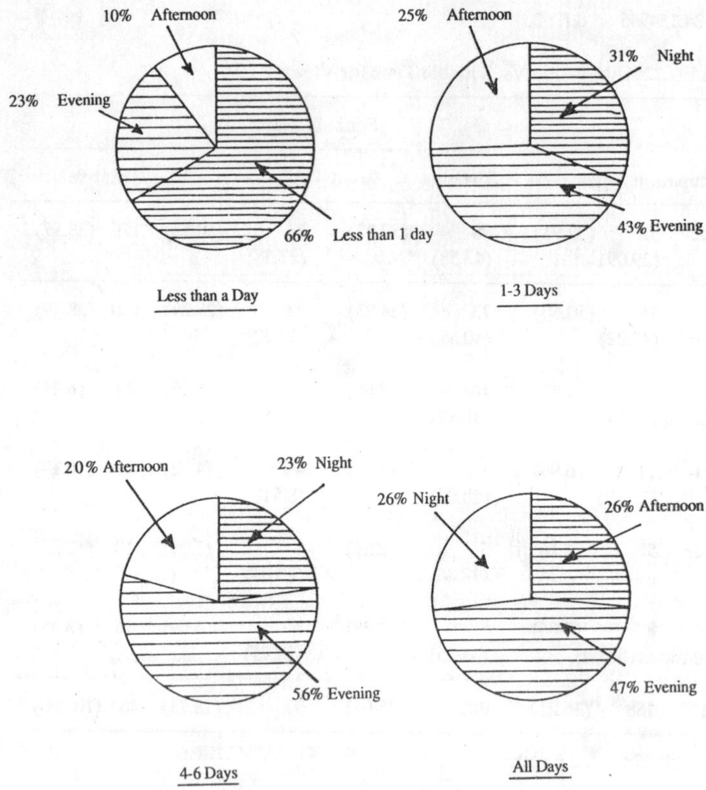

FIG. 7.4: Frequency of TV viewing Vs. suitable time.

TABLE 7.23: Age Vs. Suitable Time for Viewing TV

Age	Suitable Time for Viewing							
	Night	%	Evening	%	Afternoon	%	Total	%
Up to 30 years	73 (28.74)	(46.20)	124 (48.82)	(59.33)	57 (22.44)	(58.46)	254	(54.74)
31 to 50 years	78 (43.49)	(49.37)	76 (40.43)	(36.37)	34 (18.08)	(35.05)	188	(40.52)
51 and above	7 (31.83)	(4.43)	9 (40.91)	(4.30)	6 (27.26)	(6.19)	22	(4.74)
Total	158	(34.05)	209	(45.05)	97	(20.90)	464	(100.00)

$\chi^2 = 8.396622$ d.f.:4.

the afternoon timings are generally preferred by more frequent viewers. Our observations are indicative for a strong association between the variables, the fact also supported the obtained Chi-square value ($\chi^2 = 22.22$, d.f. =6) for figure.

In Table 7.24 it was decided to understand the strength of association between the age categories of the respondents and regularity of news viewing. As we have noted in Table 7.23 that the variable of news viewing appears to be quite 'independent' for very very few respondents are regular as it and there is no remarkable difference noted among all the three age categories. The Chi-square value ($\chi^2 = 28.05929$, d.f. =2) is highly insignificant of any association between the variables.

Table 7.25 attempts to find out whether there exists any inter-relationship between the educational background of viewers and their regularity of viewing the news programmes. It is observed that while there is no sharp difference between the respondents educated upto the primary level and the ones upto the high school level and above as regards the regularity of news viewing, the Chi-square value ($\chi^2 = 19.9254$, d.f.=1) computed for the table however, indicates a highly significant association between the variables.

Figure 7.5 attempts to understand whether there exists any association between the variables of frequency of television viewing and that of the regularity of viewing of the news programmes. It is found that the regularity of news viewing diminishes as we go from the most frequent viewers to the least frequent ones. This means that there is a very strong association between the two variables. The Chi-square value (χ^2 =12.55, d.f. =3) obtained for this figure supports our observation.

TABLE 7.24: Age Vs. News Viewing

Age	News Viewing					
	Regular	%	Irregular	%	Total	%
Up to 30 years	5 (1.97)	(20.00)	249 (98.03)	(56.72)	254	(54.74)
31 to 50 years	14 (7.45)	(56.00)	174 (92.55)	(56.94)	188	(40.52)
Above 51 years	6 (27.27)	(24.00)	16 (72.73)	(3.64)	22	(4.74)
Total	25	(5.39)	439	(94.60)	464	(100.00)

χ^2 = 28.05929 d.f. :2.

TABLE 7.25: Education Vs. News Viewing

Education	News Viewing					
	Regular	%	Irregular	%	Total	%
Up to Primary	8 (2.95)	(32.00)	222 (97.05)	(50.57)	230	(49.57)
High School and Above	17 (5.97)		217 (94.01)	(49.43)	234	(50.13)
Total	25	(5.40)	439	(94.60)	464	(100.00)

χ^2 = 19.9254 d.f.: 1.

As stated earlier that the present study was conducted in 304 villages scattered over 20 talukas of the districts of Pune, Ahmednagar and Satara. A large number of villages are essentially rural in nature.

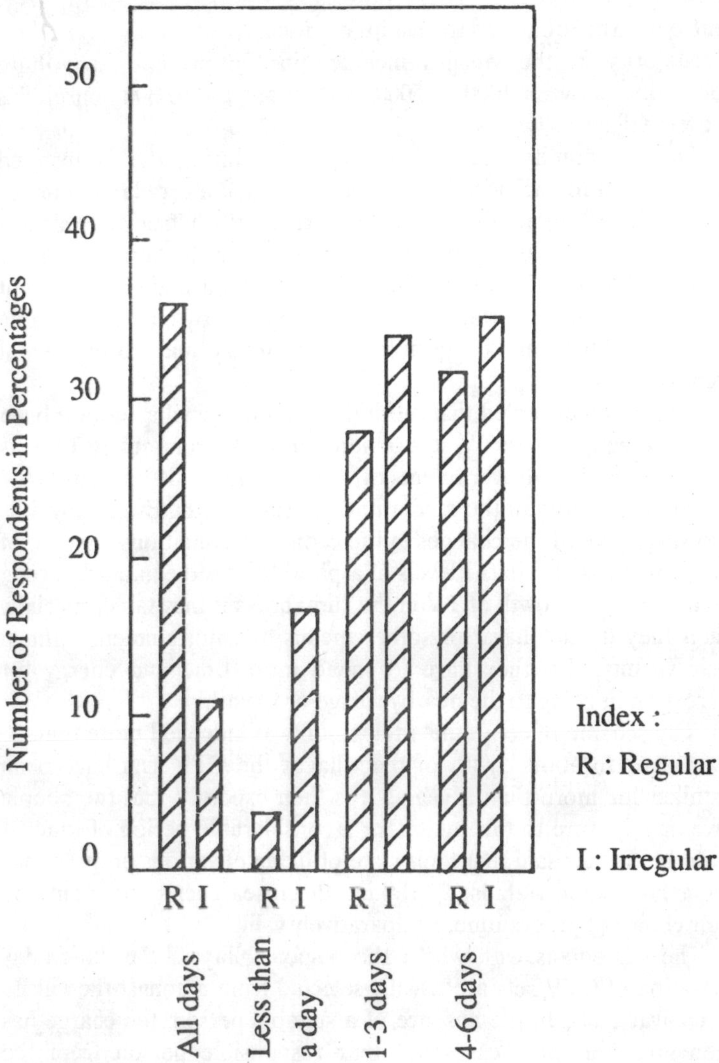

FIG. 7.5: Frequency of TV viewing Vs. news viewing.

The villagers under study thus represented a section of Indian population which by virtue of their geographical locations and at times as a consequence of inadequate development communication facilities being deprived of a good dialogue with the development centre like the urbanised townships or cities.

Majority of the villages included in the present study have population between 1000 to 5000, with about 100 to 300 households in every village.

The community radio is put to work during the noons and evenings in a few villages but it is observed that a very large number of respondents do not listen to any programmes whatsoever. This was probably an expected consequence of the introduction of a more powerful medium like TV. The villages covered under the present study have attained certain level of development by making available certain facilities and by establishing voluntary and governmental organisations.

It has been observed that more than half of the villages have been equipped with private TV sets in addition to the community TV sets provided by the Government of Maharashtra. It indicates the growing popularity of the medium in the rural areas. Eventually, it is also suggestive of the changes in the economic conditions of some of the villagers as also in the levels of aspiration. It is the author's strong feeling that the growth of TV in the rural areas is inevitable, specially when they do not have any other means of entertainment right in their vicinity, for they have to spend more time and energy for recreation in going to the nearby village or township.

The scheme of community television was launched more than 10 years ago. In about 1/4th of the villages the CTV sets have been installed for more than 5 years. It is then expected that the people have an exposure to this media for a considerable period of time. It could be further said that their state of liking of various programmes might have been stabilised. Making the researcher's comments on their choice of programme, comparatively valid.

The custodians with whom the responsibility of the day-to-day operation of CTV sets are usually selected from amongst the village Panchayat Staff. In the absence of a suitable person, the charge has been given in some cases to other responsible person from the village.

The community television sets have been installed in the village generally, at a central place, like Panchayat Office, School, Temple, Post Office etc.

It is also important to see that the community set caters to all the communities. In the present study, it has been observed that the location of the television set is such that the people belonging to all the communities stayed around it. The set, if located in a place surrounded by the higher caste people alone, can remain the property of the higher caste people only and those belonging to the lower castes may not dare participate in the community viewing of the television. It is found in the present study that the above point has been considered well enough in a desired way by locating the set in the centre of the village.

The community television is expected to cater to the largest number of people at a time. It is considered essential that the rural masses gathered around the set and shared experiences in a batter way by healthy group discussion following in an instructional and rural programme. It has been observed in the present study that the above purpose appears to have served as far as the number of viewers are concerned. The instances where more than 100 persons gathered to see a programme at a time are more common (90%) than sporadic viewers.

The enquiry regarding the viewing of the community television also included a query about the possibilities of viewing the programmes in the rainy season also. The need for such a probe need not to be over emphasized. In the village set up where the rural residence may also not be expected to the damp proof or rainproof, it was observed that the television sets could be viewed in rainy season only in about 41 per cent villages.

As far as community TV viewing is concerned it appears as if all the communities watched the programmes together and thereby a communal feeling might be surpassed in the process. With regard to the functioning of the TV set it is noted that more than 85 per cent sets are in working condition.

It might be that some of the sets could not be repaired because they are old valve sets, while there may be some other physical obstacles in receiving a clear picture in the vicinity e.g. hill surrounded etc. The other reasons attributed for keeping the TV set off for a particular period was that the village has an acute power fluctuation etc. As regards the arrangements for repair of community TV, Rural Broadcasting Department of the State Government is the major institution responsible for it. From the remaining 35 per cent, no specific arrangements have been made for repairs.

It is evident from the observations that nearly 21 per cent of the villagers indicated interruption in power supply. Due to this setback it was found difficult for the viewers to comprehend the rural programmes.

About 83 per cent of the CTV sets were put on for more that 5 days a week, and the sets were working mostly during the evening times. That meant it is necessary to utilise the evening time for rural programmes.

It is observed that 7 per cent of the villages have possessed the videos also. It may be added that the number of video sets increased with time. Videos are meant basically for viewing mainly entertainment programmes like cinema etc. If videos become popular they will be using them during the prime viewing times, namely evening, which would act as interruptor for viewing rural development programmes. This will increase the interest and liking for entertainment programmes only.

When we come to look at the rural viewers' preferences, who are now exposed to the television, we observe the following trends. Bulk of sample was composed of the male population, the female viewers being generally unwilling to respond to the researcher's inquiry. Furthermore, some of our cross-tabulations involving educational background of the viewers have fetched interesting results. It was also observed in the villages, that a few of them could afford a private television set while the majority have remained without viewing the programmes in the absence of the Community Television sets. It was also found that a good part of our respondents came from the joint family system, which retained the traditional characteristics of the village. The very structure of the joint family is such that it naturally have an indirect effect upon the viewing habits of the respondents. Although no such attempt was made, to disturb the logic of the data collection, however, the correlation established sociological thought that proved the hypothesis, viz., "the structure of the family influences the individual's television viewing habits".

As regards the frequency of television viewing we have noticed that almost all the respondents watched the television programmes at varied frequency levels every week. To this extent, the television has penetrated into the rural life. It was further found that all the respondents have a concensus over the non-suitability of the morning time for viewing the TV programmes as they were normally busy with their occupations during this time. An attempt was, however, made to obtain the data on the regularity of viewing of the rural programmes. A few selected programmes were telecaste by the Doordarshan specifically keeping in view the rural viewers. It was found that although a sizeable number of respondents watched these programmes, an alarmingly high proportion does not view them due to various reasons, like uninteresting format of programmes etc. A few questions were asked to know about the perceptions of the viewers regarding the rural programmes and it was found that a large proportion of them wanted these programmes to be telecast during their leisure time, and also an equally high percentage of the viewers were satisfied with the frequency of the rural programmes twice a week. However, many wanted these programmes more frequently. Further, a minimum of half an hour duration of the rural programmes was expressed by a good majority of the respondents.

On the whole, it is felt that the rural respondents of the present study have developed a special liking for the programmes which can relate to their own socio-cultural background. This finding is sociologically of high significance for this attracts our attention to the deep-rooted socio-cultural determinants of the individual sense of enjoyment of the television programmes.

It was also noticed that the news programmes attract the least attention of the respondents. A peculiar trend also is found in the pattern of news viewing and it showed that as people get to know the news programmes more and more in time, they became more and more disinterested and infrequent in watching them. This leads us to infer that either the monotony of presentation of the news programmes or the disinterestedness in knowledge related to the day-to-day events having no direct bearing upon their world life could be the only causes for this phenomenon. However, a further analysis was undertaken to know exactly when do they avoide news viewing. The data were computed for the task of noting down interdependence between the personal identification items and respondents' 'choice profiles' of some of the categories of televicion programmes.

It was observed that nearly 28 per cent male respondents had a tendency of deliberately avoiding the Marathi Programmes and about 10 per cent more expressed their complete ignorance about such programmes. On the other hand, we find that the women had developed much more liking for the Marathi Programme, which they expressed in the case of programmes from other languages. As regards these programmes the male population appeared to be much more disinterested. The sex differences are also quite dominant with regard to entertainment and instructional programmes. In both the instances the female population appeared to be more receptive than the males.

The students as well as teachers from our sample represented the other extreme. In case of instructional programmes the agriculturists and the businessmen respondents seemed to enjoy them most. As we have mentioned earlier that the educated category made the maximum use of the instructional programmes. However, the observation worth-noting is that the respondents from the educated category were found to be least interested in getting instructed through the television programmes. It would be worth exploring the reasons for their disliking and deliberate avoidance of the instructional programmes.

It is assumed that age of the respondents played a significant role in determining the state of liking of the TV programmes. At times one wonders whether the choice profile of our individual respondents is in such a linear relationship with the age of the person though the former is taken as a function of the latter. The elderly respondents, above fifty years of age, enjoyed the programmes in Marathi language while a much less proportion of the young respondents developed an aptitude for the Hindi programmes. While a further section of the same population (32.8%) deliberately avoided the programmes altogether. With regard to the programmes from the other languages, it is the middle aged group (31 to 50 years of age) who enjoyed these programmes. The elderly persons disliked the programmes from other languages. One apparent reason for such an occurrence was their ignorance of the other languages, particularly Hindi and English. They were either illiterate or just literates without having an opportunity to study the other languages as a part of formal education.

Strangely enough, it is the older generation who have more liking for the entertainment programmes. The young respondents have indicated their clear disapproval of the entertainment programmes, at times by deliberately avoiding the programmes. It is further striking to note that even the instructional programmes are preferred more by the old people. About half of the young respondents either disliked the programmes or they just avoided them. This observation is considered as striking because it had been the aim of the planners and the designers of the instructional programmes that their efforts are directed towards the enhancement of knowledge of the young generations. The present study has shown that from the stand point of age two inferences could be generally drawn. Firstly, the youth in general, today are either not prepared to receive the programmes directed towards them, or the programmes need certain modifications before they could be expected to achieve the desired results. Secondly, age as an important independent variable has been found to be having a significant association with the entire range of choice profiles, may it be language, entertainment or instruction.

Education of the respondents is yet another variable under investigation. The observation here is that the liking of a Marathi Programme or a programme from other languages, depended on the level of education. Pertaining to the entertainment programmes, it can be said that those with primary education liked it to be maximum. Similarly, the illiterate respondents as well as those with primary education are the ones who appreciated the instructional programmes most. Thus, a strong correlation has been found between the level of education of the viewers and their liking of the programmes from various categories.

We tried to find out the association between the frequency of TV viewing and their choice profile. Regarding the choice of Marathi Programmes, it has been observed that the most frequent viewers liked the Marathi Programmes. The same group of respondents who viewed the TV frequently, also liked the programmes from other languages as well. The association between these two variables is, however, not a significant one. The entertainment programmes are also liked by the frequent viewers. Those who do not view the TV so frequently also have registered their liking for the entertainment programmes only.

The instructional programmes are also welcomed more by the frequent viewers as compared to the less frequent viewers. The association between the frequency of TV viewing and the choice of instructional programmes is also found to be statistically significant over a period of time. Frequent viewers had developed a liking for most of the programmes. It was found that in the case of Marathi Programmes the respondents found afternoon timings suitable since they liked the Marathi Programmes, while those prefering evening times disapproved the programmes altogether. It may be due to the reason that this group has developed certain liking for the programmes from Hindi or English. But our next finding has contradicted this because here we noticed that forms group (i.e., the afternoon prefering group) is again the one who liked to watch the programmes from different languages. The viewers who preferred night timings for watching television expressed a profound dislike for the programmes from other languages. Next in the evening viewing respondents in majority did not like to watch the entertainment programmes. They seemed to find afternoon timings suitable for such programmes. As regards the instructional programmes, it was found that it is the afternoon time that the respondents found more suitable to watch them. On the whole, therefore, we found it is the afternoon timings that are preferred for the instructional and entertainment programmes.

It was found that a very large proportion of respondents who liked the Marathi Programmes also liked the afternoon programmes from other languages. Respondents generally keeping away from Marathi Programmes deliberately or due to ignorance consistently disliked the other language programmes also. Similar exercise was done regarding the entertainment and instructional programmes. It was thought that those respondents who liked entertainment programmes most may not go for instructional programmes at all. However, the data had proved otherwise. A very high number of respondents viewing the educational/instructional programmes most are from the ones who liked to watch the entertainment programmes. The other side of the picture is also quite clear. Those who avoided the instructional programmes are also found avoiding the entertainment programmes. On the whole, it was found that viewing of the eye catching Marathi Programmes by respondents gave rise to the liking for similar other language programmes. As regards the entertainment and instructional programmes, it was found that entertainment and education can very well go hand in hand and to that extent are complementary to each other.

It was found that women from our sample are more free to watch the programmes during post-dinner session, whereas men could do better during their leisure time, i.e., evenings.

Also the respondents from different age categories do not seem to be differing in their preference of timings for watching the television and watching the news programmes in particular. The educational level of the respondents, however, influenced their viewing habits to a considerable extent. It was found that there was a very strong association between educational level of the respondent and his time preferences. The more educated the respondent, the more he is likely to watch the programmes in the evening, while the less literates go for night programmes. However, as regards the news viewing habit our respondent, both literate and illiterate, showed disinterestedness. This is a very peculiar phenomenon. Commonly it is expected that the more educated the individual, the more he tries to keep track of events taking place at wider, national and international scenes. This he does through having the radio or TV news. But, here, the respondents from all the educational levels showed equal disregard for the news programmes.

Another finding worth-mentioning is that there appeared to be a strong association in this context between the suitable timing preferred by the respondents and their frequency of viewing the TV. Those who can find time for watching the TV do so mostly in the evening sessions. On the other hand, the most frequent viewers liked to watch it during the afternoons. But this does not mean that they would not watch it if the programme timings are all restricted to the evening sessions. This leads us to prescribe that majority of educational and entertainment programmes or rural programmes if telecast in the evenings, would be made use of even by the rare viewers.

Most frequent viewers were found to be attending the news programmes more than the less frequent ones. This means that as people get more and more used to the television broadcasts, they developed the liking for the news programmes also probably due to their enlightenment created by these news programmes.

It is thought proper to extend a brief commentary to evaluate whether the objectives are fulfilled. In addition to the objectives which are specific for the present thesis, the general objectives of the television in India were also born in mind while elucidating the view points.

It was decided to make an attempt to understand and explain some of the salient trends of the viewing of television in the given context. Our data has helped us to analyse the determinant features of the frequency of television viewing. It was found that a large majority of our sample has developed the viewing habit. However, the frequency of television viewing is also influenced by some of the extrinsic factors such as the pre-occupations of the villagers. It is further influenced by some technical factors like electric supply, internal faults of the TV sets etc. It was also found that the custodians of the community sets also proved to be one of the major regulatory forces of the television programmes viewing, since the duty of maintaining the TV set and the functions of operating it were assigned to an appointed custodian. In most of the cases, it was found that the custodians own pre-occupations proved to be the determinant factor of the viewing of the Community Television.

It is, therefore, suggested that at least in those villages where the CTV are the only television sets available. Some system should be evolved by which the custodian should take care of the operational part regardless of his own pre-occupations, so that the viewers would be in a position to make use of the CTV as and when they feel so, irrespective of presence of custodian. However, it was found that the majority of respondents prefer to watch the TV during the afternoons. Other timings being unsuitable to most of them, it has been felt that the policy-makers should take a note of this situation. Suitability of timings being one of the most important determinants of TV viewing and its becoming in turn an important factor influencing the choice profile of the respondents, it would be worthwhile if we could attend to the needs of the rural viewers. We must keep in mind constantly that it is the TV that has to adopt itself to the socio-cultural context of the prospective users and not the community to undergo drastic internal changes in order to suit itself to the television.

The timing of the various programmes has been one of the major concerns of present investigation. It has been found that those who watch television least frequently and also those who watch it just for 2 to 3 days per week loose hope with the explanation that the timings of the various likeable programmes are not suitable for them.

It is the mass media that had to take a constructive step to rectify the timings. It is also realised that there would be several operational and administrative difficulties in doing so but as an institution it may not be difficult to overcome them.

An attempt was made to record the viewers' responses to the programmes based on their own traditional entertainment events, such a *Tamasha, Powada*, etc. in order to illucidate on the relationship between their cultural background and these programmes. It was noted that these programmes were appreciated very much. This means that television has posed itself as a strong alternative to the channels of traditional entertainment. The informative and educational prog- rammes based on these themes of social welfare have also found to be quite effective. Such programmes are viewed regularly and by a large proportion of the respondents.

In our investigation we made an attempt to find out the relative judgement of the viewers as regards the educational/informative programmes and the entertainment ones. In this our aim was to understand to what extent doe our sample purely an entertainment media and how much do they value its instructional aspect. A very important finding was registered about this question. It was found that mostly those who go for viewing the entertainment programmes have picked up liking for the instructional or educational programmes also. It was further noticed that if there was ignorance about some of the entertainment programmes it was also for the educational ones. Furthermore deliberate avoidance by some was common to both types of the programmes. This set of findings leads us to understand one of the basic things of communication as an art as well as science. The combination of different types of programmes would be complimentary to each other. Entertainment helps education to a large extent and *vice versa*. This mutual complimentarity promotes the growth of the viewing habit and its frequency. This further leads to the expectation for a variety of programmes. In other words, it has been found that the principle of combining the programmes has been functional in the process of learning the medium itself. However, it is felt that a further research in the line might help to understand what best combinations of programmes would attract more viewers.

With regard to the relevances of the programmes to the society, the researcher has gathered some impressions which are dealt with here. The time allotted to the important programmes having predominantly educational values which dealt with social issues, the time is allotted for them is inadequate or the programmes telecast do not cover the prime time. The shift of interest on the part of the government has been from the socially relevant, instructional or educative programmes to the revenue generating, popularly entertaining sponsored programmes. The respondents opined that there are many issues which deserve coverage through the television. It is, however, observed that some of the vital issues of social significance have not received adequate attention. It is time that the media should extent itself to include the problems hitherto ignored. According to the viewers the programmes on 'grow more trees', 'deforestation', 'bride burning', irradiation of leprosy, diarrhoea common illnesses, rural indebtedness are some of the issues which could be given sufficient coverage.

The rural population is further deprived of one more aspect. The experiments related to the village development like bunding of the uneven terrains, channelling of the stream waters, new system of cheaper irrigation, the rural-based small scale industries, the rural cooperatives etc. are some of the events that are of direct consequence to the rural viewers. The coverage of such aspects of rural life is conspicuous by its absence. Such an observation stands apart specially in the Indian context where more than 80 per cent population stays in the villages.

The above type of subjects would probably receive a good feed-back from the rural population which is in readiness to know as to what happens in other villages rather than what goes on in the metropolis. When an issue on the felt needs on the viewers is discussed, it is suggested here that the above mentioned aspects should receive proportionate attention.

Conclusions

It was found that a large majority of the rural population is in the stage of getting used to TV. In other words, they are slowly but definitely developing 'viewing habit'.

It was also found that the viewing habit and the frequency of viewing are determined by two clear-cut distinct sets of factors:

(a) Firstly by the occupational structure of the population which imposes upon them only certain timings to be spared for TV viewing, and
(b) The technical factors like electric supply, functioning of TV set, time taken for repairs, suitability of time available to the custodian of community TV set etc.

The variables pertaining to the personal identification data of the viewers such as age, sex, education etc. are found to be generally neutral in determining the frequency of TV viewing.

It is generally observed that majority of the rural population preferred the afternoon timings for TV viewing.

The suitability of timings in turn influences the choice profiles of the viewer to a considerable extent.

The programmes on sports both indigenous as well as foreign, originated, were found to be growing in popularity.

The typical rural programmes have been found to be quite popular in the region and to an extent we may say that they are capable of successfully replacing the traditional entertainment programmes available at the village levels. Also it is found that the programmes in the line of ones own cultural life are more appreciated that the rest.

It has been observed that the timings of television programmes are not suitable for the rural viewers. The daily routine of the average farmer is such that he finds it difficult to view the evening programmes as well as the night programmes. The viewers therefore opted for the afternoons as the most suitable for television viewing. In the circumstances where the villagers start their work early in the morning and resume the same after a lengthy break in the afternoon, such a preference of time for viewing the TV does not appear impractical. The evenings may be suitable for the urban counterparts of the rural viewers. Presently, it has been felt that the programme timings is one of the important factors which needs to be looked into by the planners.

The traditional entertainment programmes adopted by the medium of TV are popular among the rural viewers. Rather than contradicting with the indigenous methods of entertainment the TV has been proved to be complimentary to them. The performers of 'Tamasha' and 'Powadas' benefit by viewing and the medium personnel in turn, learn from the traditional performers.

The researcher has gathered the impression that the issues of social relevance do not receive the importance they deserve. The time allotted for such programmes is either inadequate or they are deprived of coverage in prime time. Instead, a greater emphasis is given on the revenue gathering sponsored programmes. The shift of interest from the instructional/entertainment programmes to the commercially-oriented sponsored programmes is indicative of what the planners and administrators really meant by media performances.

The range of subjects covered so far is too limited. Some of the issues which have a great social significance have remained ignored or are inadequately covered. Programmes on 'grow more trees', 'dowry', 'bride burning', 'deforestation', 'rural indebtedness', 'leprosy' and 'common illness' should be given sufficient coverage.

The expansion programmes of television can meet the basic

communication needs of rural population provided it undergoes certain modifications. The exposure of TV depends upon the performances of the custodians as well as the maintenance of the community sets. Such a dependence hampers the full and free exposure of the programmes.

The traditional methods of entertainment goes hand in hand with the entertainment programmes by the television. Rather than clashing with each other, they act as complimentary to each other.

The rural viewers consider the television more as an entertainment medium rather than an instructional one. They try to avoid the purely educational programme.

It is observed that illiteracy is no barrier in communication process if the programmes are designed properly. The programmes are received well when accompanied by visuals rather than by mere words or speeches.

The television proves to be the only audio visual instrument that can cater to the large number of viewers spread over wide geographical areas. In this, it outweighs the other media of communication like the press.

The television, especially the one provided to the community television programme, caters to a large number of illiterate poor. It thus bridges the gap between the "Media haves" and "Media have-nots".

By adding to the knowledge of the rural viewers, the television broadens the horizons of the people. It helps in enhancing the political awareness of the rural masses.

By exposing to the viewers scattered in remote villages the life styles of distant people and also by attempting to educate them on various issues, the television has made people more vocal. The viewers have become more prone to discussions after viewing the programmes.

During the course of the survey the researcher had many opportunities to conduct informal interviews as well as a few case studies. Along with the other relevant information provided by the informants they had also volunteered to advance quite a number of suggestions pertaining to the TV sets the programmes, the timings, and also their preferences. A few important suggestions provided by the informants are given as under:

Regular maintenance, checking and repair of the CTV sets should be undertaken. The fee of Rs. 200 levied by the Government in the form of repair and maintenance go waste at present for want of adequate number of technicians and proper coordination in executing them. The villages in general feel that if a couple of youth are properly trained for the repair and maintenance of the above problem could be solved without much delay.

With regard to the announcement and the language the villagers generally have a feeling that they are alienated. Often they complain that the language which is used in many Marathi Programmes is either not clear or intelligible to the rural folks. It is suggested that more local dialectics should be used in the programmes especially for the rural programmes.

More time should be allotted for the rural programmes.

There is a felt need for more rural-oriented entertaining programmes viz., *Powada, Tamasha, Bhajan, Kirtan, Bharud* etc.

Rural people would also like to see on TV various forts and religious places within and outside Maharashtra. They would also like to see the details of important Jatras like Pandharapur, Alandi etc.

The agricultural programmes need to be more field-oriented following the seasonal calendars. Actual demonstration with regard to using seeds, pesticides and other modern methods should be actually shown rather than talked about in the form of interviews.

There is demand for more programmes on the eradication of social evils like dowry, superstitions etc.

8

SUMMARY AND CONCLUSIONS

The aim of the Government was to raise economic productivity and living standards of lakhs of farmers in India, which called for dissemination of technical expertise and useful knowledge among the people. India wished to accomplish this task in the shortest possible time what advanced countries took centuries to do. The conventional means of communication was felt to be inadequate. Mass media offered the greatest possibilities for effective action.

Among various mass media, television was the most potent by virtue of its unique features. It has great potential to capture and attract the attention of many. Through the compelling combination of sight, sound, motion and emotion, television brings depth and dimension to life and intimacy to most events. It can disseminate rich experiences of specialists and experts to a large number of people simultaneously. Government of India wanted to utilise this medium to herald rural development in India.

In rural areas TV is a new innovation. Majority of rural population cannot afford to purchase TV sets due to poverty. Responsibility of introducing developmental programmes rests with the government. The major burden of bringing about the desirable changes in rural life for development is attempted by Government through provision of CTVs in villages for community viewing, since the majority of the population live in rural areas. Policy planners, policy-makers and administrators have considered seriously that mass media only can enter the calculus of development and offer the greatest possibilities for effective action. This can be achieved through community viewing of educative programme broadcaste by TV.

For D.P. Mukherji (1984) "communication was neither mechanical transfer of concepts and techniques from developed to backward nations, nor was it a passive reception by a subject country of the messages transmitted to it from the mother country". He thought for India having an old civilisation, communication must be transformed into an active process of absorption/assimilation via creative format and critical borrowing. This new view of communication recognised the cultural autonomy of the Indian people and their right to assimilate and absorb as much through rejection of what was non-transferable as through assimilation of what was transferable. It also recognised that not everything inherited from the past was outmoded and desirable. "Creative communication was a process in and through which a developing country developed the will and the capability to be both at the receiving as well as at the giving end". This is proved true in the village situation wherein farmers rejected many of the programmes meant for them as they have not taken the people for whom they were meant.

Entertainment and Education Through TV

Notwithstanding the great potential of TV in imparting information to the farmers, the experience with regard to the size of audience of agricultural telecasts has not been very happy.

Why is there inadequate interest of the farmers in Krishi Darshan? We found that apart from reasons like non-availability of electricity, frequent breakdowns of the sets and the programmes are telecast when the viewers are not free. The main reason expressed by viewers is the absence of entertaining appeal of the programme which was a prominent idea in the minds of the farmers for viewing TV. The appeal most frequently associated by most of the farmers with TV set was its ability to entertain them and farmers wanted entertainment and relaxation from TV rather than the hardwork of learning alone. According to S.K. Sukla (1985) "One important conclusion that can be drawn is that to attract an audience which is free, out of school, uncaptivated and expects entertainment from TV requires, besides other measures, interspersion of technical information with items of entertainment". The programme producers should find out the 'Recreation-Education' balance for most of the farming community in which TV sets are installed.

Initially it was felt that TV would act as a source of motivation for getting information. However, we found the rural people in majority viewed TV as a source of light entertainment and for passing their spare time. Incidentally quite a bit of learning takes place. A viewer while getting entertained also changes his attitudes and stores up certain information. This incidental storing up of information proved that they developed new values, attitudes and social patterns conducive to development.

The farmers experienced language difficulties particularly regarding measurements and technical terminology used in the programmes. To illustrate this in the words of one of the respondents, "they ask us to mix 118 grams of Urea with 225 grams of Nitrates with 6 litres of water. We don't know how to do this correctly. Even the technical brands given in the programmes the shops do not have stocks".

An observation was that Agricultural Scientists in TV programmes who gave different solutions for farm problems often caused confusion to the farmers. An example may be quoted from a telecast for farmers, "to use only an improved disease-resistant *bajra* variety in preference to the existing variety". When the farmers after listening to the telecast rushed to distribution centres found that there were no stock of the type of seeds mentioned in the programme. Normally supply services do not catch up with the programme broadcasts, since the information is supplied without ascertaining the availability of the commodity in the local market.

Another example may be quoted by a woman respondent, who viewed the Women's Programmes. She said that mango pickle preparation and mango pulp are given at a time when the mango season was over.

These examples simply justify the non-interest of respondents to the educative programmes.

During the past few decades there has been in the country considerable expansion of infrastructure for agricultural information communication. It is still considered inadequate for a vast agricultural country like India. Notwithstanding the expanding facilities of information/education communication there is a big majority of farmers who need the information of the rapidly changing agricultural technology, so that they may adopt and bring forth better production thereby contributing to the development of the country. The information supplied must be effective and more readily understandable and acceptable to the farmers. Before the farmer thinks of taking action, he will require the televised information and impressions to be reinforced by local demonstration and individual personal information.

Awareness creates the curiosity about a new idea in the minds of the farmers leading them to seek more information on it.

Programmes on agriculture have an immediate effect, if the ideas come along at a time when the farmer needs them most, deals with subjects of which he had no fixed idea but was groping in the dark. This will speed up changes. This has not occurred because the programmes telecast are not space time specific hence we do not find full impact and desirable social change is not occurring. There are a sizeable number of respondents who do not view rural programmes as these do not attract their attention. There is a crying need to develop agricultural information communication infrastructure suitable for the farmers combining information with entertainment. Government is faced with a challenge. Effective information communication has a role to meet this challenge. The media should adopt to the needs and levels of understanding of the rural people.

The researcher has been closely observing the operation of the scheme in Pune District for the past three years and his experience is discouraging. There is no linkage between community viewer and the production. If it exists it is too loose to have any substantial influence. Most of the Gram Panchayats are indifferent. They have neither evolved a system for organised viewing nor for effective monitoring of the programmes. Doordarshan also seems to be happy with the pumping of the programmes into the air. Nearly three-fourths of the Gram Panchayats operate the TV sets only for the film-based entertainment programmes. Most of the sets remain invariably closed on the days the rural programmes are telecast. The Panchayat peons who are entrusted with the operation of sets are reluctant because they are not paid any additional remuneration for their presence during evening hours. The appeals of the Zilla Parishad (District Administration) for regular monitoring of the rural programmes and maintenance of records have proved futile. The argument of the Gram Panchayat is that:

(1) The power bills would be high if the sets are kept in operation daily. This does not sound reasonable because the consumption of electricity is nominal.

(2) There should be some incentive for the person who is expected to operate the set daily. This is the main problem and as the set belongs to Panchayat, no one else wants to take any responsibility. People maintain that it is the obligation of the

Panchayat to maintain the set.

Added to this are other constraints like frequent breakdown of sets, delays in repairs and power disconnections due to non-clearance of bills. While the Rural Broadcasting Department maintains that not more than six to seven per cent of the set-days are lost due to mechanical troubles, some Gram Panchayats reported closure of sets for two-three months due to defective working. The closure of sets during busy agricultural season, winter and rainy seasons is inescapable. The cumulative effect of all these operational problems is the low utilisation of the telecasts.

Information Communication Problems vis-A-vis Rural Development

In spite of the best efforts of Government and non-governmental agencies in the context of rural development, the benefits that were expected to reach the common man in the rural areas were not demonstrably in evidence. This is due to many factors, however, we are giving below communication problems encountered in rural development programmes. These problems pertain to information abundance, information flow, information organisation, information quality, lack of coordination and cooperation among information agencies, communication skills, communication channels and language barrier. Only when broadcasting policies and decisions are guided by research facts, can there be reasonable chance that the constructive potential of the television medium will be properly approached and fully exploited.

The medium of TV when properly utilised has immense power to serve the need of an efficient information system. In the words of Dr. M.S. Swaminathan (1968), regarding agricultural development, "A satellite television system together with the ground stations capable of covering all our villages should be installed as early as possible. The investment would certainly be heavy but the return we can get in the form of increased production and raising of the rights of the rural community may more that offset the total investment in a year or two". However, when we look at the performance of the TV for rural development we noticed that the hardware potential to cover 85 per cent of the villages through TV was developed, however, due to the less number of sets available to viewers and also due to the shift of

Doordarshan to make TV more an entertainment medium than educative and information dessiminative. So the expected results are not forthcoming. The viewers, responses showed failure of TV as an information disseminator and educative role for rural development.

(1) The low attendance of rural development programmes shown on TV was due to the treatment of the message. The villagers complained that proper inputs were not used by the communicators/comparers which was not always understandable. For example, in rural programmes referred to measurements of area, weight and capacity in hectares, quintals and litres respectively. They alleged that the programmes were repetitive, monotonous, dull and lacked newness.

(2) The organisational arrangement for viewing were improper, irregular and uncertain working of the TV sets, absence of the custodian, improper sitting arrangements, noise caused by children were the factors for dissatisfaction of the viewers.

(3) Prevalence of village factions, lack of general ability in some farmers to derive meaning out of visual images telecast in quick succession on TV, general aptly among the farmers to seek for useful information, lack of knowledge about particular Krishi Darshan Programmes were the reasons for non-viewing of developmental programmes.

(4) The over-whelming motive of farmers to view TV was to watch light entertainment programmes since the Krishi Darshan Programmes have no ability to entertain them the farmers do not watch these programmes.

(5) The farmers watched TV to whileaway their time, they watched TV after completing their work, so they did not find tune to watch these developmental programmes because they were telecaste in inconvenient timings.

(6) Respondents were interested in TV either for entertainment alone or for both entertainment and information, so they viewed entertainment programmes mostly and news for information.

(7) The chief irritant was sex and farmers were concerned about their children and fear the mimicking of film stars, westernised ways, creation of the feeling of sexuality and sex loaded behaviour as a result of watching TV.

(8) Since TV is independent of literacy, it showed good potential for imparting information to different categories of farmers

with almost equal effectiveness. TV proved to be a useful medium of education for illiterates as well through for its fuller exploitation formal education seemed to be an important input. TV has universal utility if exploited properly can form an important constituent of any communication strategy that may be designed to bring about agricultural development in the country. But the farmers felt the programmes lacked the component of interest and entertainment.

Notwithstanding the great potentials of TV in imparting information to farmers, the audience response to agricultural telecasts is not much which is attributed by farmers due to the absence of entertainment appeal of these programmes, since farmers wanted entertainment and relaxation from TV rather than the hard work of learning alone.

One important conclusion that can be drawn from the observations of farmers is that to attract an audience which is free, out of school, uncaptivated and expects entertainment from TV requires, interspersion of technical information with items of entertainment.

Since the viewers wanted entertainment there should be greater proportion of entertainment items to attract and compel the farmers to TV set. If higher level of the Recreation-Education balance is introduced so that a gradual tendency is built up among the audience to seek for useful information. The telecast of technical information aimed for rural development may be in the forms that are lively to the farmers. So presentation of the programmes in a variety of ways taking the help of drawing, cartoons, diagrams and other visual reinforcements could be the effective way of combining information with entertainment.

Developing Identification with TV

The entertainment which meets the cultural tastes and interests of the rural folk should be provided by TV. Even entertainment programmes are presented with imagination could provide a good deal of 'incidental learning', which may change their attitudes and can even store up informative items without seeking them. It was felt necessary to give programmes to the rural people that are not only entertaining but are also stimulating, that are not only interesting but also help develop attitudes, values, motivations and social patterns appropriate to development. The majority of viewers expressed the rural development programmes lack in these aspects, so they do not deliver the goods. The present TV rural programmes serve the interests of infinitesimally small percentage of farmers who have high need for achievement and high proneness to change only seek information from Krishi Darshan. TV with its strong visual impact and unparalleled ability to stir imagination and emotions of farmers is not properly exploited.

The farmers felt that programmes should be presented in an easily understandable manner. Majority of the farmers experienced language difficulties with metric measurements and technical words. The farmers also wanted diversified technology to suit them according to the size of landholdings and resources. They felt the programmes appear to be catering to the needs of the rich farmers.

Treatment of the Messages

Majority of the farmers felt that agricultural telecasts were repetitive, monotonous and dealt with practices the farmers already familiar with. They wanted the topics dealt with should be relatively new in character and should look new every time. The programmes should satisfy the informative needs of farmers.

The farmers wanted that the TV sets should function all the year round and the CTV hall should have enough space for all the viewers to sit in comfort.

Research Hypothesis Tested

(1) The extension of TV coverage would meet the basic communication needs of the masses in these rural villages.

The expansion of the on-going programmes of communication for rural development needs a critical look before it is accepted as a method of meeting basic communication needs of the rural population. While it appears tenable that the television does deliver the goods as far as the dissemination of information is concerned, it could achieve the objectives only when certain prevalent practices are modified. The custodians play a major role in the exposure of the community TV programmes. The technical problems involved in the proper maintenance of the sets also need proper attention, otherwise the programmes will not reach the masses for whom they are made. The expansion of TV coverage would probably meet the communication needs of the rural population if the expansion programmes are accompanied by the qualitative improvement of its delivery system.

(2) The conventional media system and the traditional media systems would not clash with the TV communication.

The traditional media system appears to be going hand in hand as far as the entertainment is concerned. The traditional media also receives newer approaches of entertainment through the television while the television attempts to represent the existing methods of entertainment. It looks as if both these media learn from each other and dwell in a kind of complimentary relationship with each other. It was noticed that these two do not clash with each other.

(3) The television media in rural areas is more popular as an entertainment medium rather than as an instructional medium.

The television media takes a form of entertainment more often than not, rather than the instructional. It has been observed in the area under study that the rural masses view the entertainment programmes and there are tendencies to avoid the purely instructional programmes. They have categorically expressed their choice of entertainment programmes. Television acts more as an entertainment medium in the rural population rather, as an instructional one.

(4) Illiteracy is a barrier to understand and appreciate TV communication or not.

The visual programmes are better enjoyed than mere speeches or verbal communication. The programmes are received well if accompanied by visuals, and they are understood when presented in the language of their mother tongue. Television thus demonstrates that illiteracy is no barrier in communication process, if properly designed programmes are shown. This is an important consideration for a country like India where literacy is still very low and television appears to act as an important medium of information.

(5) The Community TVs in the villages act as a boon to the masses who do not have other medium of communication.

The methods of mass communication are gaining popularity in the Indian sub-continent. The radio, for example, has reached the remote villages in India, including the tribals in the hilly regions. Similar is the case with newspapers. The Community TV still acts as a boon to the masses, in spite of their access to other means of communication, because it is probably the only audio-visual instrument that can cater to a large number of rural masses.

(6) Community TV bridges the gap between the "media haves" and "media have-nots".

The television appears to be useful when considered from yet another view point. The illiterate and poor who do not have access to the other means of mass communication, can view the news programmes on community TV and can also be benefited by the programmes like "Amachi Mati Amachi Manse". The Community TV acts as an agent to bridge the gap between the 'media haves' and the 'have-notes'.

(7) Television helps in the process of political socialisation of the illiterates.

It is also apparent that the television broadens the horizons of knowledge. The hitherto limited knowledge about the political aspects of local groups now expands to include the information about the political parties, leaders and activities of national and international levels. The TV thus helps in enhancing the political awareness of the rural masses.

(8) It is beneficial for transferring the technical know-how of agriculture to the rural population.

Television made a headway in imparting technology, particularly the agricultural technology to the illiterate farmers. Various programmes dealing with seeds, fertilizers, pesticides and irrigation methods have gained popularity. The TV has proved beneficial to transferring the technical 'know-how' of agriculture to the rural population.

(9) It adds to the knowledge and awareness of the people.

The role of television in disseminating the knowledge and expanding the horizons of rural viewers needs a specific consideration. By imparting relevant facts, it has not only made the rural people more aware of the world around them but has also made them prone to discussions on the matters of their interest. It has demonstrated to them the ways and life styles of distant and different people as also the tools and techniques hitherto unknown to them. Television thus, acts as an important means of enhancing the general knowledge of the people, so also of creating awareness among them.

(10) Educational Programmes help in rural development.

Agricultural programmes are aimed at providing knowledge for the farmers. Some of these suggestions are implemented by some of the farmers, these resulted in better yields. Educational programmes thus helped in rural development.

Inter-relation between the Village TV and Viewer

On the basis of the data collected from the field it could be inferred that the state of development of the village influences the pattern of viewing among the villagers. It could be said that the community television sets are operated mainly to view the entertainment programmes in the villages which appear to be more developed than the other. When there are good facilities of communication like the motorable roads, State Transport Buses, Railway Stations and so on, it could be observed that there are a large number of privately owned television sets. The local choice regarding the television programmes falls more on the entertainment than on the instructional one. If the village is located at a relatively isolated place, the people view the news programmes with some eagerness while they also choose to view the entertainment programmes. The custodian in the developed villages seldom give a prime significance to the responsibilities bestowed on him. For them, the community television appears to be an additional work which they do with a comparative half heartedness. The custodians in the remote, undeveloped villages appear to be more concerned about their being selected as custodians and they do try to give services that were expected from them.

Villages equipped with the health care delivery do also show a marked up to dateness in their utilisation of the facility of community television. Villagers here develop the habit of viewing instructional programmes and the news in addition to the entertainment programmes.

Women viewers appear to be different in many ways as far as the television viewing is concerned. They tend to watch all the programmes that they can and they do not seem to dislike programmes even from other languages. They watch the instructional programmes tirelessly and so also the rural programmes. They appear to retain what they view on the screen. As a result, they appear to show a greater awareness about many vital issues of their importance like agricultural technology, family welfare, bio-gas, rural indebtedness, health, immunization and so on. Their interests somehow do not include social forestry, hard-core subjects related to agriculture, and higher technological issues etc.

The custodians, bias is a vital issue in the community television programmes. The custodians often act as the filter between the programmes and the viewers. It may so happen that a relevant programme could not be seen by the viewers just because the custodian was not available or just because he was tired. The custodian may switch on the set only when there were programmes of his choice thereby influencing the choice of others too. This element probably causes a great hinderance to the smooth functioning of the community television programme.

Suggestions

(1) *Video Library*

If the target audience is rural people to provide information, education and entertainment to them right kind of software will have to be produced. This has to be considered in relation to wide divergence in language, social customs and tastes. Preparation of software to suit specific groups involves decentralisation of productions.

(2) Doordarshan at present does not have the facilities nor the personnel to undertake the responsibility of maintaining CTVs in the villages; hence it has been given to State Governments. But State Government's Rural Broadcasting Department do not have efficient personnel to handle the equipment. Hence the need for training maintenance personnel is acutely felt.

(3) Mobile production facilities with portable equipment that can easily be handled, with productions originating in the village can be the best way of disseminating information and ideas.

(4) More programmes of social awareness should be produced.

(5) Identification with the local environment and culture be used by using local dialect; and planning Area Specific Programmes to improve the utility of the programmes to rural people.

(6) Lecture format should be replaced by group discussion method, demonstration, drama, puppets, muppets, animation, film episodic presentations. These formats depending upon the type of theme especially for agricultural programmes were found to be very useful. Hence these formats should be introduced.

(7) Important episodes of interstate agriculture should be telecaste once in a month.

(8) O.B. Vans should be used for more live coverage of important current farm operations, outbreak of diseases, natural hazards etc.

(9) Technical words and theoretical information in Rural Programmes should be simplified keeping in view the level of education of the viewers.

(10) Information relating to services for farmers such as imported seeds, fertilizers, pesticides, credit facilities should be telecaste at appropriate time and seasons.

(11) Success, stories of individuals and rural based projects undertaken by a community, voluntary organisations should be telecaste.

(12) Coordination between Doordarshan and agricultural universities should be strengthened.

(13) A video cassette library at national, regional and taluka level should be created and the cassettes can be used for regional stations. 1/2" VHS versions could be made available at BDO with VCPs. The Agricultural Extension Workers should show the programmes and clarify the doubts and quarries of the viewers.

(14) Projection type community sets should be provided by Government at nominal costs to the villages. These sets should be kept with a responsible person preferably at a central place.

(15) Continuous Audience Research is necessary.

(16) Evaluation of programmes should be done at regular intervals.

(17) Awards to best rural programmes should be initiated.

(18) Renowned film and theater artists should be invited to participate in rural TV productions by giving special incentives and awards.

(19) The TV programmes would be coupled with entertainment component particularly with folk songs.

(20) There should be adequate remuneration for the CTV operator. Also fix the timings and responsibilities of the operators to keep the CTV sets on at the time of telecasts. There should be periodical surprise checks by Rural Broadcasting Department officials to see that the CTVs are switched on at the time of the telecast and deterrent punishment should be imposed for default.

It is suggested that the educational programmes should have higher level recreation so that the audiences are drawn to these programmes. Technical information may be made lively by using drawings, cartoons, diagrams and other visual reinforcements. We can use the traditional mode of imparting information through *Harikatha*, *Lokagatha* and *Lavani*, which rural people are accustomed to viewing. The programme planners should make the programmes not only entertaining but are also stimulating.

The needs of the different user groups are quite diverse and any information system must cater to these needs. The TV should give information in terms of use and transfer.

Know - Why information - more scientifically oriented.
Know - How information - more technically oriented.
Show - How information - more operationally oriented.
Know - Why information - more personally oriented.

The most effective means of rural development is through participatory approach in rural communication.

TV Communication should be participatory and time space specific and not universal. This participatory approach poses a question whether the programmes in Hindi dished out by Doordarshan are of any use for rural folk? They are neither entertaining nor educative, which are the aims of the people and government respectively. If we want to achieve these twin aims, we should have a participatory approach. TV cassettes should be prepared about the various problems faced by farmers and loaned to viewers whenever they face a need. After showing these, there should be extension educators present to answer the farmers querries, so that they comprehend the programmes and implement them. Programmes should be made in such a way that the rural community identifies the people as one of their village folk. The language used should be native dialect, which makes villagers identify as their own. One can say if the programmes have no entertainment content, the villagers are not going to view them. Hence the need for making these programmes entertaining. For example, a programme on family planning should be broadcast in such a way as it will appeal to their taste. The knowledge can be imparted in an interesting form of Harikatha rather than in the form of a monotonous monologue. Since the rural folk are traditional this form of communication will be more effective.

Also if we want to exploit the mass media, TV properly to bring in socio-economic development, the programmes can't be universal, but should be based on the needs of the people. Bottom to top approach should be used, whereby the villagers ask for programmes on topics which they feel that they should be enlightened on. The urban based elite producers cannot produce programmes to suit the rural people and hasten the socio-economic development in rural society. This means that the process of communication should not be initiated from the top, but should draw as much as possible from rural resources. The communication strategy in this approach would be to use interpersonal channels found at the grass-roots level. Participation is the key concept that has emerged as being of considerable importance in recent times.

Ideally, people would be encouraged and opportunities should be created so that they can participate in their own developments. They must be free to develop as individuals. However, the present system is not geared to this form of participation. There are many bottlenecks that prevent genuine participation from the people.

Primary principle of participatory communication is to involve the people themselves in the design of the media. One should not misunderstand by people's participation as particular community. As is seen from the present situation, elites are having a say in the decision making. But majority of the poor have little access to resources. These groups should become the principal actors of the media design effort. Unfortunately the entire media system negates participation in the real sense of the word. The prevailing system no doubt encourages competition and hierarchy and not cooperation and unity The existing educational system is encouraging the individual for his development but not stressing the cooperative efforts. This attitude is leading to inequality. The media system should stress to develop a spirit of solidarity and unity.

No doubt, the poor are branded as 'irrational, lazy and irresponsible'. Every one looks down with contempt their 'traditional' knowledge. The urban oriented middle class professionals think that they are best suited for the media system. Unless there is a degree of humility on the part of the professional staff and a desire to listen and understand others, will not be in a position to relate to other through the media.

There is a general assumption on the part of the media professionals that they can disseminate a particular idea without a dialogue with the grass-roots people because they consider themselves as 'specialists'. A majority of them show little or no respect for the experience and knowledge of the people – the creative potential of the peasents or slum dwellers. They fail to understand that the poor people are more suited to depict and present their own lives. What the media system would have to do in order to achieve participation is to establish consultation, cooperation and effective mobilisation of this community for depicting the issues concerning them.

Extensive training programmes would have to be organised to build up capability of the community members in the use of various communication media. They should make concerted efforts to make media more accessible to people by deprofessionalisation of media efforts.

Participatory communication should help people to understand the oppressive structure that are responsible for perpetuating poverty. They should be made to learn to make more effective demands on government so that change in their life is brought about by consentisation and organisation building of the poor. They should be made aware about the structural causes of their oppression. The participatory communication demands that the poor should form organisations with leadership emerging from within, so that they can exercise more control over their lives.

By participatory communication one should not be guided away by the idea of one-way communication of a section of one community, but it should be kept in mind that participatory communication is a two-way interactive and dynamic process. Participation should start from the stage of planning and then go on through all stages of implementation, monitoring and evaluation. By this process one should accept the fact that the elements of power should be shared instead of bestowing it in the hands of one section of people. The communication can become truly participatory if it depends largely on the confidence and trust that the government and media system have in people. If the aim of participatory communication is redistribution of resources and decision-making powers in order to make ordinary citizens to have more of a say about their own lives. This will have a political underpinnings.

If participation of people in rural development through mass media is to be achieved an important factor is to be kept in mind by the planners i.e., that any communication dished out by the media people will not be acceptable to all the viewers at the same rate and same enthusiasm.

The greatest need of the present times if money is not to be wasted in producing programmes meant for rural masses for rural development is evaluation research. Even before launching the programmes one must assess which group appreciates that type and format of a programme. Then we can plan programmes for target groups who will benefit from them.

Lately an approach that is gaining ground is characterised by its explicit emphasis on the ideas of self-reliance on natural and human resources available and the ability of individuals to define developmental problems, set goals, make decisions independently and in accordance with one's own social and cultural ethos. Self-reliance to succeed, popular participation is absolutely essential.

Suggestions for Development of Software in TV

Television must be utilised in the development process as an instrument of social change and national cohesion by upholding progressive values and involving the community in a free dialogue. We noticed that Indian TV has an elitist approach without bothering about the consumer value systems.

It was noticed that majority of the rural development programmes cater to education and information disseminating, hence the rural audience are not interested in them. With the available resources TV should try to cater to the needs of the general audiences, high priority should be given to the information and entertainment needs of the rural people ensuring their active participation.

The Government should invest enough money in providing adequate community TV sets as a capital outlay. There should be enough financial investment to maintain the TV sets in working order as part of recurring expenditure.

The bureaucratic procedural constraints and restraints should be reduced so that the TV personnel develop their own individual identity.

The infrastructure should be flexible enough to ensure sharing of interdisciplinary experiences in other communication media and innovative approach with the widest participation of outside talent.

Television as a support to better education should assist the teacher effectively. The experience of countrywide classroom and

Shalleya Chitravani showed that these TV programmes are not useful, instead of TV Cassettes should be prepared and supplied to students and teachers so that they can use them when they experience any need for them. TV could disseminate information about aspects of science and technology, agriculture, health, family planning through video cassettes. These cassettes could be shown to village audiences at appropriate time, with some expert discussant who will clear the doubts of the rural audiences.

There should be continuous evaluation and research of the different programmes in order to improve the quality of the programmes. This evaluation should be done by researchers who are not the members of Doordarshan.

TV programming should be built into the total solution at the planning stage. For example, (a) if fertiliser is assessed as the top priority need, supply, distribution and extension communication strategy should be interlinked. A programme detailing how to use fertiliser is telecast when no fertiliser is available adversely affected the subsequent credibility of the medium and the audience figures. (b) The rural audiences complained that the programme on how to build far fences to keep cattle out when drought has claimed the crop and lives of most of the cattle. This assessment of the farmers' problems is totally inapt and incredible in bad taste.

The female audiences complained that women's programmes on working etc. are telecast at the time when the raw materials shown in the programme are not available in their village or they are not in season.

BIBLIOGRAPHY

Agarwal, Binod, C. (1977) *SITE Social Evaluation Consultans and Implications of Holistic Study.* Ahmedabad: Space Application Centre. ISRO.

Agarwal, Binod, C. (1981) *SITE Social Evaluation Results, Experiences and Implications.* Ahmedabad: Space Application Centre. ISRO.

Ahmed, Y.L. (1975) Administration of Integrated Rural Development — A Note on Methodology. *International Labour Review.*

Aiyey, S.P. (1973) *Modernization of Traditional Society*, Bombay: Macmillan Company.

Altbach, Philip G. (1986, Sept. 13) Knowledge Enigma Copyright in the Third World. *Economic and Political Weakly,* 21(87), pp. 1643-1650.

Aurora, D. (1975) Communication for Development, *Communicator,* pp 23-26.

Barman and B.K. Roy (1986, August, 12) Rural Development in Seventh Plan: A Restatement of the Issue. New Delhi: *Mainstream,* 24(32), pp. 21-25.

Barnett, P.W. and Vernon, E. Cronen (1980) *Communication Action and Meaning*, Beverler Hills : Sage.

Beals, Alan R. (1962) *Gopalpur — A South Indian Village.* N.Y. : Hotle Rinebort and Winston.

Belson, W.A. (1975) *The Impact of Television:* London : Crosby Lookwood.

Black, Cyril E. (1966) Change as Condition of Modern Life in Modernisation. In Myron Weiner (Ed), *The Dyanamics of Growth*. New York.

Bordenave, J. Diaz. (1976) Communication of Agricultural Innovations in Latin America. The Need for New Models. In E.M. Rogers (Ed), *Communication and Development — Critical Perspectives.* CA: Sage Publications.

Borra, Ranjan (1972) TV in India. *Vidura* 52, pp. 46-48.

Boyd, Paul D. (n.d.) Causes and Cures of Communication Neglect in Development Planning. *Educational Broadcasting International,* 8, pp. 5-9.

Bowers, John (1974) Rural Extension and Information Systems. *A.G. Communication,* 57, pp. 22-31.

Burstein, Leigh, *et al.* (1985) *Collecting Evaluation Data: Problems and Solutions.* New Delhi: Sage.

Chakrawarthy, Nikhil (1983) *Communication should Indicate the Direction of Development* Address: Insitutes Annual Convocation, New Delhi.

Chandani, Lala Karam (Ed) (1973) *A.G. Communication.* Farm Information Units. Director of Extension. Ministry of Agriculture New Delhi.

Chandani, Lala Karam. (Ed) (1974) Action Research in Information Communication. *Farm Information Unit Directorate of Extension Ministry of Agriculture.* New Delhi.

Chawla, N.L. (1984, February 19) Video Technology Speed for Communication Policy. *Patriot,* New Delhi.

Chawla, N.L. (1985) TV as Catalyst of Social Change. New Delhi. *Public Opinion Surveys,* 33(11 and 12), pp. 31-32.

Chawla, N.L. (1986) Three Tier Television: Integrating the Modern and Traditional. Delhi: *Statesman* (May 18).

Class, Gene V. *et al.* (1981) *Meta Analysis in Social Research.* London : Sage.

Clifford, Geertz (Ed). (1963) *Old Societies and New States.* N.Y.: Free Press of Glencoe.

Cook, Thomas D. *et al.* (1983) Implicit Assumptions of Television Research: An Analysis of the 1982 NIMH Report on Television and Behaviour. *Public Opinion Quarterly,* 47(2), pp. 161-199.

Cowtan, Burt (1973). Thinking Small: Some Comments on the Role of Mass Media for Economic and Social Development. *Educational Broadasting International,* 6, pp. 79-83.

Crickman, R.D. (1976). Community Communication Patterns in Chicago. In Kochen M. and Donohul J.C. (Eds.), *Information for the Community.* American Library Association, pp. 237-48.

Dankworth, A. Rustow (1967) *Towards a Theory of Economic Growth.* New York: Brookings Institution.

Das, Amalkumar and Raha, Manish Kumar (1963) *The Oraons of Sunderban Cultural Research Institute.* Calcutta: Tribal Welfare Department, Government of West Bengal.

Dean, T.J. (1972) Television in India: Investment Alternatives. *Educational Broadcasting Review,* 6, pp. 244-250.

Desai, M.V. (1983) *Communication Policies in India.* Paris: UNESCO.

Deutschmann, P.J. and Ellingsworth. H. (1968). *Communication and Social Change in Latin America.* New York: Freedquick. A. Praeger.

Deutschmann, Paul. J. and Orlando, Fils Bonda (1962) *Communication and Adoption Patterns in an Andean Village.* Costa Rica: Programme Interamericano de Information Popular.

Deutschmann, Paul. J. and Wayne, A. Danielson (1960) Diffusion of Knowledge of Major News Story. *Journalism Quarterly,* 37, pp. 345-355.

Devito, Joseph A. (1986) *Communication Handbook : A dictionary.* New York: Harper and Row.

Dissanayke, Wimal (1981) Development and Communication : Four Approaches : *Media Asia,* 8(4). pp. 217-227.

Drinkwater, Jane. (1984) *Get it on: Radio and Television: A Practical Guide to Getting Air Time.* London: Pluto Press.

Dobb, Leonard W. (1969) *Communication in Africa: A Search for Boundaries.* N.Y: Yale University Press.

Dubey, S.C. (1967). Communication, Innovation and Planned Change in India. In Lerner and Schramm (Eds.), *Communication and Change in Developing Countries.* Standford : Standford University Press.

Dubey, S.C. (976). Mass Media and National Development. In Schramm. W. and Lerner D.(Eds). *Communication and Change in the Developing Countries.* Honolulu: University of Hawaii Press.

Duby, V.K. and Bharja, S.K. (1986, Aug. 12-16). *Using Video in Rural Development.* Paper presented at International Seminar on Media Development, Pune.

Easterlin R. (1968). Economic Growth: Overview. *Encyclopedia of the Social Sciences.*

Easton, David and Jack, Dennis. (1969) *Children in the Political System* N.Y: McGraw Hill.

Education for Our People. (1978) Citizens for Democracy, Bombay : Allied Publishers Pvt. Ltd.

Etienne, Gilbert. (1985) *Rural Development in Asia, Meetings with Peasant.* New Delhi : Sage.

Fergusson, Marjoree (Ed) (1986). *New Communication Technologies and Public Interest, Comparative Perspective on Policy and Research.* London: Sage Publications.

Fernandes, W. (Ed) (1980). *Peoples Participation Development.* New Delhi: Indian Social Institute.

Fink Ariene and Kosecroff, J. (1985). *How to Conduct Surveys.* Los Angeles: University of California.

Foote, Dennis. Heather, E. Hudson and Edwin, B. Parker (1955) *Telecommunication Planning and Rural Development.* IEEE Transaction, pp. 67-106.

Foster, C.M. (1962) *Traditional Cultures and the Impact of Technological Change.* N.Y.: Harper and Row.

Fowler, Floyd, J. (1984). *Survey Research Methods.* New Delhi: Sage.

Frey, Frederick, W. (1968) *Development Aspects of Administration, Behavioural Change in Agriculture.* N.Y: Cornell University Press.

Frey, Frederick. W. (1973) Communications and Development. In Itheil de Sola Pool *et al* (Eds), *Handbook of Communications.* Chicago: Rand Me nally College Publishing Company.

Feed Back on Alcoholism Series and Other Programmes. (1978). F.T.I.I.

F.T.I.I. (1973) TV Programme Production and Prototype Research Unit. *New Letter,* 1978.

Gastron, Roberge. (1982) *Visual Communication and Development.* Seminar and Exhibition on Rural Communications, Calcutta.

Gokhale, S.D. and Sohoni, N.K. (Ed) (1979) *Child in India.* Bombay Publications Pvt. Ltd.

Goulet, D.A. (1971) *The Cruel Choice: A New Concept in the Theory of Development.* New York : Atheneum.

Government of India. (1973) *Planning Commission Report of INSAT Hardware Working Group (Final Draft),* New Delhi.

Gumpert, Gavy and Catheart, Robert (Eds) (1986) *Intermedia, Interpersonal Communication in a Media World.* (3rd ed.) New York: Oxford University Press.

Hagen Everett H. (1962) *A Framework for Analysing Economic and Political Change in Development of Emerging Countries.* In Robert. E. Asher (Ed). Brookings Institution, Washington.

Hassan, Salleh. (1986) Human Resources Development for Broadcasting. New Delhi: *Asia Gazette,* 38, pp. 187-250.

Holemberg, Allen R. (1960) Changing Community Attitudes and Values in Peru: A Case Study in Guided Change Council of Foreign Relations. In *Social Change in Latin America Today.* N.Y: Harper and Brothers.

Hornik, R. (1980) Communication as Complement to Development. In G. Gerbner and Seijert, M. (Eds). *World Communications.* New York: Longman.

Huntington, P.S. (1971) *The Change to Change: Modernisation, Development and Politics, Comparative Politics.*

Inayatullah (1967) Towards a Non-Western Model of Development. In Daniel Lerner and Wilbur Schramm (Eds), *Communication and Change in Developing Countries.* Honolulu: East-West Centre.

Jain, L.C., Krishnamurthy, B.V. and Tripathy, P.M. (1985). *Grass Withouth Roots: Rural Development under Government Auspices,* New Delhi : Sage.

Jha, R.C. (1978). *A Study of Delhi TV : Retrospect and Prospect.* M.Sc. Thesis, IARI, New Delhi.

Jha, R.C. (1982). *A Study of the Organisational Performances of Farm and Home Units of All India Radio.* Ph.D. Thesis, IARI, New Delhi.

Jones, Nicholas (1986) *Strikes and the Media Communication and Conflict.* Oxford Publishing Services.

Joshi, P.C. (1984) Communicator and Social Transformation. New Delhi: *Communication,* 11(27).

Joshi, P.C. (1985) *National Development, Culture and Communications: The Interface Between Development and Communication Planning.* Seminar on National Goals and Mass Media Communication : New Delhi.

Joshi P.C. (1985) Communication and National Building Perspectives and Policy, Delhi. *Public Opinion Surveys,* 33(11 and 12), pp. 18-20 and pp. 21-28.

Joshi. S. (1986) Community TV : The Kheda Experience, *Delhi Gazette,* 38, pp. 4357.

Joshi S.R., Manjuri Shah and Radha Mishra (1984), *What Went On Air,* Ahmedabad, Indian Space Research Organisation.

Karl de Schweinitiz, Jr, (1965) *Economics of the Underdeveloped Economics,* American, Behavioural Scientist.

Khanna, Amit (n.d.) Video and Cinema : Allies or Adversaries 10 IFFI. Seminar on Cinema, TV and Video. New Delhi: IIMC.

Khurna, B.K. and Choudhary S.V.S. (1986) Insat Communication through, TV Paper presented at the international Seminar on Communication Development, Aug. 12-14.

Khurana, B.K. (1986) *"Television India"* Audience Research Unit, Directorate General, Doordarshan, New Delhi.

Kincaid, D. Lawrence. (1975) *Fundamental Human Communication: A Professional Development Module.* Honolulu, East-West Centre.

Klapper, Joseph T. (1960) *Effects and Mass Communication.* Free Press.

Kosecoff Jacqueline and Fink Arlone (1982) *Evaluation Basics: A Practitioner Mannual,* New Delhi : Sage.

Kroeber, A.L. (n.d.) *Anthropology.* N.Y: Harcourt, Brace and Wond, Inc.

Lakshmana Rao, Y.V. (1973) Regional Conference on Communication and Change in Rural Asia, New Delhi, A-G Communication, No. 3.

Lassey, W.R. (1979) *Planning in Rural Development.* N.Y: McGraw Hill.

Lele, Uma (1973) *The Design of Rural Development Lessons from America.* Baltimore: John Hopkins.

Lerner, Daniel (1958) *The Passing of Traditional Society.* Glencoe, Illinois, Free Press.

Levine Robert, A. *et al.* (n.d.) *Evaluation Research and Practice: Comparative and International Perspectives,* London : Sage.

Listening to News Current Affairs. (1982) A Study conducted in Bihar District, Bangalore Audience Research Unit, All India Radio.

Lucien. W. Pye (Ed) (1963) *Communication and Political Development.* New Jersey: Princeton.

Lucien. W. Pye and Sidney Verba (Eds) (1965) *Comparative Political Development.* Princeton University Press.

Maamen, John Van (1985). *Qualitative Methodology.* New Delhi: Sage.

Madan, G.R. and Madan Tara (1983): *Village Development in India : A Sociological Approach,* New Delhi : Allied Publishers.

Maheswari, S.R. (1985). *Rural Development in India,* New Delhi : Sage.

Marsh, Patricia, O. (1983) *Messages that Work : A Guide to Communication Design.* N.J.: Englewood Cliffs Educational Technology Publications.

Masani, Mehra (1976). *Broadcasting and the People.* New Delhi : National Book Truth of India.

McBride J.C. (1986) *The New Interactive Video Disc Technology,* Pune, Paper Presented at the Development Communication Seminar. University of Pune.

Mcluhan, Marshall (1984) *Understanding Media : The Extension of Man,* New York : McGraw-Hill.

McQuil, Dennis (1969) *Towards a Sociology of Mass Communication,* London: Collin Macmillan Ltd.

Menon, Narayana (1976). *Communication Revolution.* New Delhi. National Book Trust of India.

Mickiewier, Ellen Propper (1981) *Media and the Russian Public.* New York : Praeyor Publications.

Middleton, John (1978) *Using theory in Communication Planning:* Development Communications Report, 33 : 1.

Miller, George A. (Ed) (1967) The Psychology of communication: Seven Essays, Battimane : Penguin Books Inc.

Mishra, V.M. (1972) *Communication and Modernisation in Urban Slums.* New York : Asia Publishing House.

Mohammod, Khalid (1986) Serial Time, Scrndol Time, *The Times of India*, April 24.

Mohanty, J. (1984) *Educational Broadcsting Radio and Television in Education*, New Delhi : Sterling Publications.

Murthy, N.V.K. (1983) *The State of Cinema, TV and Video in India* 10, IFFI., Seminar on Cinema, TV and Video, New Delhi.

Nair, K.S. and Shirely White (1985) *Operationalisation of the Development Communication Research Project,* UNI, Pune/USA Pune : University of Poona.

Narula, Uma (1985) *Development Bureaucracy and the Masses will they change*? : New Delhi : *Patriot,* 29th June.

Narula, Uma and Pearce Barnett, 1985 : *Development as Communication*, Southern Illinois : University Press, Carbondale.

Palkhivala (1986) 75th Convocations Address delivered at University of Poona, Pune 25th October.

Panda, Sricharan, (1978) *Viewes of the Viewers of Sambalpur TV : Some Specific Programme Assessment,* ISRO, SAC.

Patra, Swampanand (1978) *Social Change Through Education:* Its Dyanamics, Need Assessments, Program Briefs, Strategies and Instrucational objectives. SITE.

Parthasarathy, C. (1984) *Human and Cultural Values in Communication.* New Delhi, Address at the Plenary Session of the Namedia Conference.

Padnekar, Vandana (1986) Doordarshan Strikes Goldmine in TV Commercials, *Economic Times*, Bombay April 24.

Phillip, Robert. T. and Johansen, Patricia A. (1977). *Series in Telecommunications and Satellites for Public Service II.* Washington: Agency for International Development.

Pool, Ithiel de Sola. *et al* (1963) *The Mass Media and Politics in the Modernisation Process in Communication and Political Development.* Lucian Pye University Press.

Premdasa, R. (1985) Mass Media, Putting the Message Across, New Delhi : *Media Asia* 12(4) pp. 183-84.

Prasad L.V. (1969) *Opportunite Available to Developing Nations Through the use of Communications Satellite – The Delhi Project in Space Research in India*. ISRO SAC Ahmedabad.

Pye Lucien W. (1966), *Aspects of Political Development little.* Brown, Baston.

Rahim, S.A. *Diffusion and Adoption of Agricultural Practices : A study in a Village in East Pakistan,* Comilla : Bangladesh.

Ramanamma A. 1985: Women in TV in sponsered programme. New Delhi. National Seminar on Mass Common organised by ICSSA.

Ramanamma A. (1986) Participatory Approach to Rural Development Through Community Development Communication, 12-14, August, 1986.

Ramesh Chandra (1972 Dec, 17) *Problems of Programming for SITE.* Paper Presented at V.M. Panel Meeting on Satallite Instructional Television.

Rameshray, Roy, Srivastava R.K. (1985) Dialogues of Development Delhi : Sage.

Rao, Y.L. (1963) *The Role of Information in Economic and Social Change: The Study of Two Asians Villages,* Unpublished Doctoral Dissertation, University of Minnesota.

Rao Y.V. Lakshamana (1966) Communication and Development. A Study of two Indian Villages, Minneapolis : University of Minnesota Press.

Rawal, Jyoter (1986, March) Role of TV in Agricultural Broadcasting in India, *Combroad* 70; pp. 39-41.

Rogers, E.M. (1968) *Mass Economic Exposure and Modernization Among Clombian Peasents in Mass Communication and Development Among Nations,* ed, David. K. Berlo : East Lansing, Michigan State University.

Rogers E.M. and Shoe Makco F. (1971) *Communication of Innovations : A Cross Cultural Approach.* New York : Free Press.

Rogers E.M. and D. Lawrence Kincaid (1981) *Communication Networks Towards a New Paradigm for Research.* New York : Free Press.

Rogers E.M. (1986) *Communication Technology : The new media in Society*. New York : Free Press.

Roy Bunker (1986, May 3) Media : T.V. and Rural audiences, *Mainstream*. New Delhi, 24(35) pp. 32-33.

Roy Prodipto. (1968) *Agricultural Innovations Among Indian Farmers*. IIRD, Hyderabad.

Rutan Leonard (Ed) (1984) *Evaluation Research Methods: A Basic Guide,* 2nd edition : New Delhi, Sage.

Sarabhai, Vikram A. (1969) *TV for Development,* Paper presented at the 11th World Congress, Society for International Development, New Delhi.

Schramm, Wilbur (1964) *Mass Media and National Development : The Role of Information in the Developing countries*. Stanford : Standford University Press.

Seetharama S. (1986) *Information Analysis and Consolidation in Defence contexts* paper presented at the National Conference on Scientific Information Defence, New Delhi.

Seminar Proceeding, (1980) Rural Development and Communcia-tion Politics, New Delhi : IIMC.

Sharma, G.K. and Singh. J. (1972) *TV in Agricultural Transformation Mimeographed*. New Delhi : ICAR.

Sinha. B.P. (1974) *TV in Diffusion of farm Information : A motivation Study.* Delhi : New Heights Publishers and Distributors.

Sinha, B.P. (1974) *TV in India : Retrospect and Prospect.* International Seminar on Development Communication. Pune, Aug. 12-16, 1986.

Singh, J.P. and Dean, T.J. (1969) *The Satellite Instructional Television Experiment in India: A Case History* : St Louis, Missouri, Washington University.

Singh, J. (1971) *A Study of Factors Influencing the Viewing Behaviour of Farmers Towards Agricultural Programme on Television,* Unpublished Ph.D. Thesis, IARI, New Delhi.

Singh, Swaraj Pal (1986, May 16-31) What Fails Rural Development? *Yojana,* 30(9), pp. 11-12 and 19.

Sood, Rahul (1986, August) *Message Design in Development Communication,* Unpublished Paper presented at International Seminar on Project Development Communcation, Pune.

Sperber, Dan and Wilson, Diordre (1986) *Relevance, Communication and Congnition* Oxford, Basi., Balckwell.

Srivastava, Anil. (1983) *Cinematography in an Electronic Age.* 10 IFFI Seminar on Cinema, Television and Video, Indian Institute of Mass Communication, New Delhi.

Sujan, D.K. (1986) *Traditional Folk Media for Rural Development.* Paper presented at International Seminar on Communication Development, Pune : University of Poona.

Swaminathan, M.S. (1968, Jan. 4) *Presidential Addresses in Agricultural Science Section,* 55th Indian Science Congress, Varanasi (U.P.)

Todaro, M.P. (1977) *Economic Development in the Third World,* New York : Longman.

Varalakshimi, T. (1985) *TV Viewing Behaviour and Consumption of Rural Telecast by the Rural Audience of Range Reddy District of Andhra Pradesh.* M.Sc. Thesis, IARI, New Delhi.

Vilanilam, J.V. (1986) *Basic Indicators of Development in Underdeveloped Societies: The Need for a New Approach Among Communcations.* Seminar on Communication Development, Pune : University of Poona.

Wilbur, Schramm (1964) *Mass Media and National Development* California: Stanford University Press.

Wong, J. and Edward, Reed. (1978) *Teaching and Research Forum,* 17, 1290 Avenue of America. N.Y. 10019 USA.

World Bank (1975). *Rural Development Sector Policy Planning,* Washington.

Yadava, J.S. (1985). *Multi-level Information System for Intgrated Rural Development Programmes in India,* New Delhi : IIMC.

INDEX